I0795831

IMAGES
of America

ERWIN AND UNICOI COUNTY

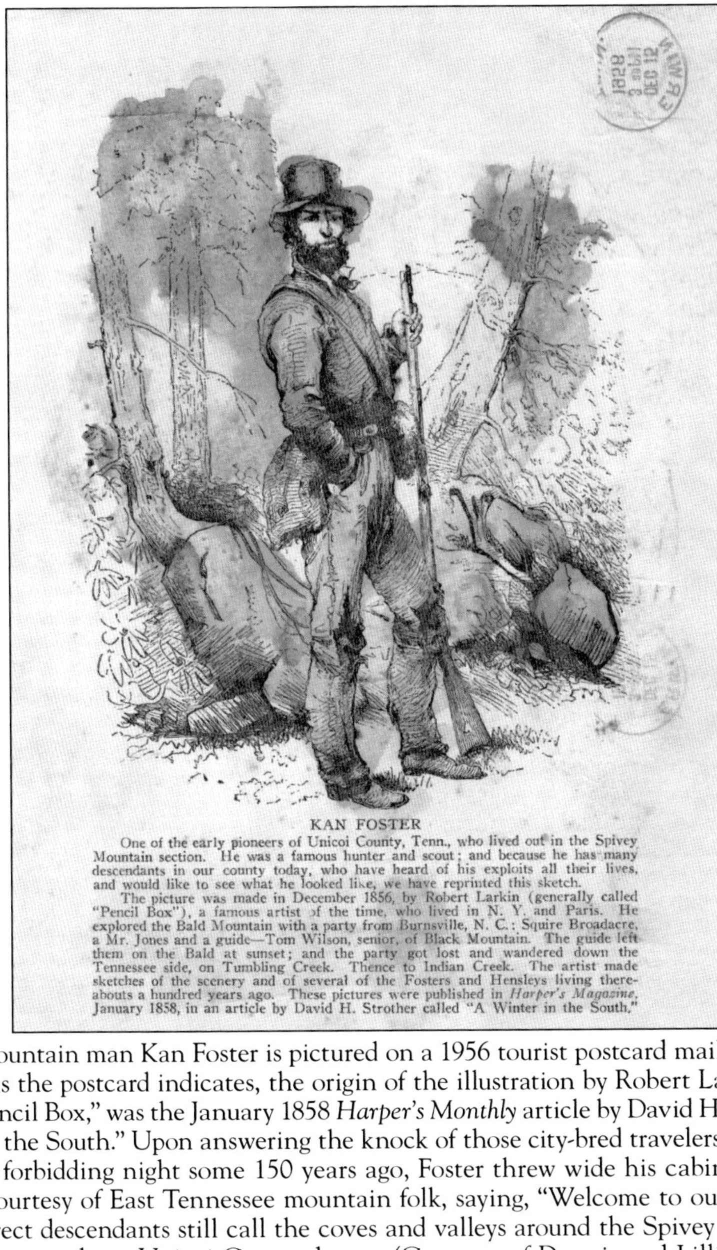

Legendary mountain man Kan Foster is pictured on a 1956 tourist postcard mailed from Erwin, Tennessee. As the postcard indicates, the origin of the illustration by Robert Larkin, the artist known as "Pencil Box," was the January 1858 *Harper's Monthly* article by David H. Strother titled "A Winter in the South." Upon answering the knock of those city-bred travelers-in-distress one bitterly cold, forbidding night some 150 years ago, Foster threw wide his cabin door, offering the typical courtesy of East Tennessee mountain folk, saying, "Welcome to our home!" Many of Foster's direct descendants still call the coves and valleys around the Spivey Mountain area of Flag Pond in southern Unicoi County home. (Courtesy of Dennis and Lillian Foster/Jakie Foster collection.)

On the Cover: Jakie Farnor, at left, was a schoolteacher in Unicoi County for 60 years. Her own photo albums offer a personal documentary history of the diverse and remarkably efficient rural schools of the first half of the 20th century. Pictured one late summer day about 1950, Farnor and her 10-year-old niece Ruth Chandler stack wheat on the Chandler family farm in Flag Pond. The old Clear Branch School is in the background. Today Ruth Chandler Gonce recalls the simplicity of that Clear Branch School with great affection. (Courtesy of Dennis and Lillian Foster/Jakie Farnor collection.)

IMAGES
of America

ERWIN AND UNICOI COUNTY

Linda Davis March

ARCADIA
PUBLISHING

ISBN 978-0-7385-5264-4

Published by Arcadia Publishing
Charleston, South Carolina

Printed in the United States of America

Library of Congress Catalog Card Number: Applied for

For all general information contact Arcadia Publishing at: 2007922638
Telephone 843-853-2070
Fax 843-853-0044
E-mail sales@arcadiapublishing.com
For customer service and orders:
Toll-Free 1-888-313-2665

Visit us on the Internet at www.arcadiapublishing.com

To my son Adam and my son Drew—who have both always been my inspiration for everything.

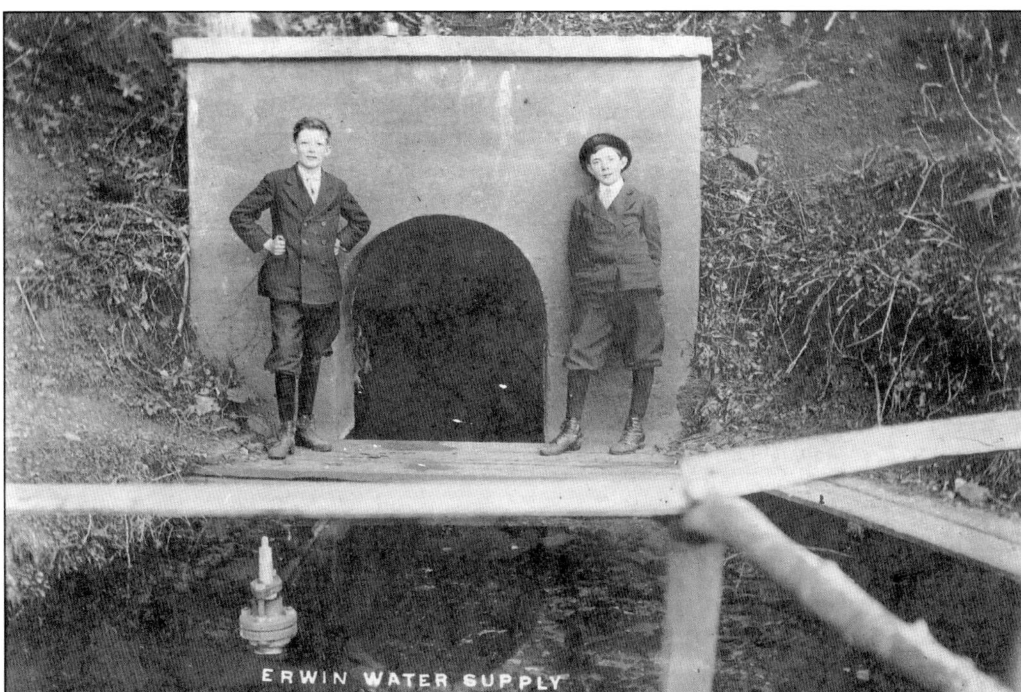

Young Carl Pritchard (left) and George Woodward pose at O'Brien Springs, the source of Erwin's first commercial, public water supply, initiated in the early 1900s by local Erwin businessman A. R. Brown. (Courtesy of Martha Brown Stromberg/A. R. Brown collection.)

Contents

ACKNOWLEDGMENTS

I wish to express my deepest thanks to the descendants of the many families who settled Erwin and Unicoi County. This book about my home has been a labor of love, made all the more wonderful by the incredible kindness and generosity of the folks who freely opened their own family albums to me. The Unicoi County Historical Society kindly gave me free access to its invaluable photograph collection. My aunt Lucille Booth and my cousin Juacquetta Davis Edwards shared unseen family photographs with me, which fed my soul. Writer and historian Lewis Thornberry opened the pages of Erwin's day-to-day history for me in his wonderful book *Remembering Old Erwin*. My special visit to the Unicoi County Heritage Museum, courtesy of Curator Martha Erwin, made these historic photographs come to life. From Judy Moss, Hilda Padgett, Chris Tipton, James Goforth, Martha Erwin, Bert Thompson, Anderson Pate, Kathy Thornberry, George Hatcher, Sylvia and Arnold Banner, Sharlotte Jones-Rynders, Carole Tilson, the Arnold Williams family, the Sam Keesecker family, Betty Cox, F. B. and Marie White, Violet Kelley, Mick and Jean Bergendahl, Joan and Bob Sams, Debbie Tittle, Jim Gladson, Rupert Brannon, Jan Hendren Parsley, Patsy Alderman Tittle, Dr. Nat Ed Hyder, W. A. Wilson, Bob and Dolly Gilbert, Betty Griffith, Myra Anne Sellars Murray, Myra Edwards Sellars, Vicki Harris, Becky Love, Pat and Johnny Lynch, Greg Lynch, Kent Garland, Margaret Sue Range, Lisa Range, Kim Arwood, Dennis and Donna Seagroves, Betty Chandler, Margaret Swingle, Noel Muhn, Marie Kegley Deyton, Ruth Chandler Gonce, Guy Street, John Edwards, Lisa and John Pilkington, and Dennis and Lillian Foster, I was given the gift of wonderful photographs and an open door, allowing me to hear the little stories of each special family that made the years fall away and made Unicoi County's history all so very real again, so very close to home. Special thanks go to Martha Brown Stromberg for allowing me to spend an entire day within the walls of the historic A. R. Brown family home on South Main Street. Her generous loan of many rare Brown family photographs gave me the opportunity to share a largely unseen view of local history. The Brown house was truly a family home, a beloved sanctuary that embraced its family for 100 years, much the same way the Valley Beautiful has sheltered its families for some 250 years. Thank you all for the rare opportunity to step inside the lives of these families of old Erwin and Unicoi County, if only for just a moment to witness, as did the camera, the rare infinitesimal snapshots of life, which, when pieced together, reveal that we are all part of the same universal family.

Finally, to my own dear family: my two sons Adam and Drew; my mother, Eulala Davis; my Aunt Lucille and Uncle Bill Booth; my cousin Juacquetta Davis Edwards; and my extended Davis and Hensley clan for their tender care and loving kindness—I know now even more clearly the importance of family.

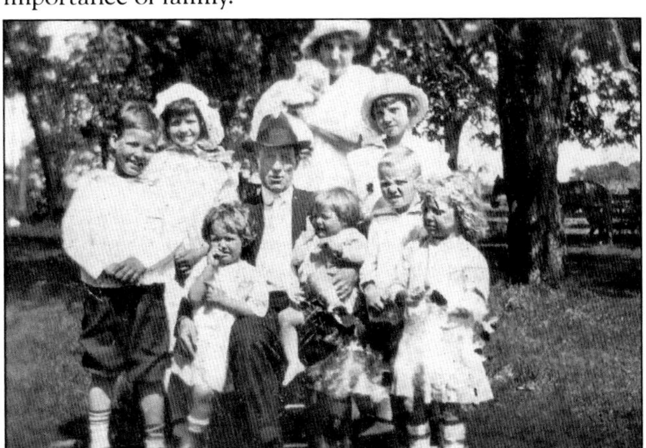

This photograph of a proud papa in the midst of his large, loving family is from the early 1900s and was found in the photo albums of the author's own Davis family heritage. Although these Davis kin are unidentified, this image seems to represent all the wonderful families of Erwin and Unicoi County—past and present—whose marvelous collective photographic history is illustrated in the pages that follow. (Courtesy of Juacquetta Davis Edwards.)

INTRODUCTION

Erwin and Unicoi County are twin jewels that are part of the same sparkling strand of the Blue Ridge Mountains. Sheltered by the shimmering folds of the Blue Ridge, the Big Bald, and Unaka mountaintops, this alluring valley tempted the legendary Long Hunters, who, in the early 1700s, followed the sunset in search of the abundant game of this rugged Tennessee country. Watered by the mighty Nolichucky River, the area soon welcomed settlers in the mid-1760s to the place then called Greasy Cove—a place where hunters cleaned game and met for trade.

The Civil War in East Tennessee and what later became Unicoi County was a bitter conflict of divided loyalties. Tennessee was the last state to secede but the first to experience the heartache of brother against brother. The area which became Unicoi County was heavily Union and suffered from Confederate "bushwhackers," who unceremoniously conscripted farmers from their own fields for service with the South.

After the war, old bitterness was put aside as progress made its way into the mountains. Unicoi County was established in 1875, taken from parts of Carter and Washington Counties. The railroad was linking northern markets to southern seaports and a short, profitable route was needed. By 1890, railroad track had reached the village that was to become the town of Erwin. Once headquarters for the Carolina, Clinchfield, and Ohio railroad were established in Erwin, the population exploded and a boom time was on the way. From 1909 to 1914, Unicoi County was bursting at the seams with new business, new ideas, and the latest in modern convenience. However, the streets remained dusty and unpaved until 1917, and the sidewalks were made of planks.

But the continued success of the railroad in the 1920s was a boon for the entire county. The Ohio-based Southern Potteries, makers of hand-painted china dinnerware, set up a factory in Erwin and became the second largest employer in the county besides the railroad.

Good times went bust in 1929 when the ripple effect of the stock market crash finally reached Unicoi County. Railroad freight demand was cut back, jobs were scarce, and families had to feed their own with large gardens. Camp Cordell Hull gave young men temporary work in the Civilian Conservation Corps, and the railroad offered farmland to out-of-work men and rail shipments of free flour for families. New Deal agencies provided relief, and community churches and local civic groups offered respite and communion, as well as economic aid to those in hard times. Local ladies' sewing circles gathered weekly in Erwin to stitch up garments for distribution.

But World War II took many of Unicoi County's own away from the valley, and some did not return. But others, like the nine Erwin boys who miraculously found each other in the same German POW camp, returned to Erwin and Unicoi County, living quiet lives of service to the community, their churches, and their families.

After war's end, the 1950s and 1960s in Unicoi County was a heady time of exultant joy in everyday life. The social life of young and old was full and rich in Unicoi County, with rousing high school sports events, community concerts, a local drive-in movie theater, Rock Creek Park, a golf course, and more churches, it seemed, than the local population.

By the 1970s and 1980s, however, the pervading national trend of downtown drain and the flight to suburbia was also being felt in Erwin and Unicoi County. The landmark A. R. Brown Department Store was sold in the mid-1980s. Its absence left a huge void in downtown Erwin, and other shops fell by the wayside in favor of the strip malls of nearby Johnson City.

But fortunately the last decades of the 20th century have witnessed a renewed interest in historic preservation of the unusually rich architectural heritage of downtown Erwin and the county at large. In 1995, the hamlet of Unicoi finally incorporated and has a fast-rising economic future. Also in northern Unicoi County, Tanasi—the proposed regional cultural arts and performance facility—set to be constructed off the new I-26 highway, which bisects Unicoi County.

The future seems bright for this beautiful little East Tennessee county, whose greatest heritage is its rich and resilient pioneer past.

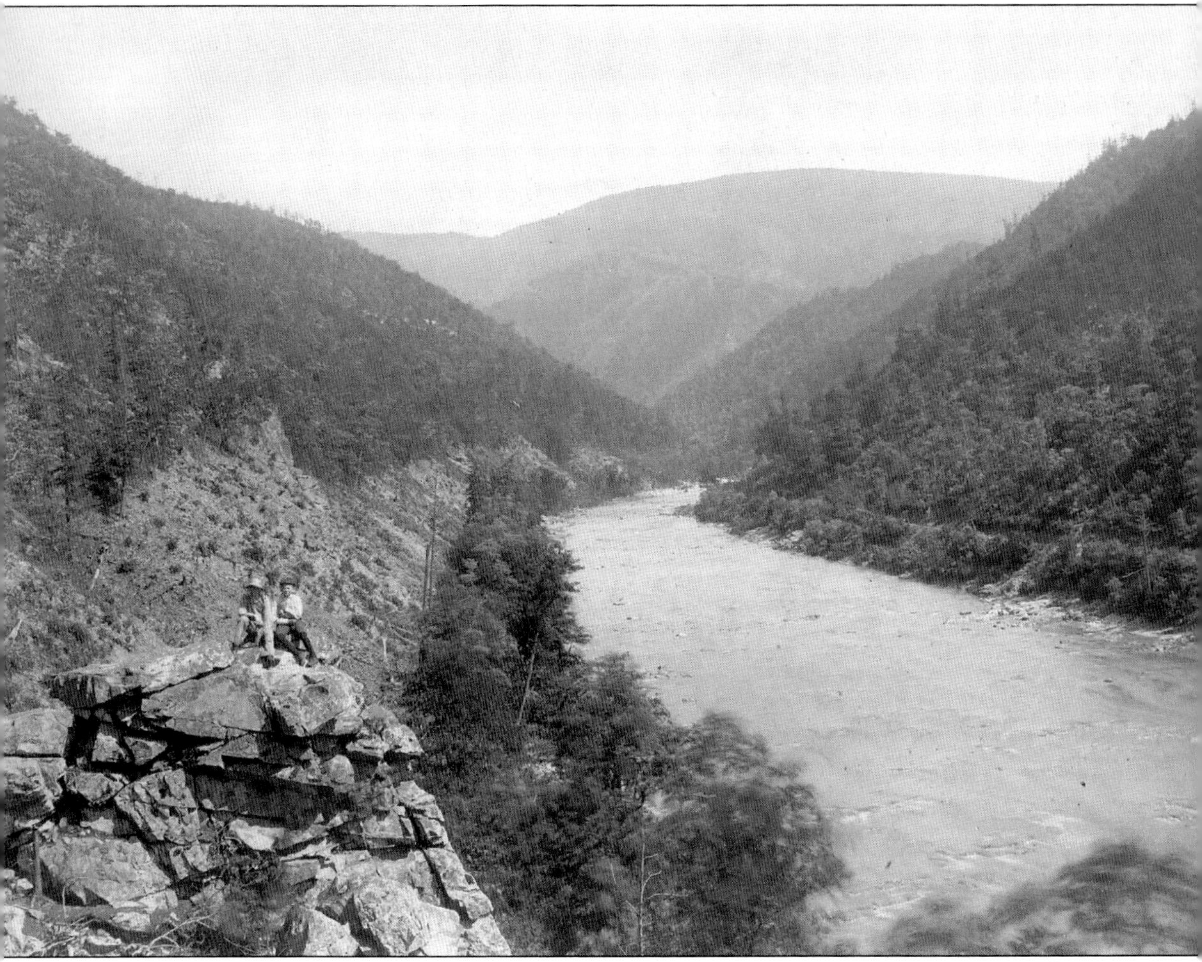

This is a view that would have opened itself to the pioneers of East Tennessee: wave after wave of undulating mountains fed by an ancient river under a pristine sky. These young boys, perched unexpectedly atop the chimney outcrop above the river at Flat Top Mountain at the end of the 19th century were luckier than they knew. (Courtesy of Marie Kegley Deyton.)

One

Into the Mountains

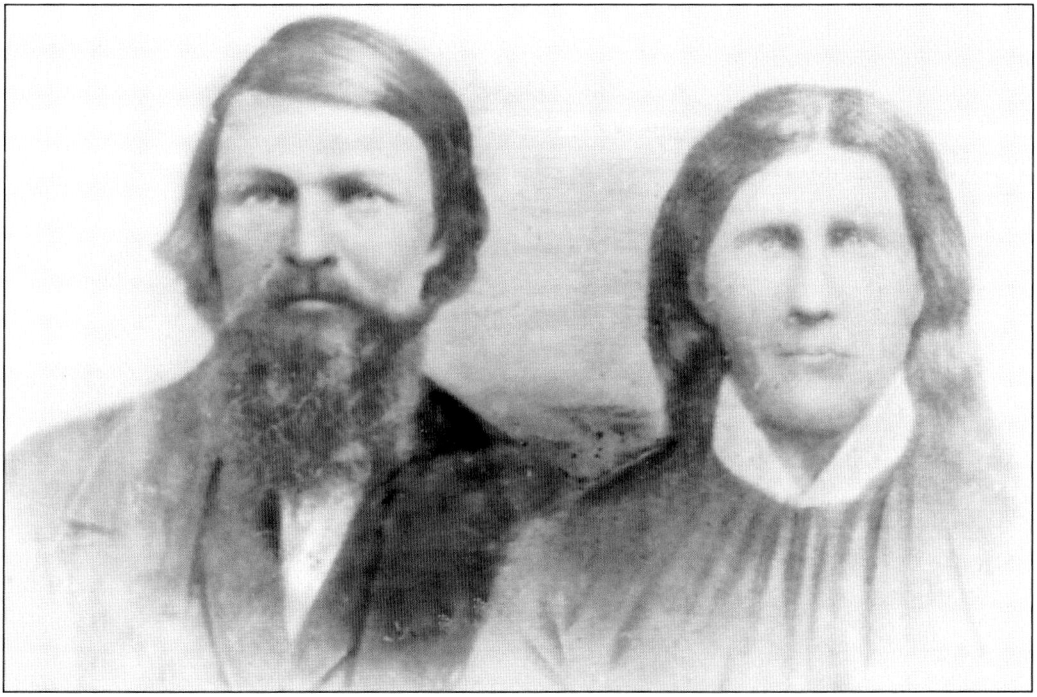

William Allison Hensley and his wife, Lucinda Maney, are recognized as the first settlers on Spivey Mountain, located in southern Unicoi County. Hensley, born in North Carolina in 1798, moved up and over the mountain in the early 1800s from what is now Yancey County, North Carolina, establishing himself and his family on Spivey Mountain. His grandmother Elizabeth Washington Angel was a first cousin to Pres. George Washington. Maney, born in 1803, was part Cherokee. Her half-Cherokee grandfather John Joseph Vann, born in 1740, was noted as an able scout and translator for the settlers of this rugged frontier region. (Courtesy of Betty Chandler.)

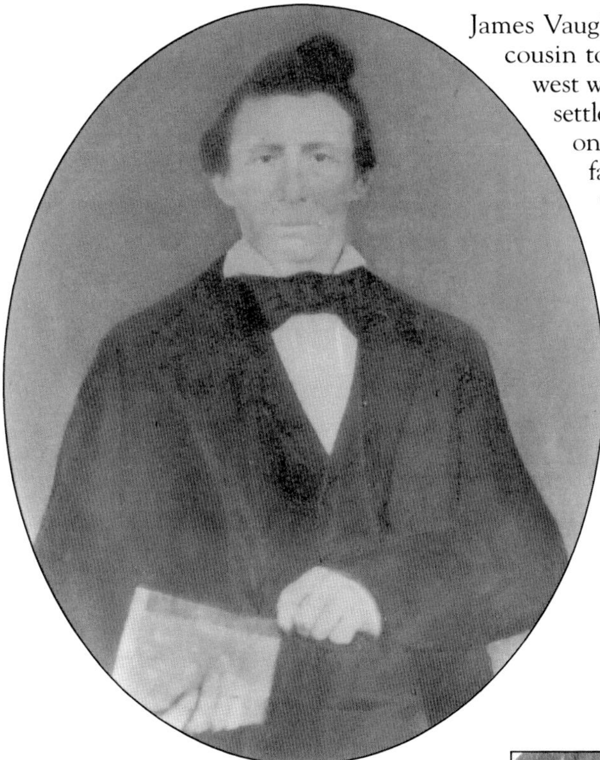

James Vaughn Johnson (1810–1876) was a second cousin to Pres. Andrew Johnson and had come west with him to Tennessee about 1824. James settled in what became Unicoi County, carried on a blacksmith trade, and owned a large farm in what is now north Erwin. Johnson was one of the original commissioners charged with organizing the new county of Unicoi. He is buried in the rock wall family cemetery on North Main Street. (Courtesy of F. B. White.)

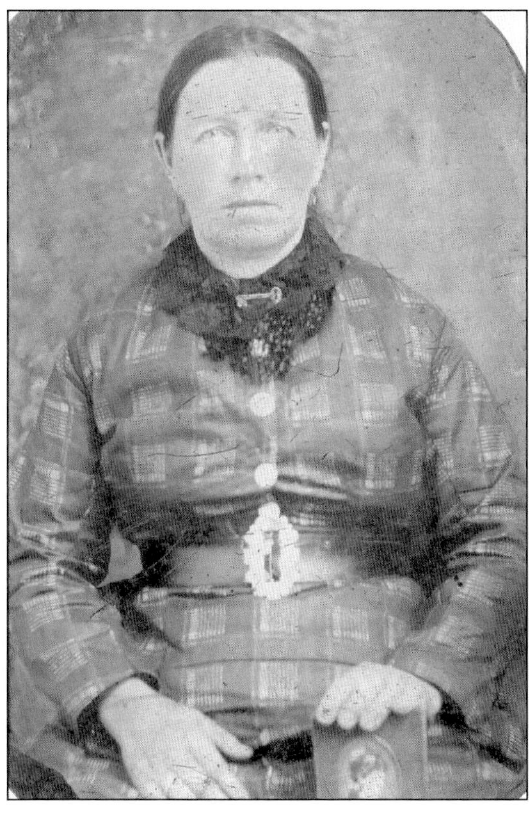

Cassa Laws Davis was born in 1828. Shown here in a tintype image from the late 1860s or 1870s, Davis gazes into the camera with the fixed expression characteristic of the era. Interestingly Davis holds in her hand another tintype image or painted miniature of a child—perhaps one who died too young. (Courtesy of Juacquetta Davis Edwards.)

Jesse P. Tinker fought in the Civil War. Like so many of East Tennessee's Union sympathizers, Jesse had been unwillingly conscripted into the 64th N.C. Confederate unit by bushwhackers. Men who were not conscripted were pressured by the occupying Confederates to enlist or, in some cases, pay with their lives. In those desperate circumstances, many hid out in the hills and coves, waiting for the tide to turn. (Courtesy of Christine Christy Tipton.)

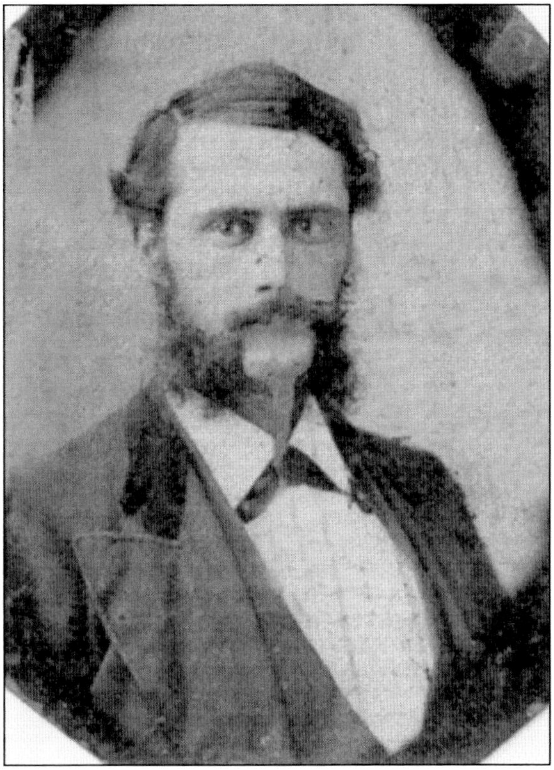

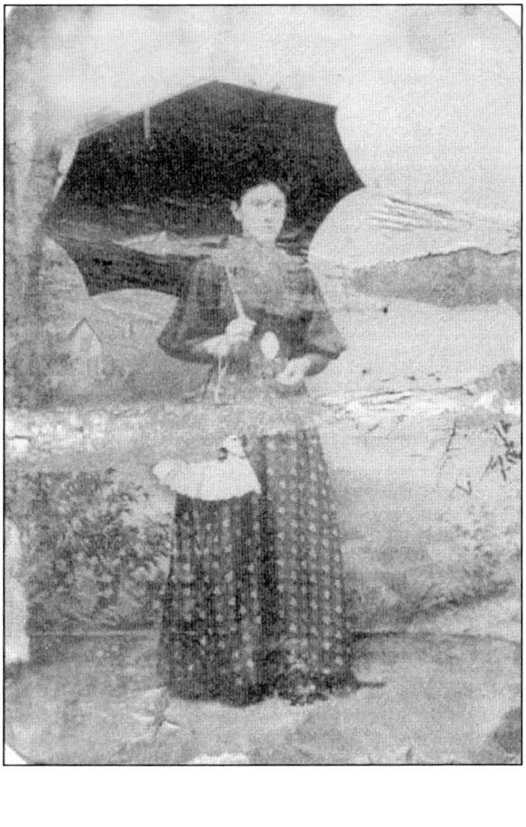

When the Confederates took off Jesse P. Tinker to serve in their army, his wife, Sarah E. Moore, like so many other East Tennessee women, was left alone with the family farm to tend and children to feed. Tensions were high and provisions were scarce. Sarah Tinker, reflecting years later on East Tennessee's Civil War conflict, could only relate the deep desperation of the circumstances by saying that "times were so hard that we were just lucky that there were fish in the river." (Courtesy of Christine Christy Tipton.)

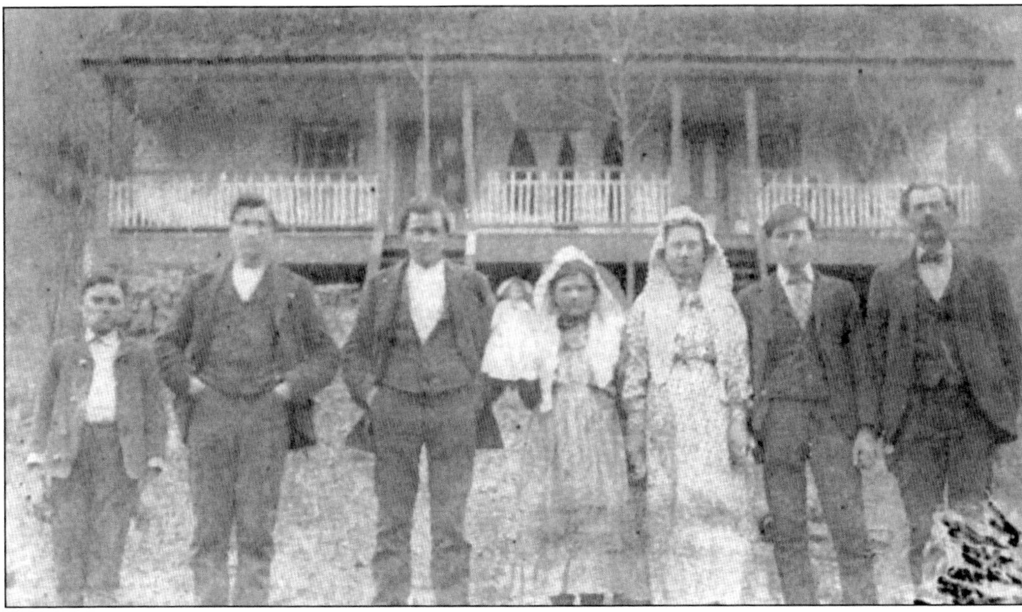

In this wedding portrait from the early 1900s, groom Jason Ledford and bride Mary Lovett hold hands as they pose in front of the Ledford family home place in the Flag Pond community. Mary wears a crocheted wedding headdress. Minty Ledford holds a doll. To the extreme right is Amos Ledford, father of the groom, and to the extreme left are Jason's brothers Pet and Omega. (Courtesy of Juacquetta Davis Edwards.)

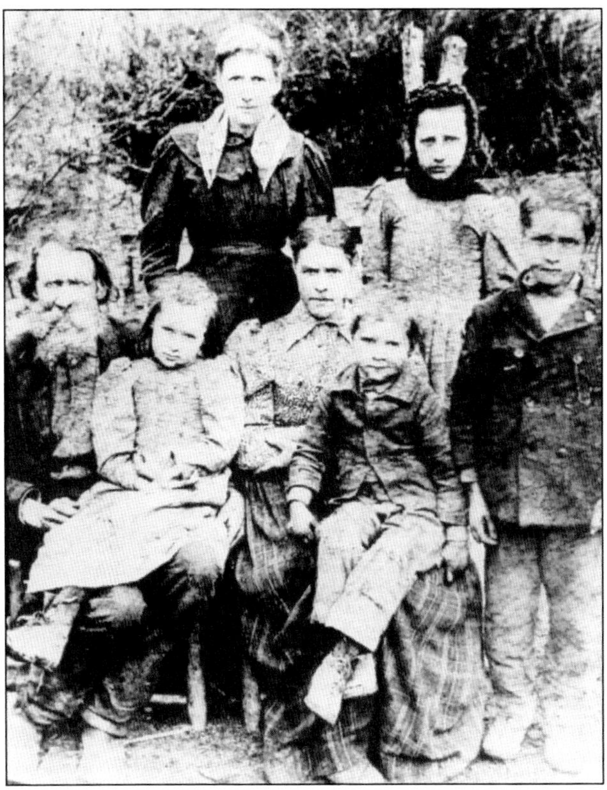

William Grannison Chandler lived in the Spivey area of southern Unicoi County. This family portrait from about 1860 includes his wife, Mary Elizabeth, who is seated in the center with son Lucius. Standing from left to right are sister Ellie and daughter Jane, and son Wolford. William Grannison Chandler holds daughter Becky Ann. Chandler also had four sons—William, Andrew, Joseph Henry, and Isaac—from his first marriage to Mary Drucilla Rice. (Courtesy of Betty Chandler.)

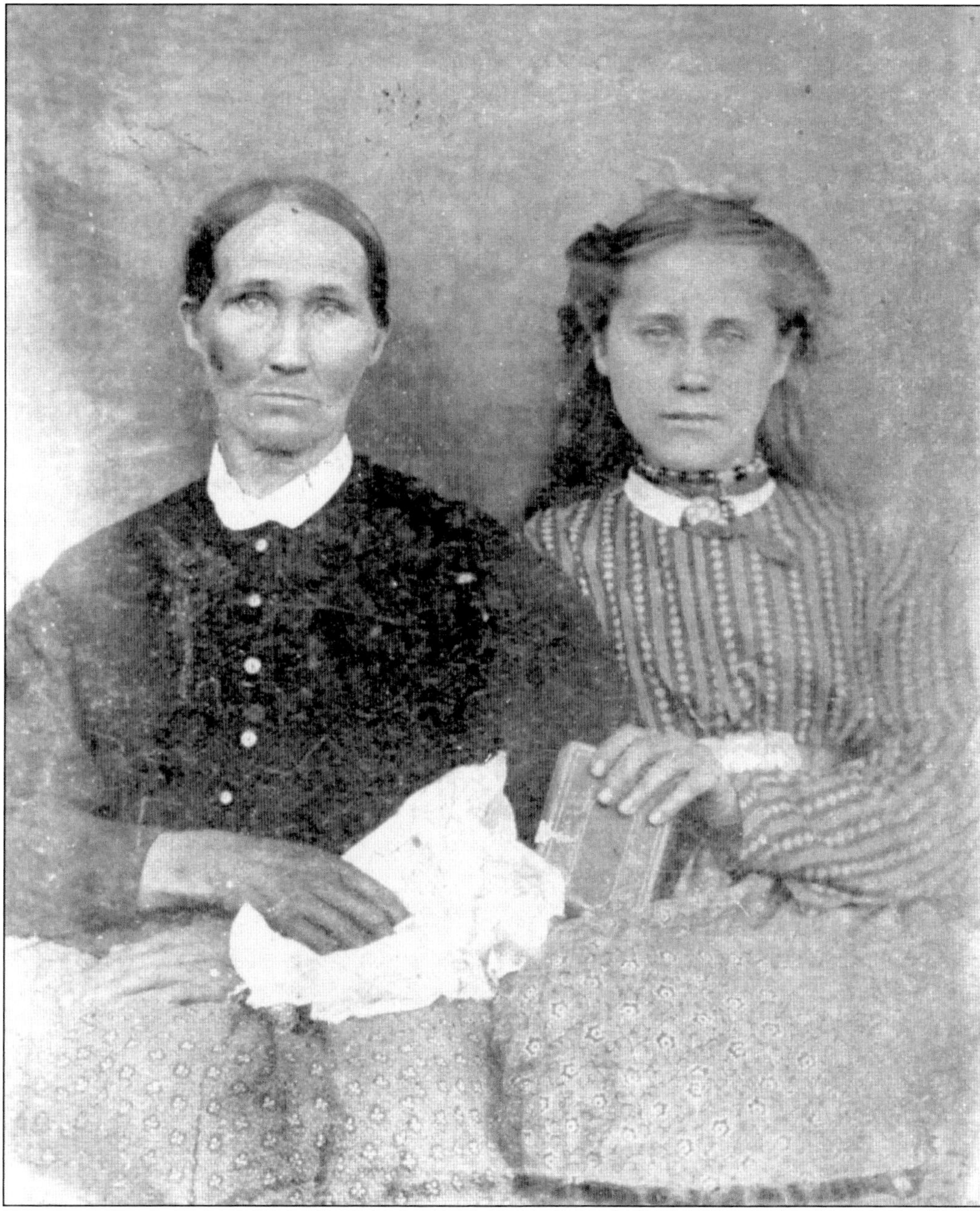

Martha Tilson Farnor, shown with her mother, Rebecca Bayless Tilson, about 1875, was descended through her Tilson family line from Mayflower pilgrims John Alden and Priscilla Mullens. Martha, at right, wears a strand of lustrous dark and light glass beads and holds a gilt-edged volume sealed with a clasp. (Courtesy of Dennis and Lillian Foster/Jakie Farnor collection.)

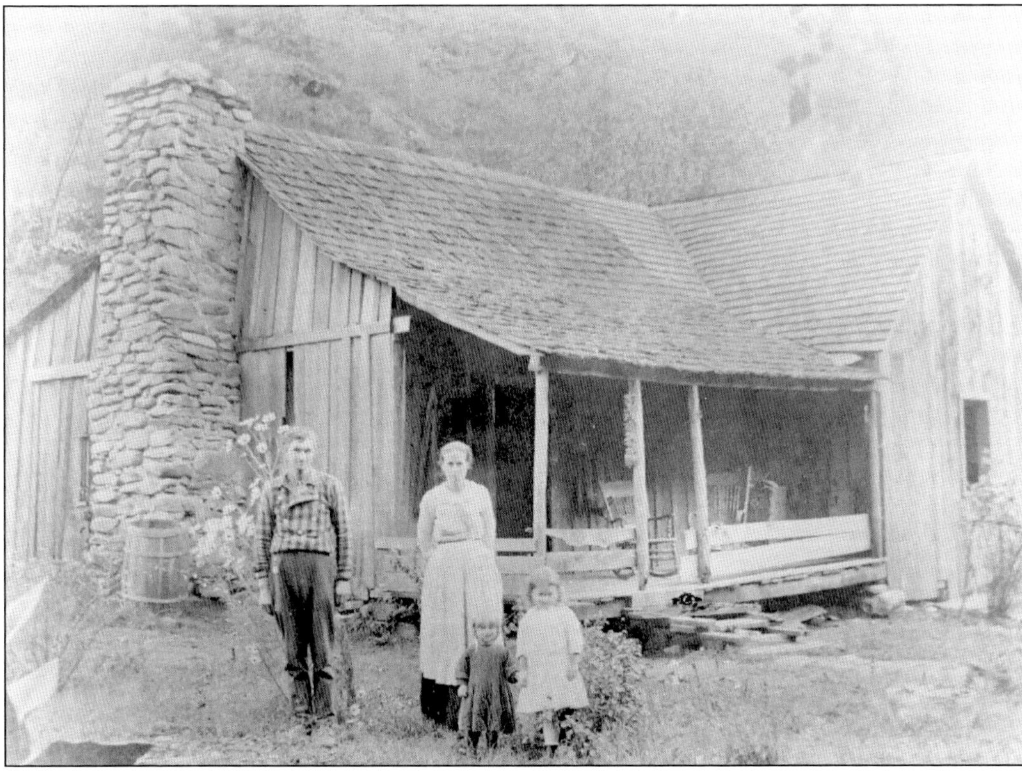

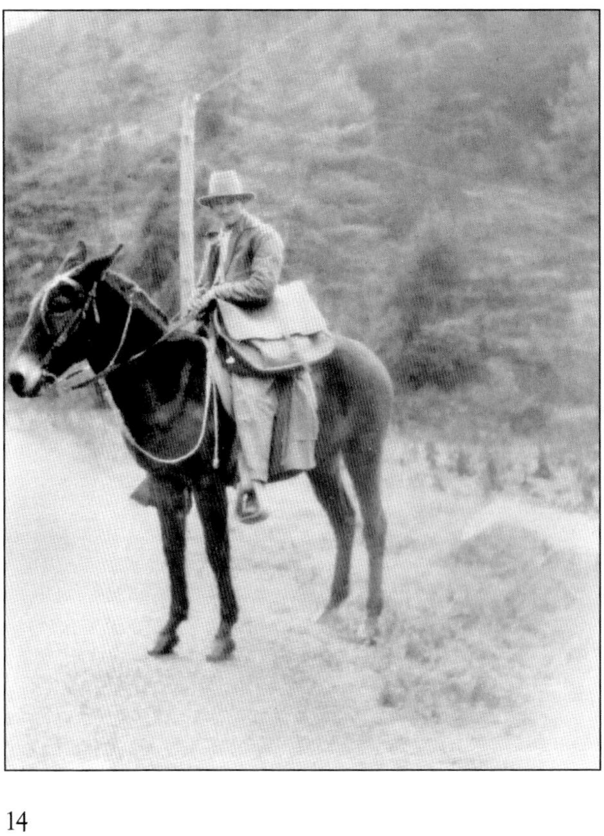

Allison Woodville Hensley and Mariah Cordelia Foster raised their family in this board-and-batten house at the fork of Coffee Ridge and Spivey Creeks. In addition to being a farmer, Hensley was also a rural mail carrier, delivering by mule to the Flag Pond, Clear Branch, and Kittyton communities. Hensley carried the mail well into the 1930s, when automobiles took over. (Both images courtesy of Betty Chandler.)

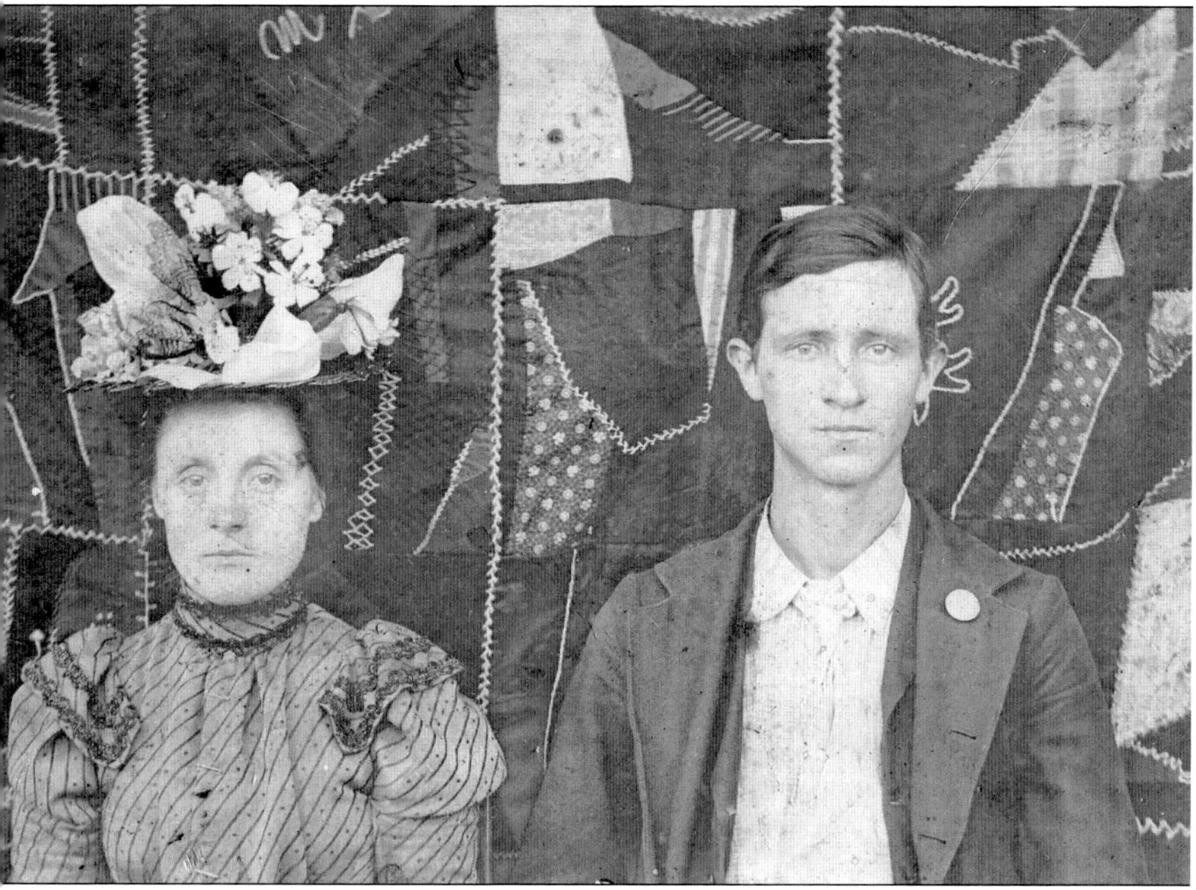

The remarkable blossoms of Martha Tilson Farnor's hat were, no doubt, a source of great pride when she and husband, Dave P. Farnor, sat for this photographic portrait about 1898. The elaborate, crazy quilt backdrop is a splendid example of the exquisite fancywork and needle arts accomplished by the women of Unicoi County in the late 19th and early 20th centuries. (Courtesy of Dennis and Lillian Foster/Jakie Farnor collection.)

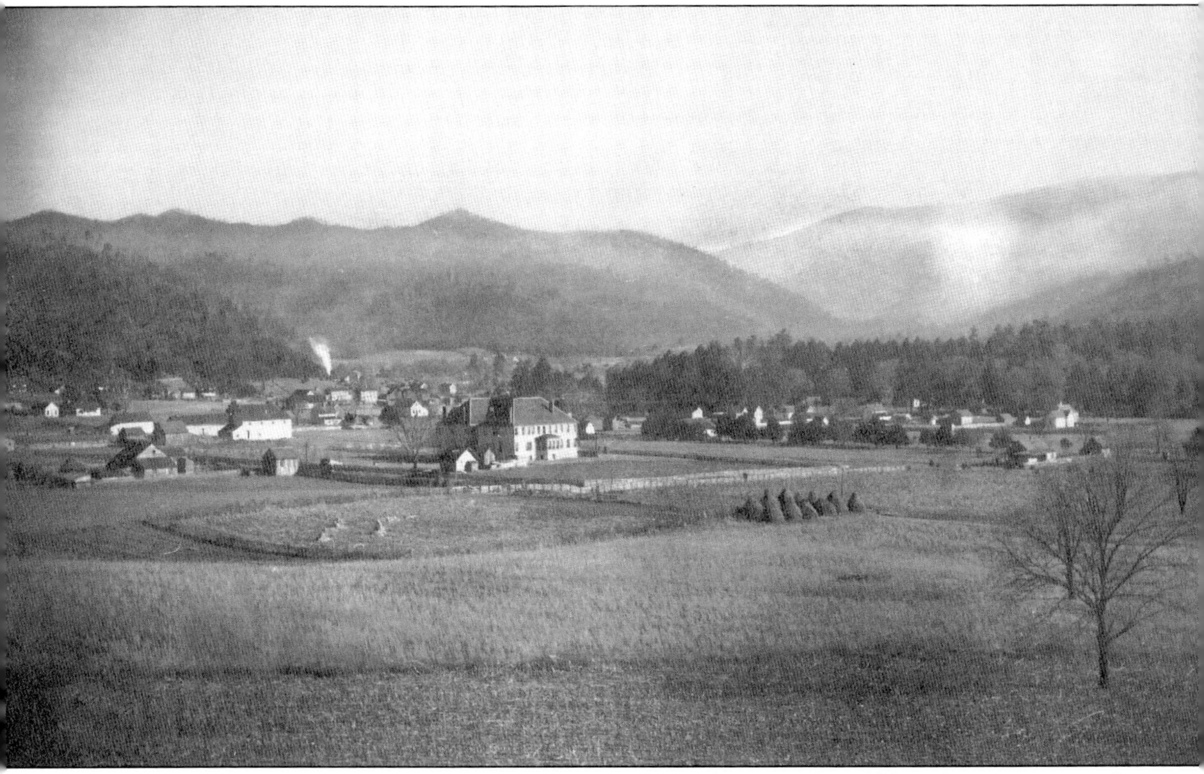

This view of the village of Unicoi was taken around 1900. The old hotel, now gone, takes center stage in this bucolic portrait of the valley. (Courtesy of Kent Garland/Judge Walter Garland collection.)

Popularly known as the "White Elephant," this mercantile, located in the hamlet of Unicoi and owned by the McInturff brothers, was also used as a post office and a community gathering place. (Courtesy of Kent Garland/ Judge Walter Garland collection.)

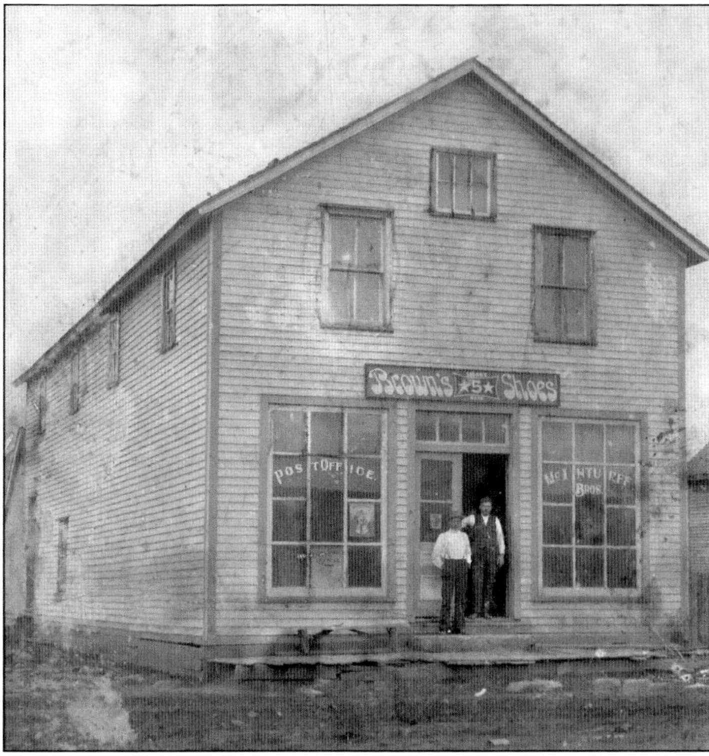

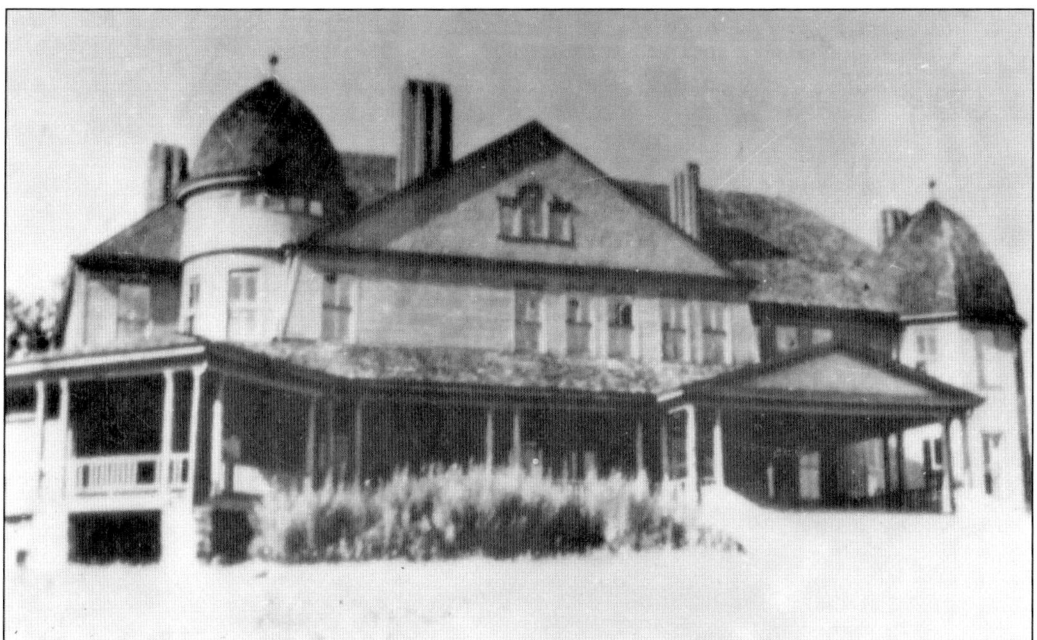

This hotel was built in Unicoi in the late 1800s with expectations that the village would be chosen by the railroad as its headquarters. Erwin was chosen instead. The hotel was eventually used for church services and later as an elementary school. It was destroyed by fire in the winter of 1935. (Courtesy of Kent Garland/ Judge Walter Garland collection.)

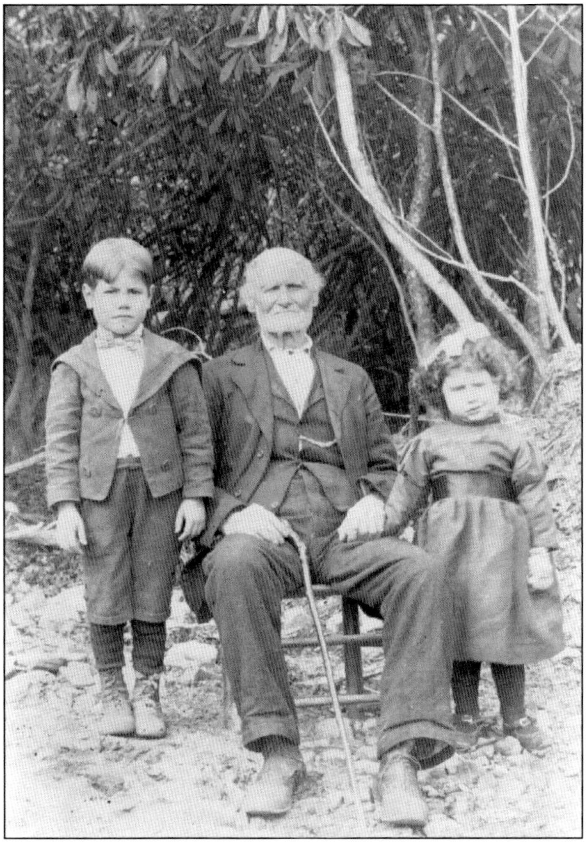

W. P. Brummett and his grandchildren pose in the natural light of an outdoor setting at his home place on Scioto Road in Limestone Cove around 1890. The old cabin, seen below, was a sturdy, two-story affair that showed a bit of affluence in its rustic setting. (Both images courtesy of Hilda Padgett.)

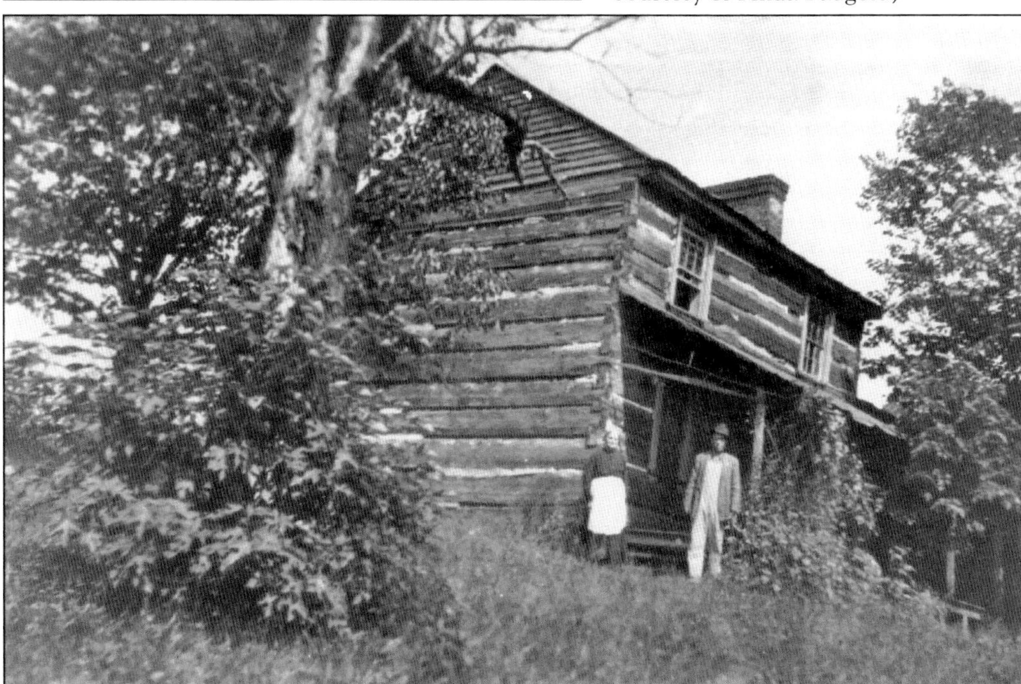

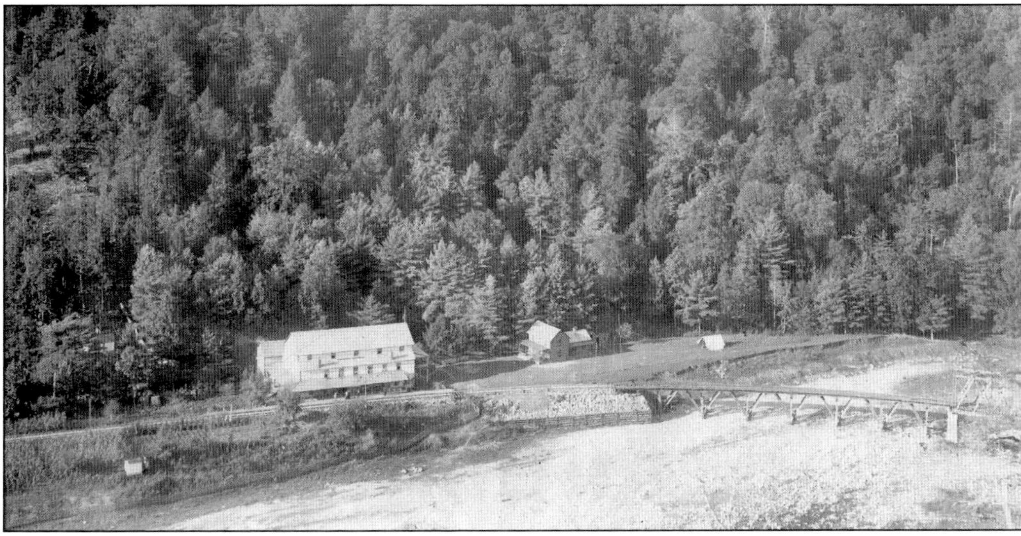

Taken by photographer Dick Deyton around 1905, this bird's-eye view of the Unaka Springs Hotel shows the remote nature of the location. A rough road through expansive woods led to the hotel. The major form of access was the CC&O railroad, which skirted the edge of the hotel alongside the Nolichucky River. (Courtesy of Marie Kegley Deyton.)

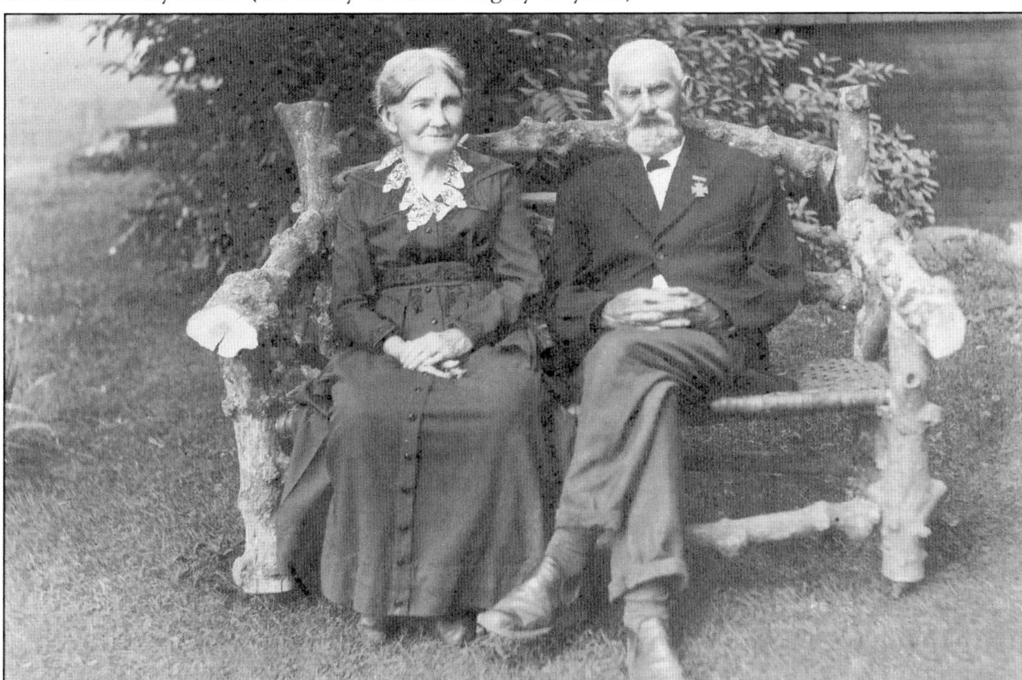

Mary A. and Arthur V. Deaderick were the proprietors of the popular Unaka Springs Hotel, built in 1899. The Deadericks advertised their establishment as being a place "where fishes swim and mosses grow," a place with "pure air that blows through the tops of the tall pines," and one that produces the "sleep and rest that Nature alone can provide." The spring water was promised to "greatly benefit any case of indigestion" and could be purchased for $5 a barrel and shipped by railroad to "all points" upon request. (Courtesy of Christine Christy Tipton.)

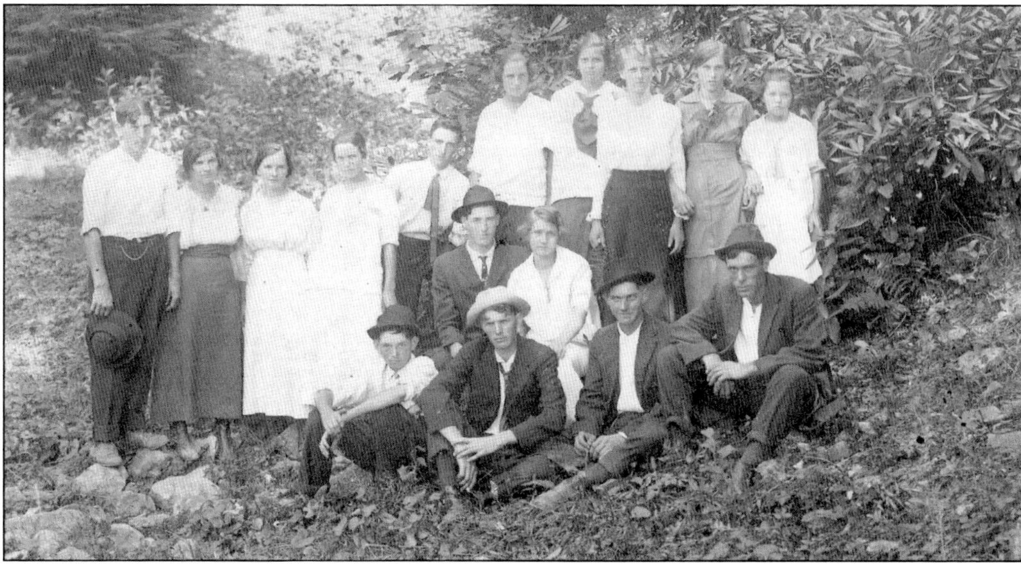

These fresh young faces were the hired help at the Unaka Springs Hotel in 1916. They worked a variety of jobs, from kitchen staff, to domestic and wait staff, to grounds maintenance. Many lived nearby, and some came from families who regularly supplied the hotel kitchen with fresh produce and other edibles. Lydia Tinker is pictured second from right in the back row. Her sister Cora is beside her, third from right. The others are unidentified. (Courtesy of Christine Christy Tipton.)

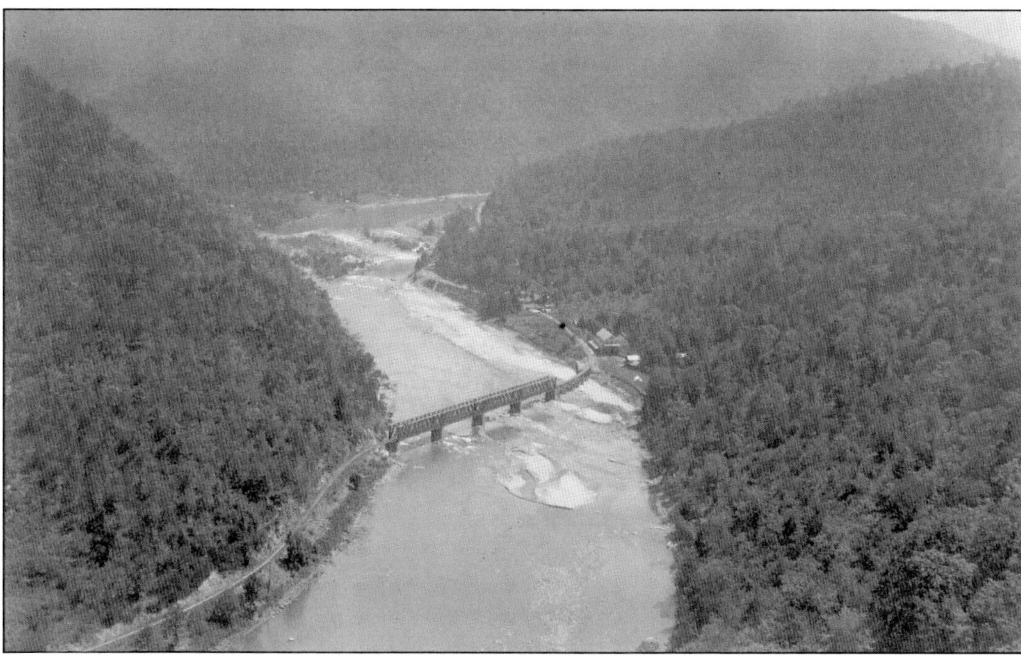

The mighty Nolichucky River makes its way through the mountains of Unicoi County at Unaka Springs in this photograph by Dick Deyton from about 1900. The rough-timbered CC&O train trestle bisects the river at the location of the Unaka Springs Hotel, seen to the right. A more efficient and far safer steel train trestle replaced the rough-cut wooden one about 1908. (Courtesy of Marie Kegley Deyton.)

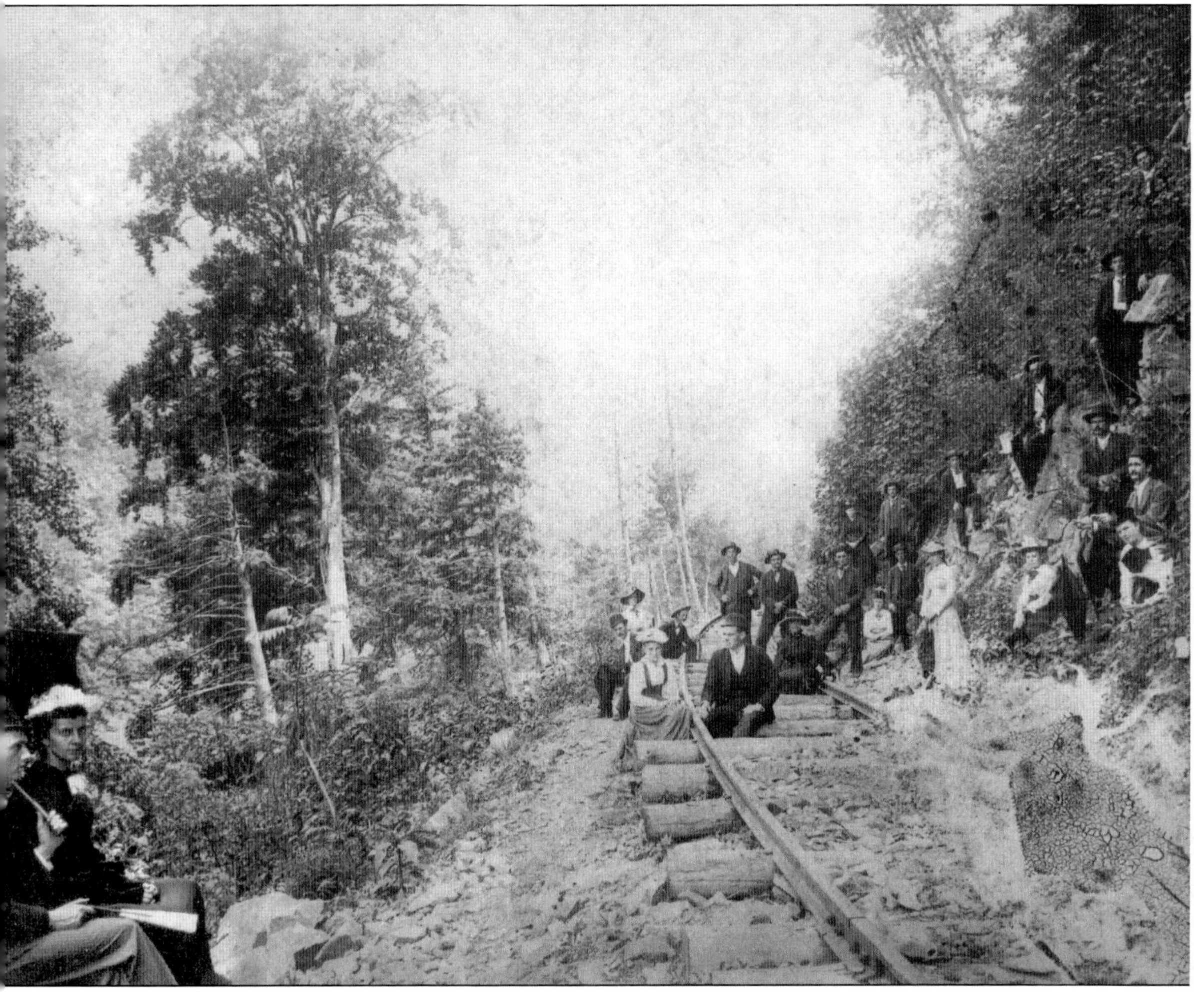

The young lady in the foreground of this 1890s photograph, shaded by her parasol-wielding beau, stares uncompromisingly at the camera from her unlikely seat alongside these railroad tracks located in southern Unicoi County near the Unaka Springs Hotel. "Taking the waters" of the invigorating mineral springs for which the hotel was named and embarking on rigorous outdoor frolics were popular pursuits for guests, who arrived by train from distant parts to experience the charm of the rustic setting. (Courtesy of the Unicoi County Historical Society.)

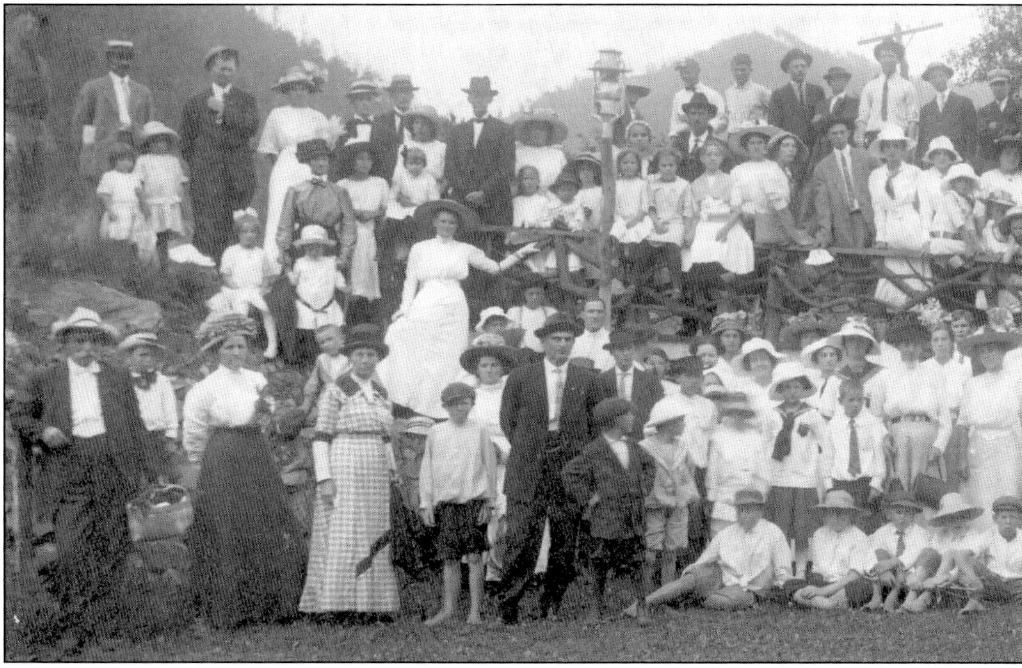

In this *c.* 1905 panorama photograph of a Sunday school picnic at the Unaka Springs Hotel, the enormous "Merry Widow" hats worn by the ladies of the Erwin First Baptist Church are as voluminous as any picnic basket. This well-attended gathering was typical of the many church-related "socials" that provided welcome fellowship and entertainment for rural communities a century ago. Everyone is dressed, naturally, in his or her Sunday best. But the lively little barefoot boys in the front row, no doubt, shed those hats, ties, and stiff collars by day's end. (Courtesy of Martha Brown Stromberg/A. R. Brown collection.)

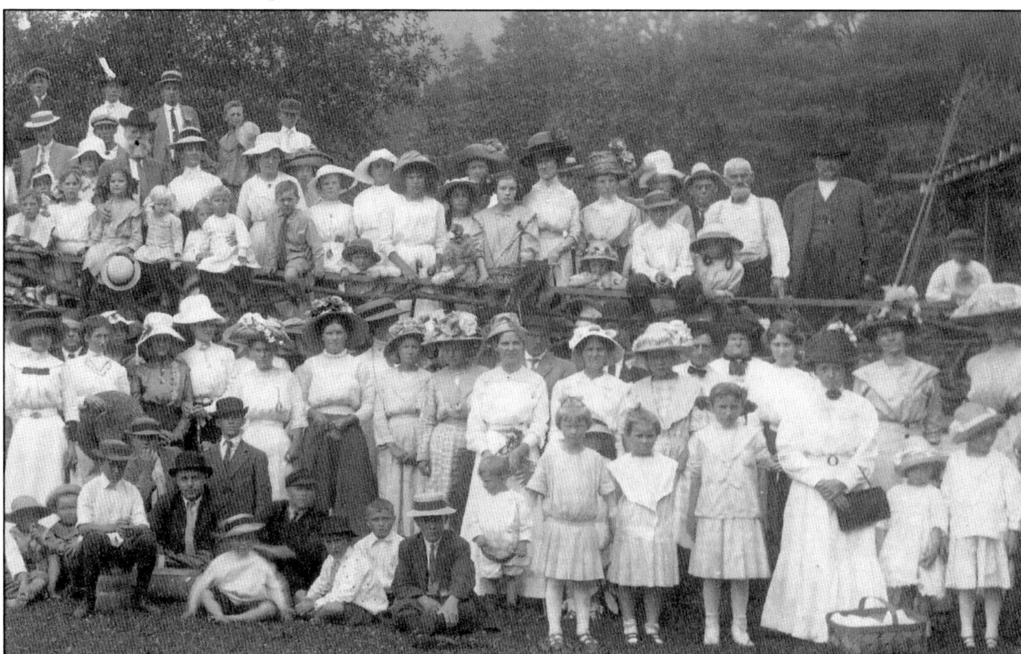

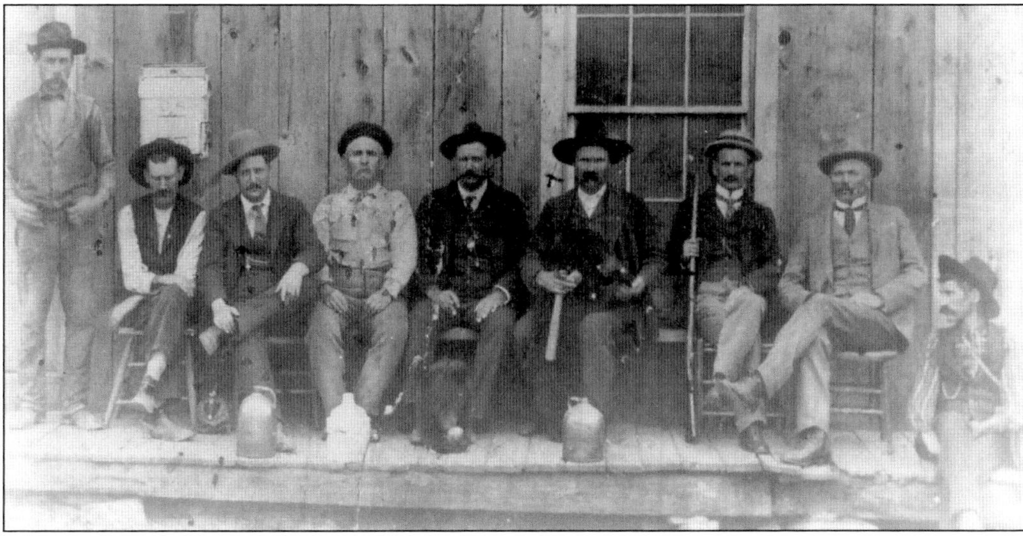

These early-1900s gents are the constabulary, the constituents, and the drinking public of the now defunct town of Rock Creek—all accomplished from this single spot, the Rock Creek Saloon. The legal sale of alcoholic spirits was only allowed in Unicoi County in the confines of an incorporated town. To get around this sticky point of law, distiller and entrepreneur Bill McNabb, fifth from the left, decided that he would create his own town—with his own saloon as the seat of the government. With McNabb as saloon owner, sheriff, mayor, and judge, his was a self-perpetuating enterprise. (Courtesy of F. B. White.)

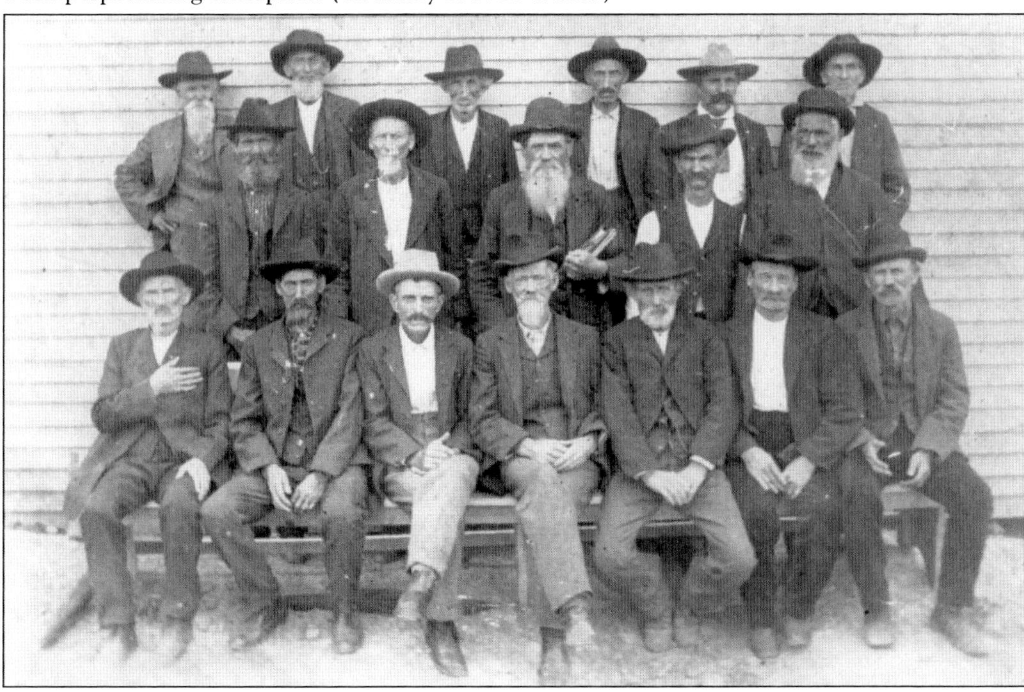

Unicoi County's Civil War veterans gathered for a photograph in the late 1890s. Most had set aside the differences that had torn East Tennessee in two. Although Tennessee had seceded, upper East Tennessee and what later became Unicoi County were heavily Union. (Courtesy of the Unicoi County Historical Society.)

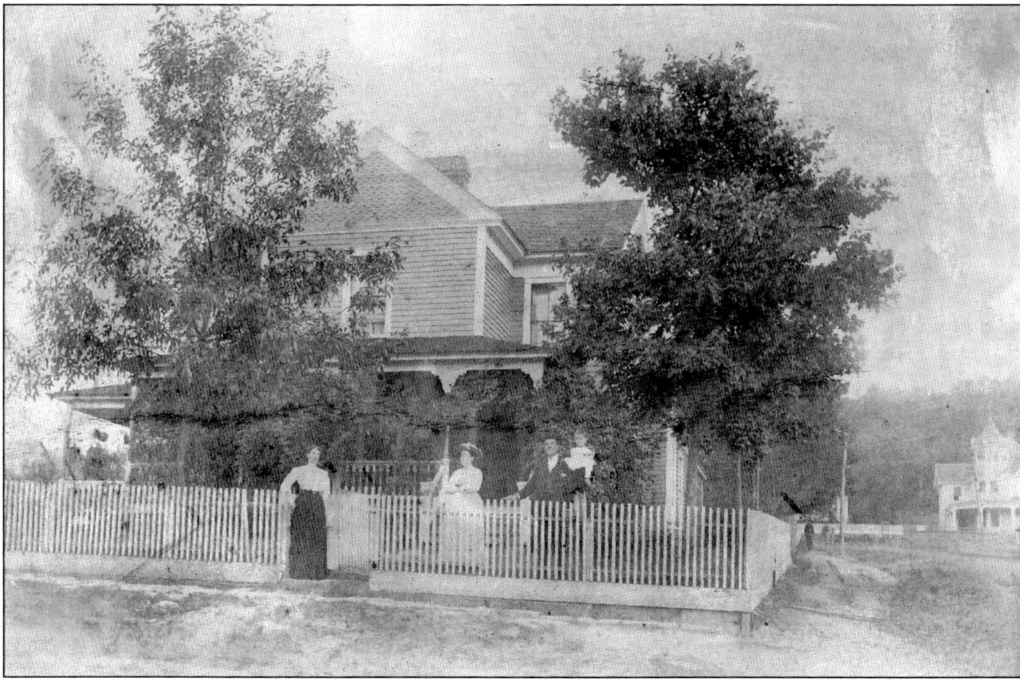

The Thomas D. Davis family lived in this house at 206 Second Street well before Unicoi became a county in 1875. Thomas served in the Union cavalry in the Civil War. His wife, Cassa Laws, bore four children: James, William, Robert, and Mary. Thomas was registrar of deeds for Unicoi County in 1887. (Courtesy of Juacquetta Davis Edwards.)

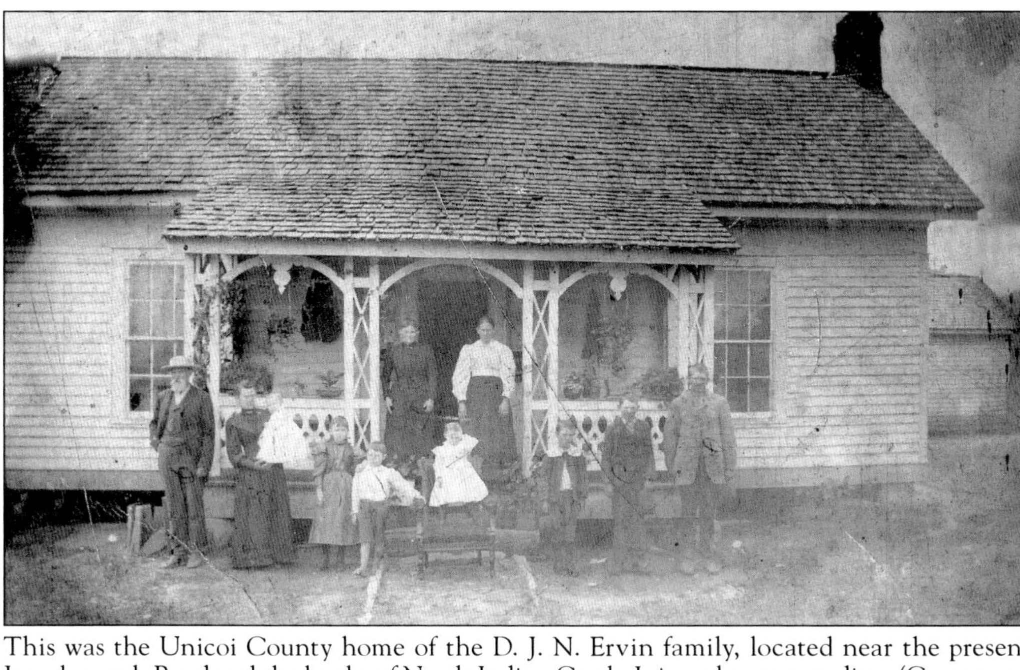

This was the Unicoi County home of the D. J. N. Ervin family, located near the present Jonesborough Road and the banks of North Indian Creek. It is no longer standing. (Courtesy of Margaret Swingle.)

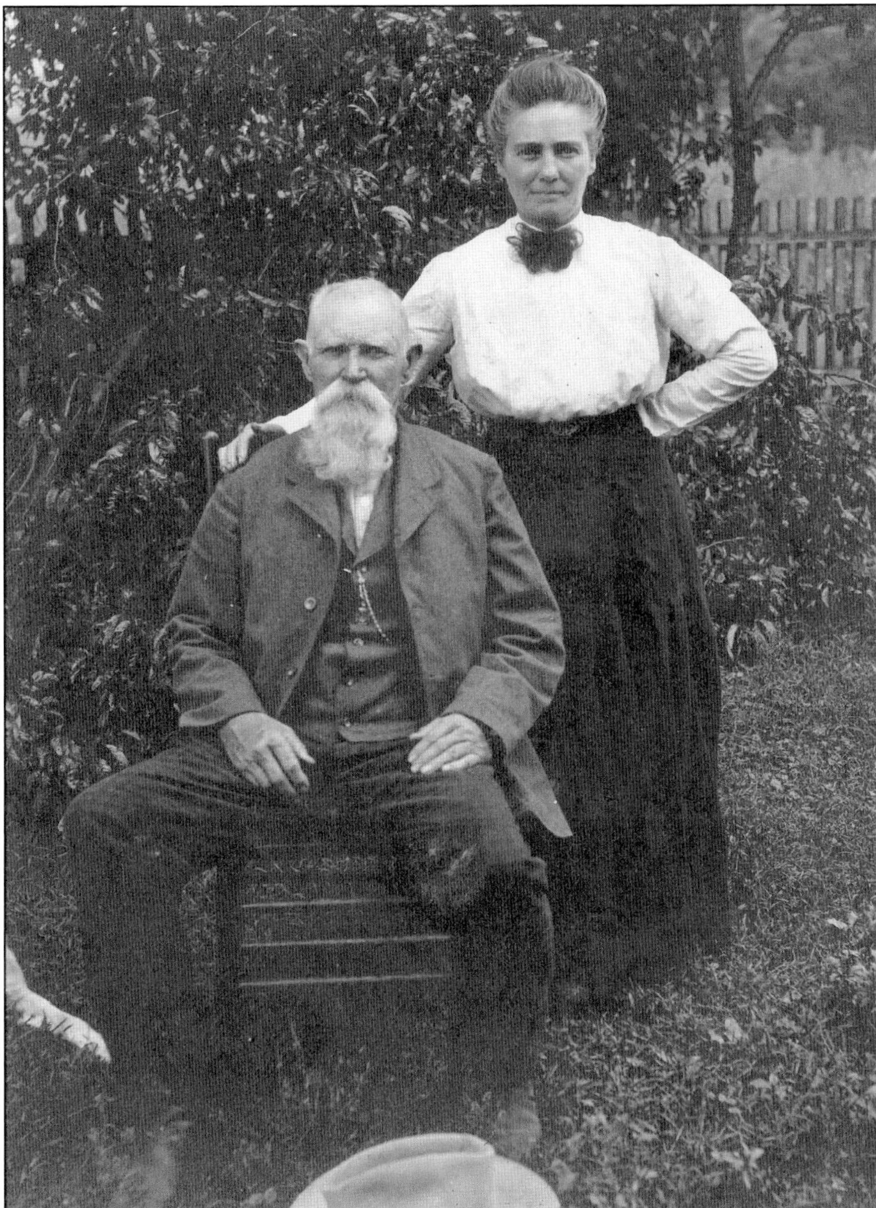

David Jasper Newton Ervin was educated at Washington College in Greene County and fought in the Civil War for the Union. After the war, he married Susan Catherine Jones, who came from a prominent Jonesborough family. According to Viola Ruth E. Swingle's book, *Ervin*, the wedding was an event of great interest in Vanderbilt (now Erwin), with the entire village turning out for the grand "infare" at the Wheelock Hotel. In 1876, Ervin donated 30 acres to Unicoi County for the establishment of a county seat. The name of the village was changed to "Ervin" in 1879 to honor Ervin's generosity. The passage of time has clouded the definitive reason why the town, initially named for Ervin, later took on the spelling of "Erwin." Some accounts refer to a mistake in a single letter by the post office. Others say the town took on the name of postmaster Jesse Erwin. Regardless of the name's evolution, D. J. N. Ervin was a key figure in the development of the town. (Courtesy of Margaret Swingle.)

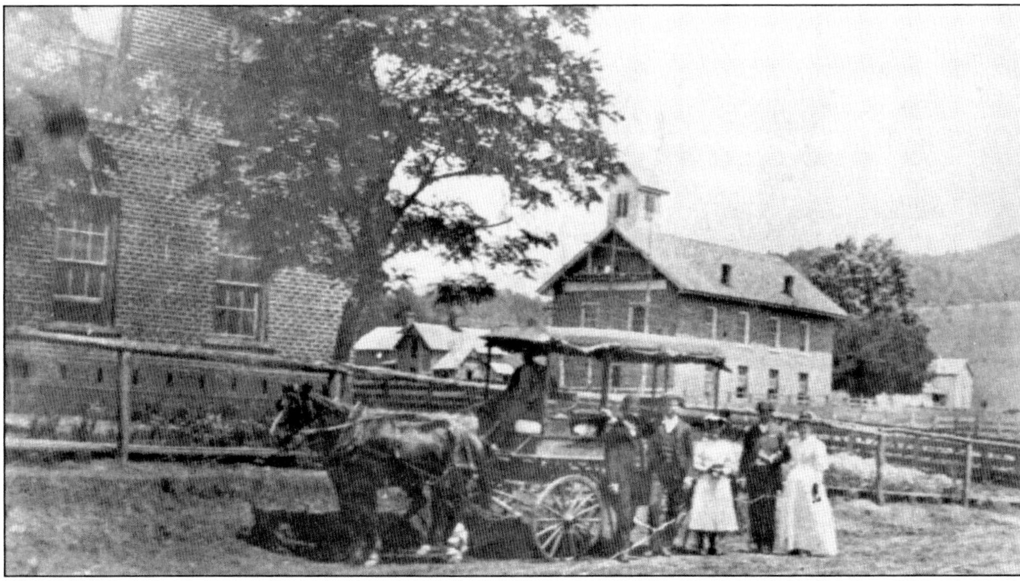

This charming 1892 wedding party chose to document the union with a photograph taken on present-day Gay Street adjacent to the first Unicoi County Courthouse. The June 6 edition of the *Erwin Magnet* reported, "Mr. N. T. Miller and Miss Ida Ray were united in marriage at the residence of the bride's uncle, Mr. Barney Ray, Reverend O. G. Jones officiating. Mr. Miller is a worthy young merchant of Limestone Cove and his bride is one of Erwin's most charming young ladies. May their lives be as bright as their wedding day." (Courtesy of Kent Garland/Judge Walter Garland collection.)

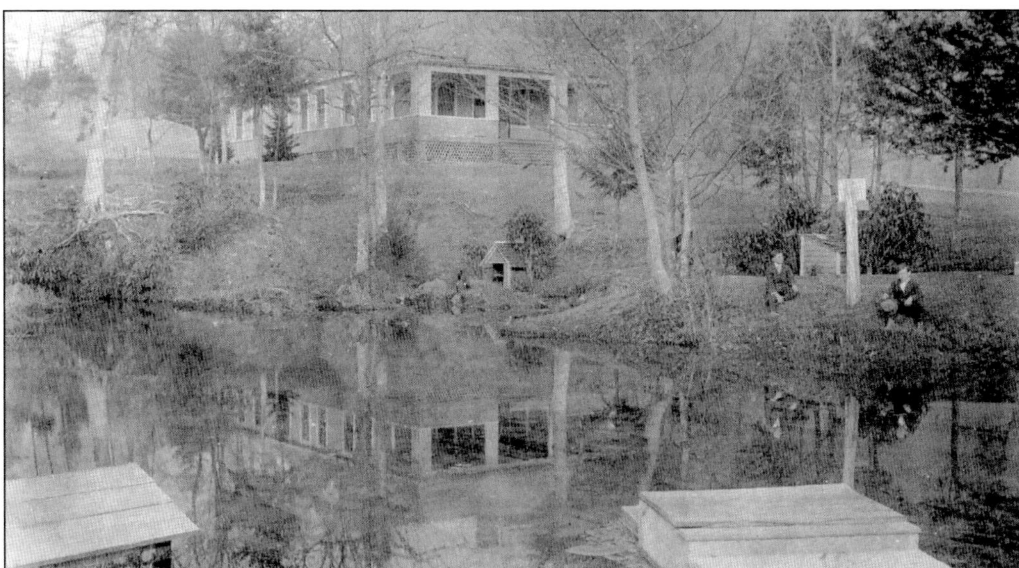

The 42-acre Erwin National Fish Hatchery was established in 1894. This view from the early 1900s shows the pristine nature of the ponds and an early residence on the grounds. The official hatchery superintendent's residence was built in 1903 and today houses the Unicoi County Heritage Museum. The Erwin Fish Hatchery currently produces 10 million disease-free eggs annually for federal, state, and tribal fish-management needs. (Courtesy of Martha Brown Stromberg/A. R. Brown collection.)

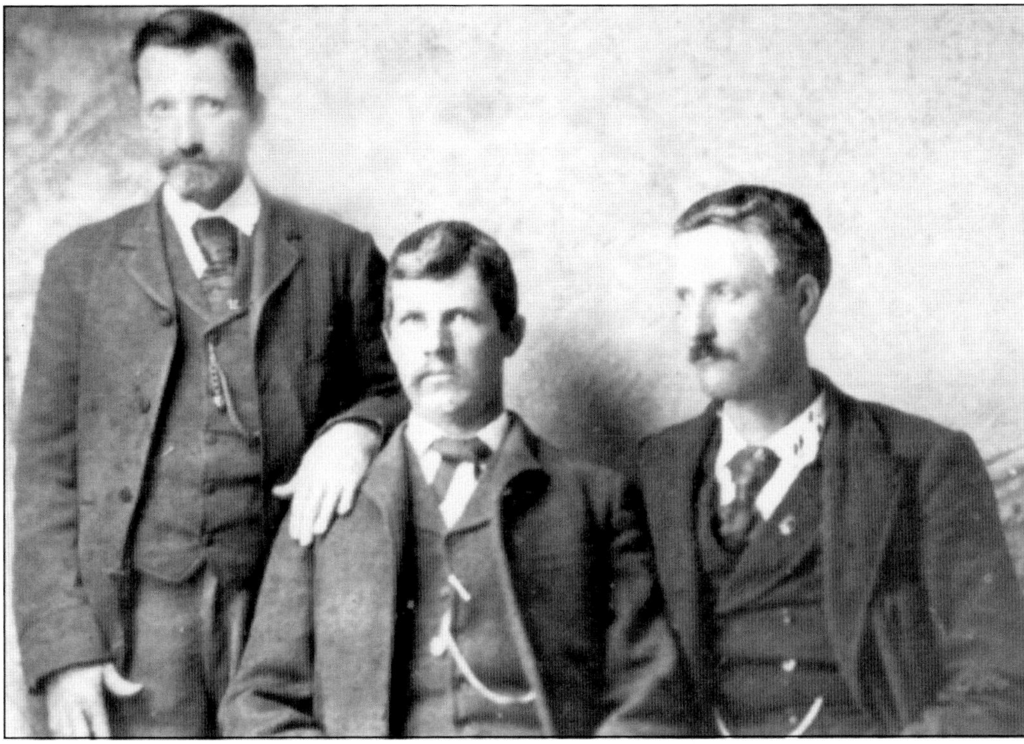

Shown from left to right, Dr. G. C. Williams, Dr. L. S. Tilson, and Dr. Harry Banner all practiced medicine in Unicoi County around 1900. These country doctors were a welcome sight on the dusty back roads, traveling on horseback with handy medical bags full of remedies and implements of the trade. (Courtesy of the Arnold Williams family.)

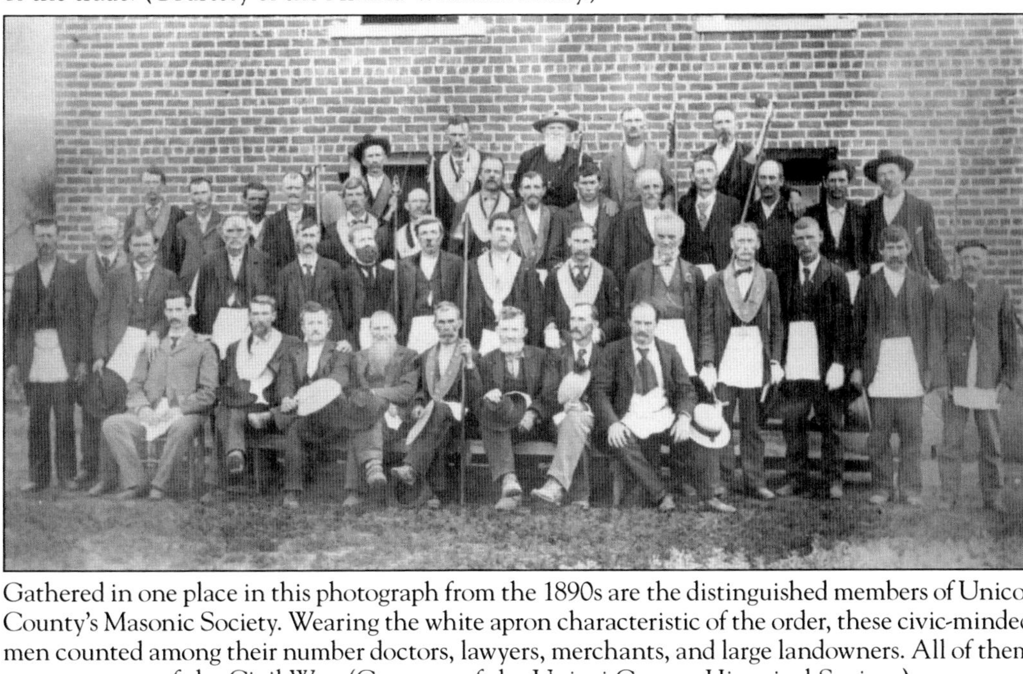

Gathered in one place in this photograph from the 1890s are the distinguished members of Unicoi County's Masonic Society. Wearing the white apron characteristic of the order, these civic-minded men counted among their number doctors, lawyers, merchants, and large landowners. All of them were veterans of the Civil War. (Courtesy of the Unicoi County Historical Society.)

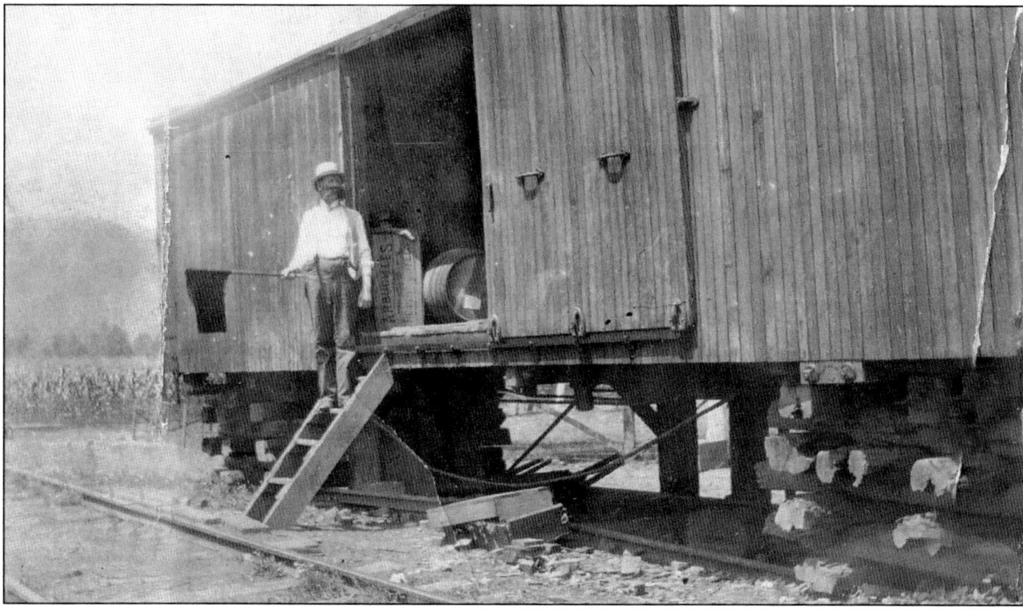

A very young Albert Rosecrans "A. R." Brown, with an admirable display of mutton chop whiskers, stands with flag at the ready on the ladder steps leading into this boxcar-on-timbers—the first official train depot in Erwin. Brown, pictured here about 1895 as the official depot agent, served his adopted hometown ably in many capacities, becoming one of the region's most prominent businessmen, as well as a distinguished state legislator and education advocate. The barrels seen in the doorway of the boxcar advertise "Arbuckle's Roasted Coffees." (Courtesy of Martha Brown Stromberg/A. R. Brown collection.)

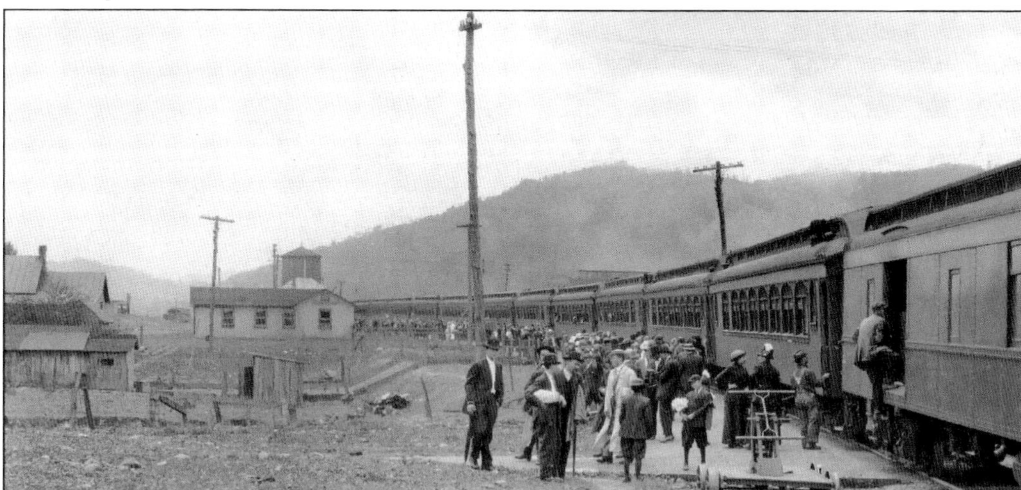

Passengers from Erwin get ready for an excursion to Altapass, North Carolina, about 1912. Two well-dressed matrons stand at right with hands on hips, presumably discussing the merits of their journey. A railroad worker loads the boxcar as a young lad cocks his head to one side to examine the camera. A dapper fellow in a slick straw hat strides confidently away from the train, the folds of his white duster catching the wind. To the left, a handsome young dandy, his bowler hat at a rakish angle, leans casually on the handle of his umbrella as he poses unselfconsciously for the photographer. (Courtesy of the Unicoi County Historical Society.)

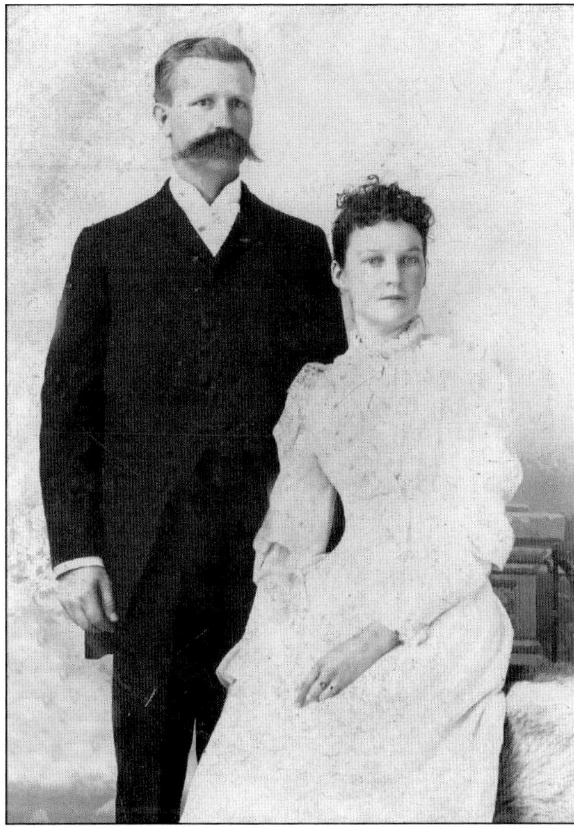

A. R. Brown was a traveling salesman in a horse-drawn wagon when he met his future bride, Tuppy Burleson, of Plum Tree, North Carolina. After their marriage in the 1890s, the young couple settled in Erwin, a town that Brown had traveled to many times in his sojourn as a drummer. Brown started a mercantile business that blossomed as the town grew. Brown is shown below perched on a steel girder of the new construction of what would become the landmark A. R. Brown Department Store. (Both images courtesy of Martha Brown Stromberg/ A. R. Brown collection.)

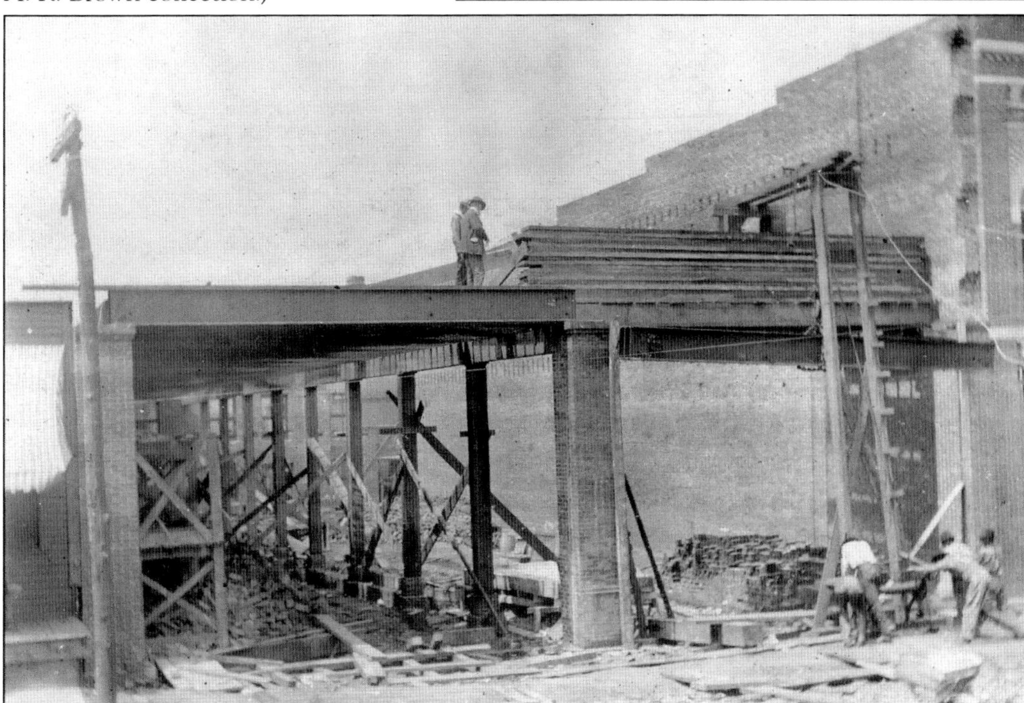

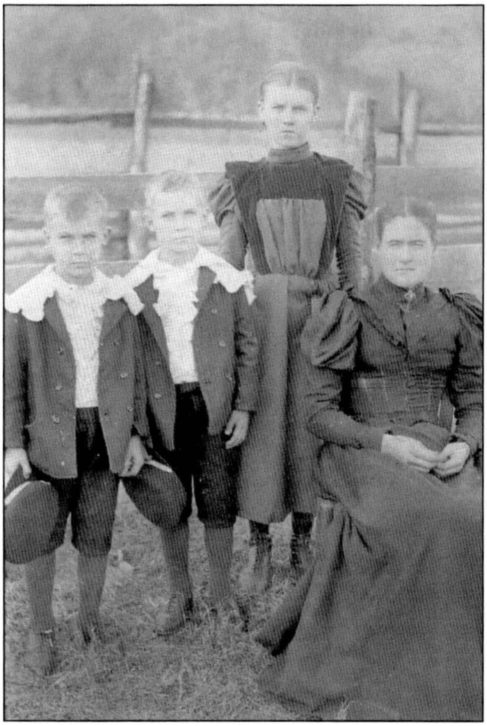

Mary Elizabeth "Mollie" Booth married James C. Davis in 1889. When James died in 1916, Mollie found herself in need of an income to feed her children. The enterprising Mrs. Davis then decided to open her Second Street home to boarders. Mollie Davis is shown about 1899 with her twin sons Wesley, at left, and Bob, at right, and daughter Pearl, in the center. (Courtesy of Juacquetta Davis Edwards.)

The rigid, formal composition of this John W. Price family portrait, *c.* 1908, shows Price at left; his daughter Edith and niece Enolia Lindsley flank the doorway. Annie Ryburn Price watches over her youngest, Albert, who is posed in the best settee, while grandmother Anne Feathers Price takes her place beside the healthy snowball bush at right. The elegant Price house, now gone, was located on Nolichucky Avenue. (Courtesy of Martha Brown Stromberg/A. R. Brown collection.)

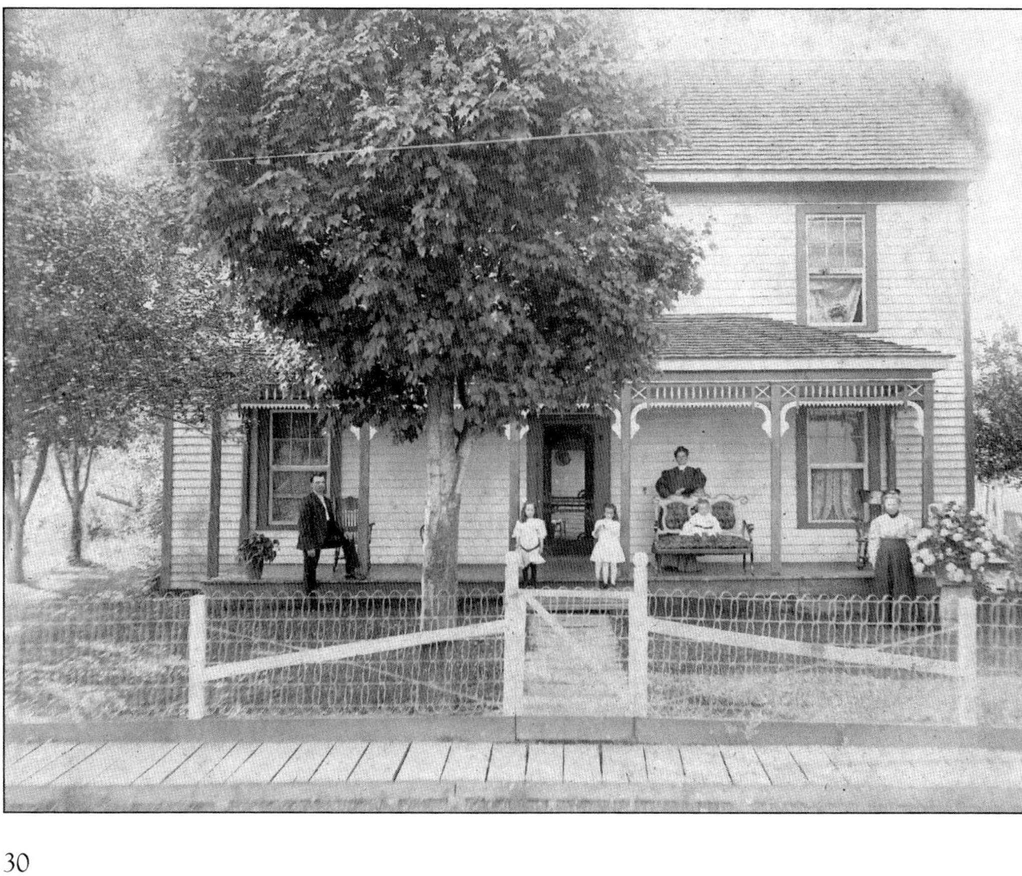

Sam Duncan, at left, worked as an engineer for the railroad in the early 1900s, settling with wife Lula and son Casey on Carolina Avenue. A devoted member of the First Baptist Church in Erwin, Duncan was also active in politics and business, serving a stint as a county magistrate and on the Unicoi County Board of Mayor and Aldermen. In later years, he owned Duncan Coal Company on Carolina Avenue. During hard times, Duncan generously supplied coal free of charge to those in need. Duncan's friend is unidentified. (Courtesy of Kathy Thornberry.)

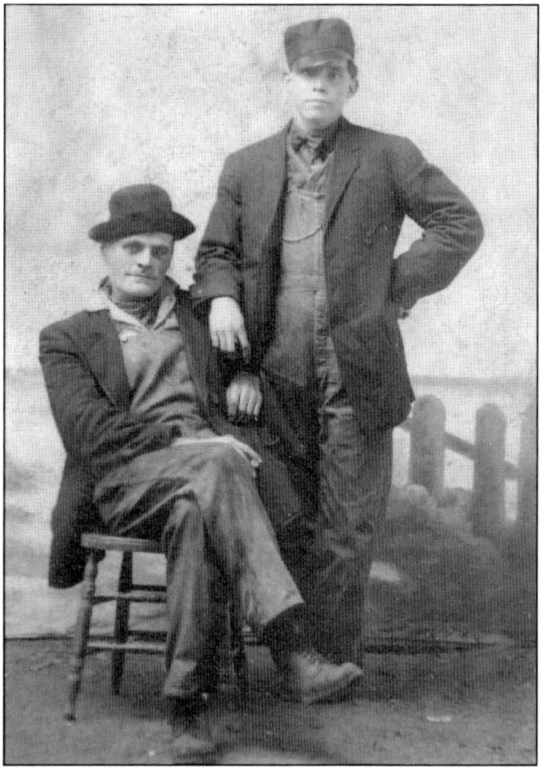

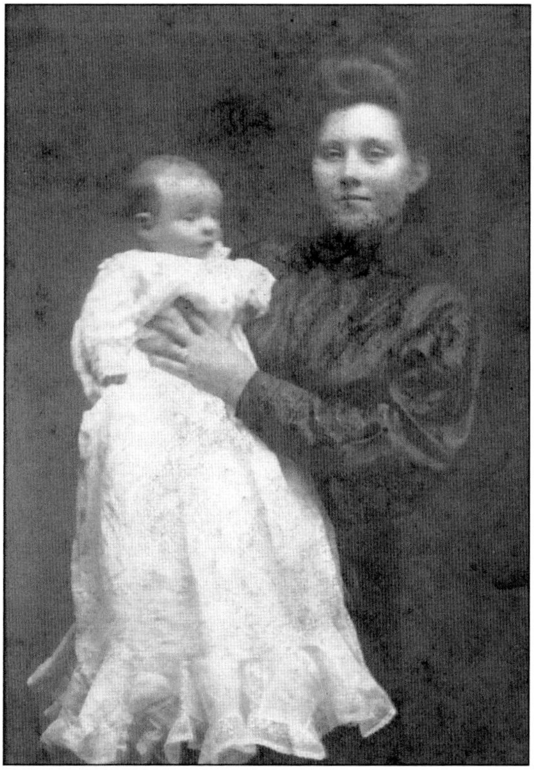

Lula Duncan cradles her son, Casey, in this lovely mother-and-child image from about 1907. Lula's religious devotion was marked by her fervent desire to see a church built for the Pentecostal Holiness community of Unicoi County. Her husband, Sam (above), fulfilled this wish by his instrumental influence in the construction of the Pentecostal rock church building on the corner of Carolina Avenue and Academy Street. (Courtesy of Kathy Thornberry.)

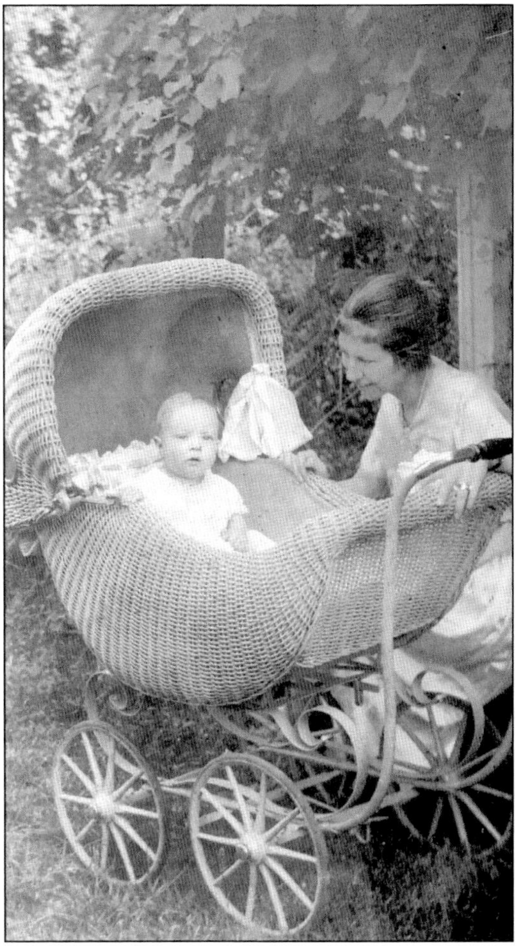

"Mother Booth's Baby Boy!" was the loving inscription and the only identification on this charming photograph from the early 1900s. The delicately ornate wicker perambulator and the vine-covered porch are reminiscent of the early 20th century, but the love shown by the radiant young mother for her angelic child is timeless. (Courtesy of the Juacquetta Davis Edwards.)

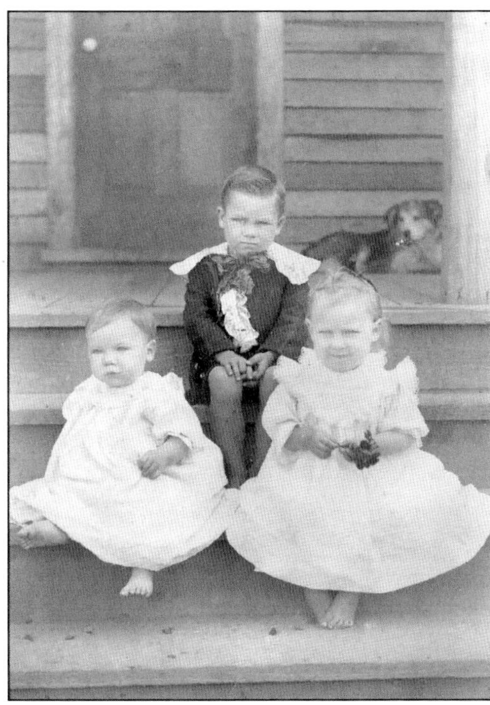

Cecil, Charlie (upper step), and Etta Davis are dressed for a special occasion in this photograph from about 1903. Dainty little Etta, who clutches a tiny sprig of blossoms, is obviously the only one of this trio comfortable in the ruffles and lace chosen by their mother for this formal portrait. Old Wheeler, the family dog, looks on with keen interest from his spot on the porch on Second Street. (Courtesy of Juacquetta Davis Edwards.)

Two

Boom Time and the New Century

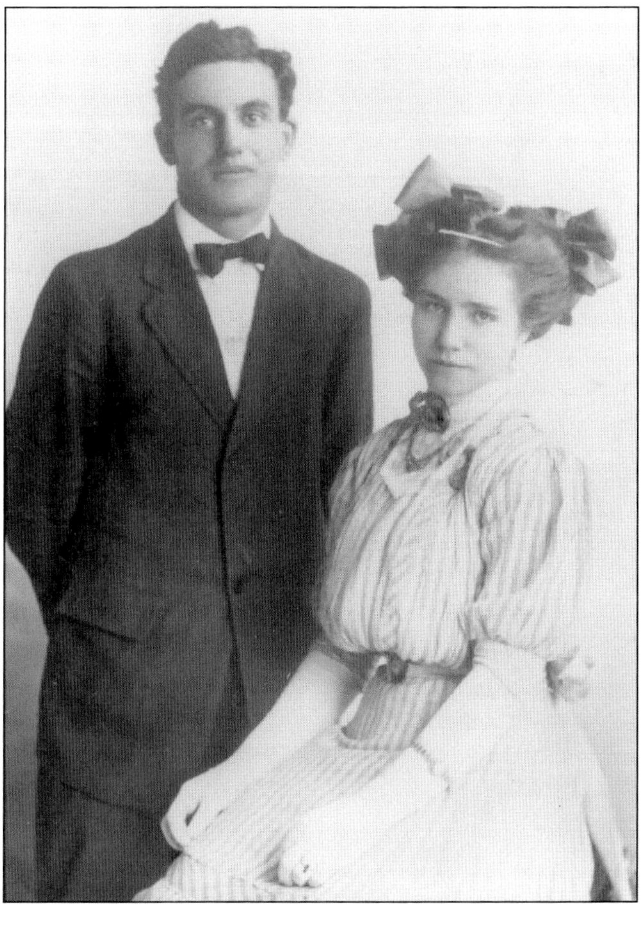

Wade H. Kegley and wife Ada Allen look very young on their wedding day in 1912. Ada, a native of Greene County, Tennessee, had moved with her family to Illinois at age six. After their marriage, the Kegleys returned to Tennessee and settled in Erwin. Since travel was difficult in those days and Wade and Ada eventually had 11 children to raise, Ada was never able to return to Illinois to see her parents again. Wade, a brick mason, soon found his talents in great demand for the fast-developing town of Erwin. The enterprising young man helped build the old city hall, the Erwin Post Office, the 1925 YMCA, and the 1929 Unicoi County High School. Also a trained violinist, Wade played hymns for his family and in church on Sunday, taught music, and was a violin accompanist for the silent movies shown at the Lyric Theater in town. (Courtesy of Marie Kegley Deyton.)

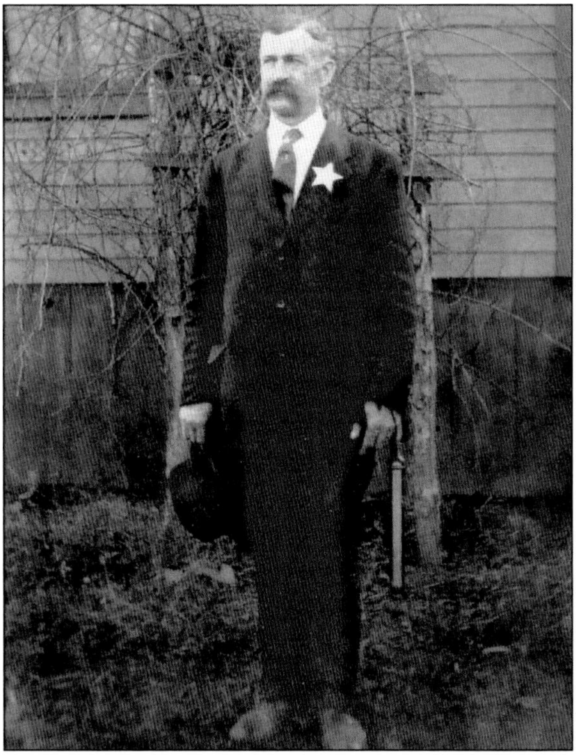

Daniel Calloway was the first marshal of the town of Erwin back in 1910, when livestock frequently roamed the dusty› streets of Erwin and when raucous Saturday night horse swaps often kept the marshal from a good night's sleep. Marshal Calloway was known for his diligence as a lawman and his unflappable ability to keep the peace. He was elected to the post several times. (Courtesy of Betty Cox.)

The occasion for this exuberant gathering of the citizenry in Erwin on Main Street was the anticipated political oration by gubernatorial candidate Ben W. Hooper one hot day in July 1910. Hooper was elected to two terms as governor of Tennessee. (Courtesy of the Unicoi County Historical Society.)

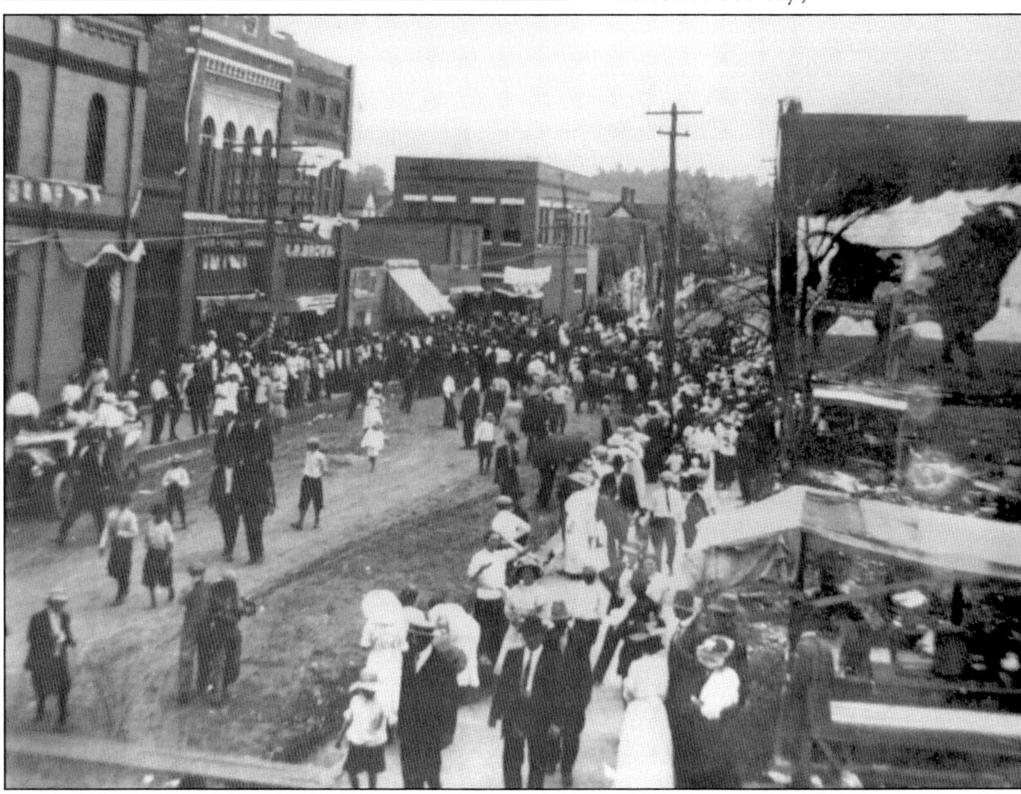

In 1910, Lula Rice came with her mother to Erwin from Yancey County, North Carolina, when the streets were still dirt and the sidewalks were made of planks. She married Bob Davis at age 16 and helped run a boardinghouse for railroad workers. She bore seven children, two of whom died in infancy. A third died of strep throat in 1937. Lula lived to be 87 and is buried in Jobe Cemetery, surrounded by her beloved children. (Courtesy of Juacquetta Davis Edwards.)

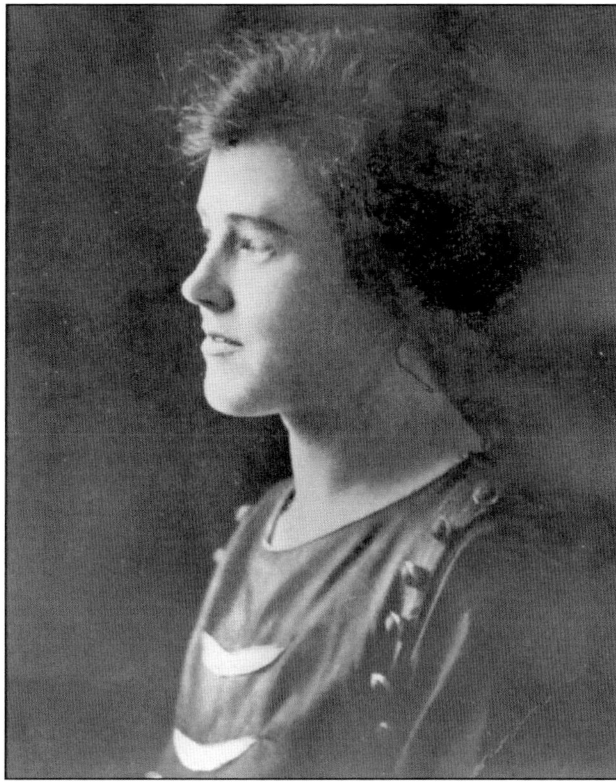

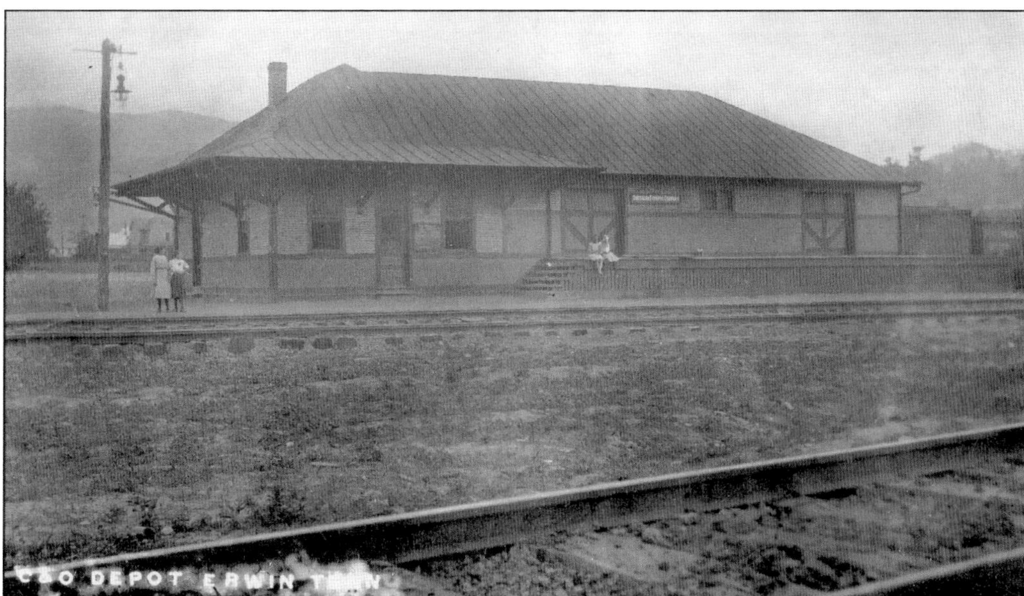

Built in 1913, this low-slung frame building was the first train depot in Unicoi County to comfortably accommodate the traveling public of the Clinchfield Railway, succeeding the county's first boxcar depot. In this vintage postcard, two girls, about age 10, look to their left where they have spotted two younger girls sitting on the freight platform playing with a cat. (Courtesy of Martha Brown Stromberg/A. R. Brown collection.)

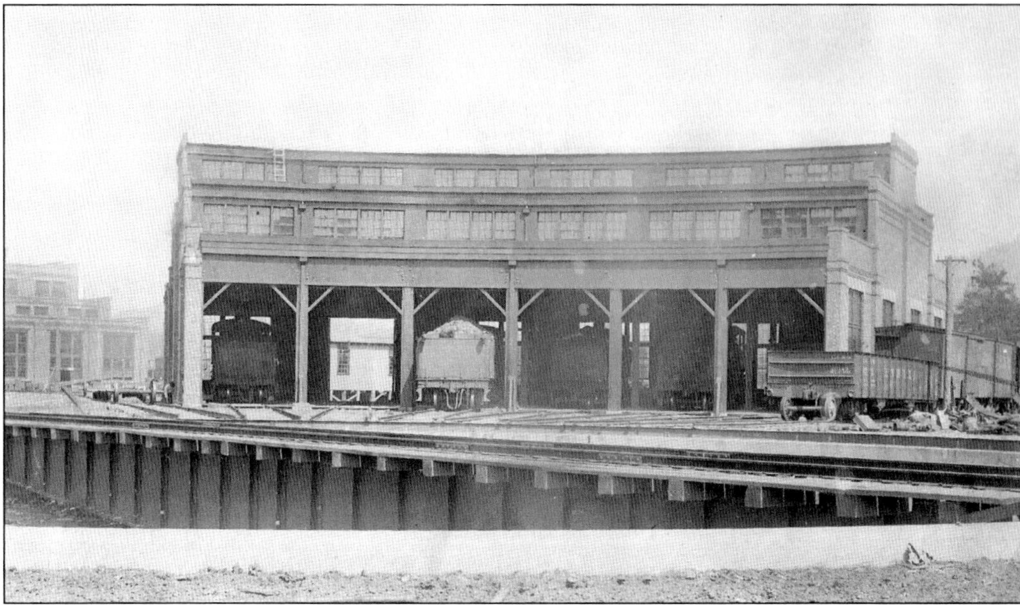

The railroad roundhouse offered an efficient method by which to service the Clinchfield's diverse rolling stock. In this photograph from the early 1900s, a locomotive is in the first bay, loaded freight cars are in the third and fourth bays, and another locomotive is in the last bay to the right. The intricacy of the track system can be seen in the foreground. (Courtesy of Martha Brown Stromberg/A. R. Brown collection.)

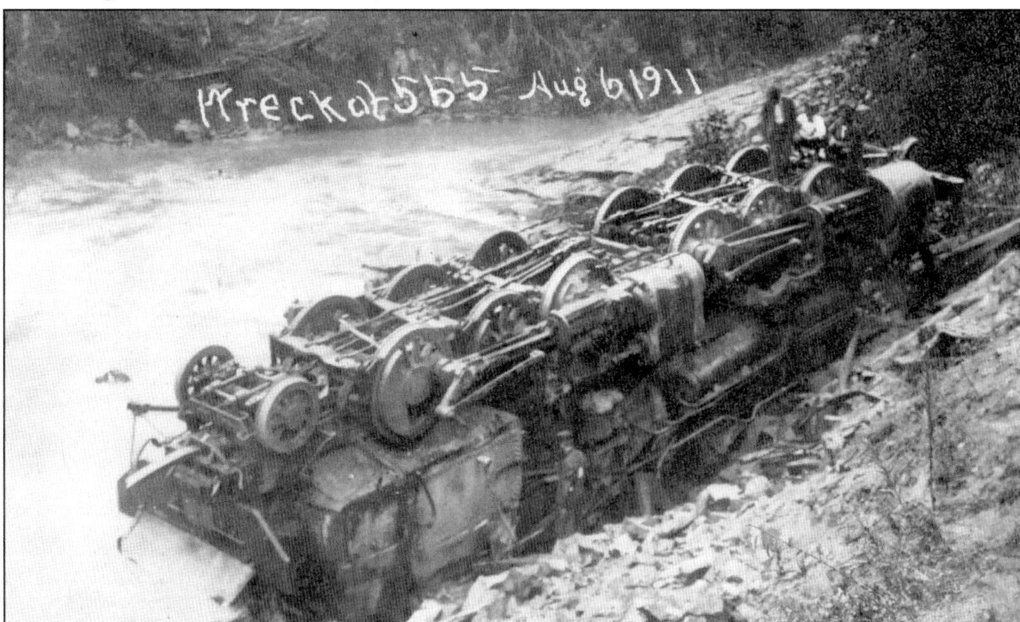

August 6, 1911, was the date that the old Clinchfield No. 555 met its fate, tumbling upside down into the waters of the Nolichucky River. With the train tracks running along the base of the perilous Nolichucky Gorge, the rugged chasm claimed many lives, locomotives, and heavy freight. Clinchfield Railroad men can be seen checking the damage to the No. 555. (Courtesy of Violet Kelley.)

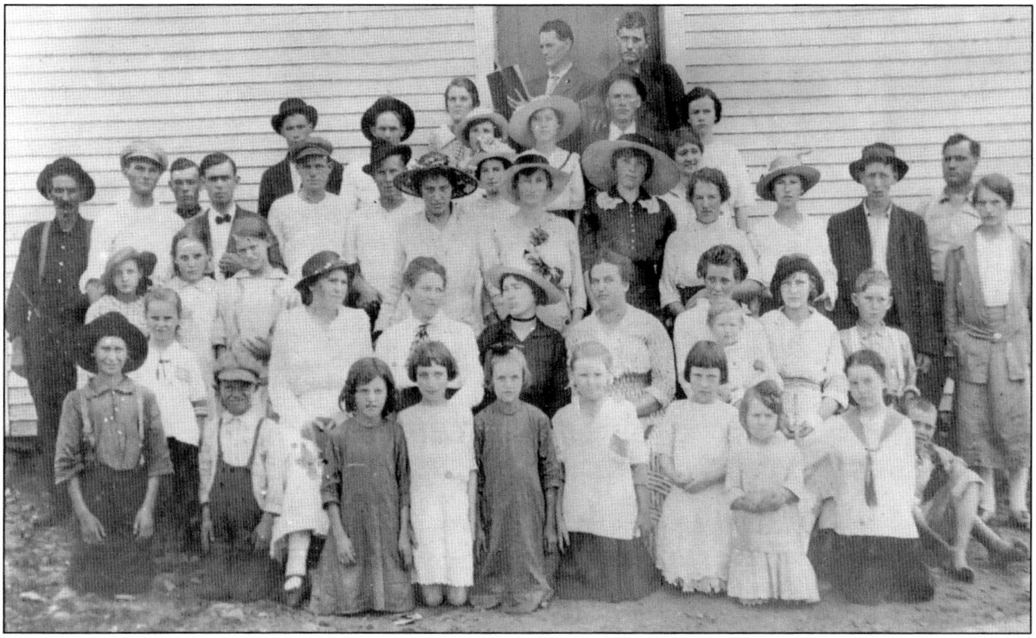

These members of the Rock Creek Singing School, shown about 1914, would have been familiar with shape-note singing—an a capella performance without the accompaniment of a musical instrument. Singers relied on sight-reading geometrically shaped note-heads from such sacred hymn songbooks as *The New Harp of Columbia— 1846–67.* The Rock Creek Singing School was led by Dock Davis, the gentleman in the fifth row at the doorway perusing the dog-eared songbook. (Courtesy of F. B. White.)

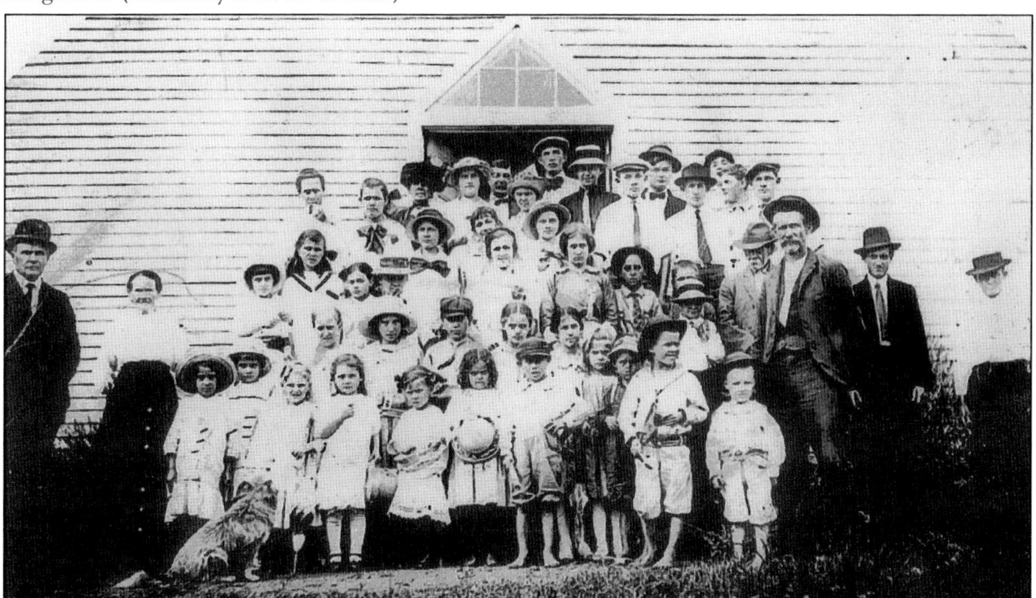

Fishery Community Church was organized in 1906 as a nondenominational congregation. The land adjacent to the Erwin Fish Hatchery was donated by Robert Tapp and his nephew Thomas with the stipulation that the building be used as a house of worship, a school, or for any other purpose for the "upbuilding of the community." (Courtesy of F. B. White.)

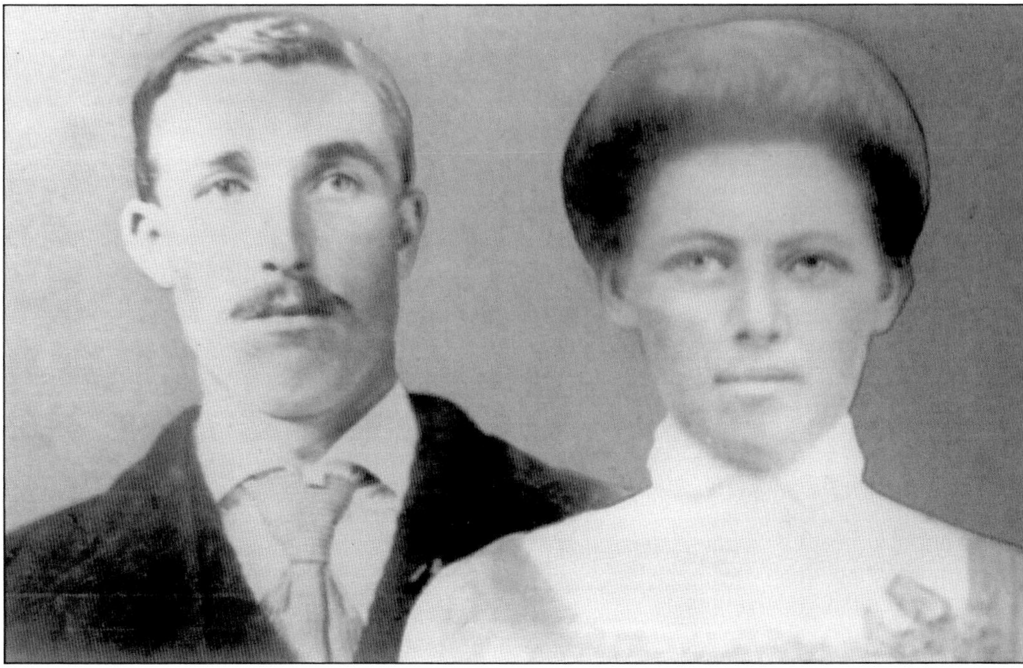

Isaac "Ike" Banner and Julia Tapp wed in 1899. Julia died in 1914. Left with seven children, Ike turned to his parents, Matt and Mollie Banner, for help and then followed a love of tinkering to a job opportunity at Thomas Edison's lab in New Jersey. When the independent-minded Ike found that Edison's "muckers" could not lay claim to their own inventions, he returned to Erwin, where he put his talents to work as a furniture-maker, among other vocations. (Courtesy of Arnold and Sylvia Banner.)

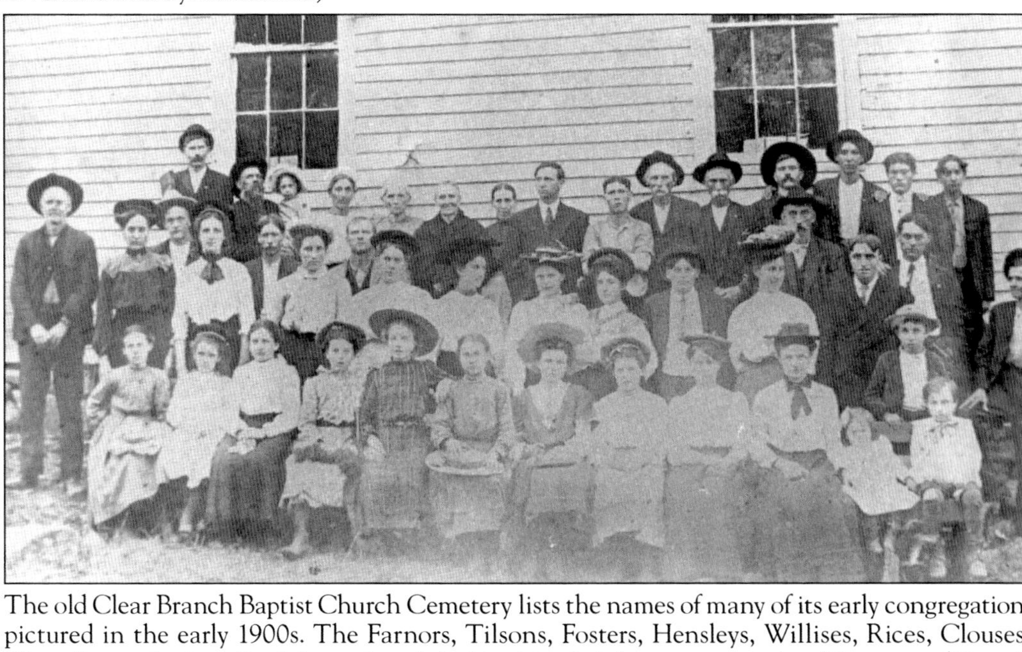

The old Clear Branch Baptist Church Cemetery lists the names of many of its early congregation, pictured in the early 1900s. The Farnors, Tilsons, Fosters, Hensleys, Willises, Rices, Clouses, Chandlers and others lived, farmed, and died in this, their home community. (Courtesy of Dennis and Lillian Foster/Jakie Farnor collection.)

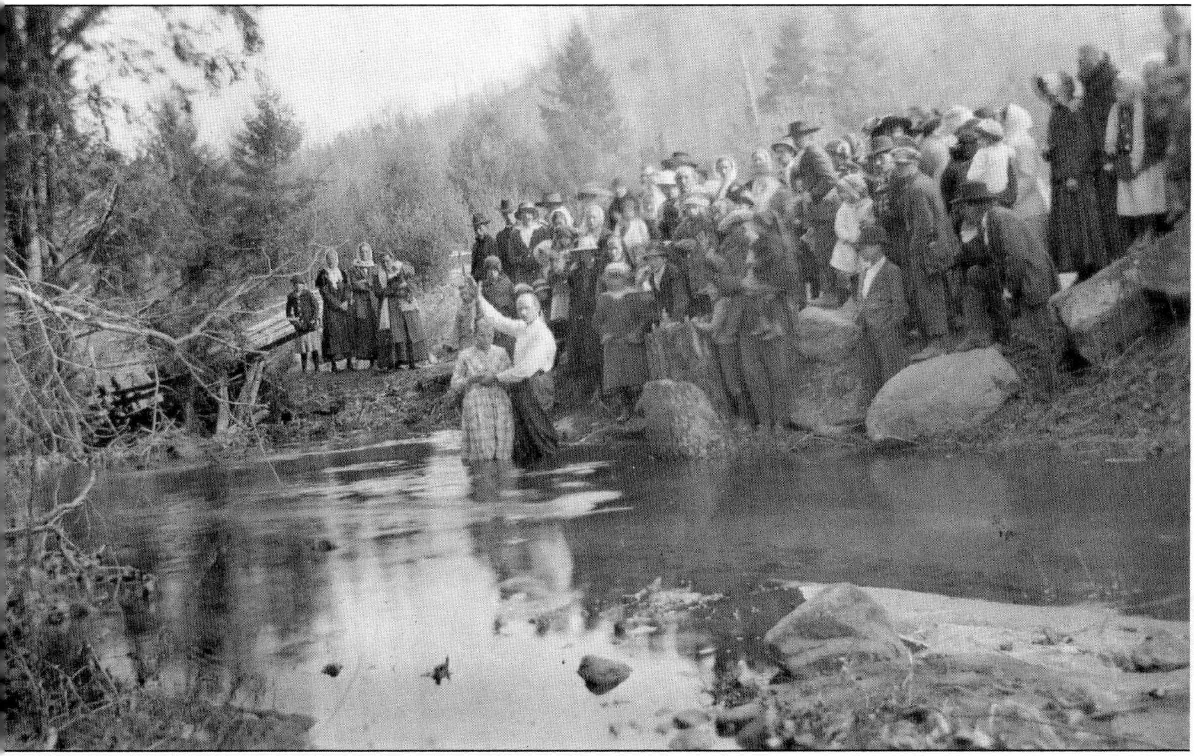

This solemn scene from about 1910 records the baptism of a young girl in the icy creek waters near Clear Branch Baptist Church. The congregation, dressed in the jackets and woolen scarves of late winter or early spring, look on from the creek bank. Standing in the frigid water, the young woman waits, hands clasped in prayer, for the benediction of her pastor and her moment of salvation. (Courtesy of Dennis and Lillian Foster/Jakie Farnor collection.)

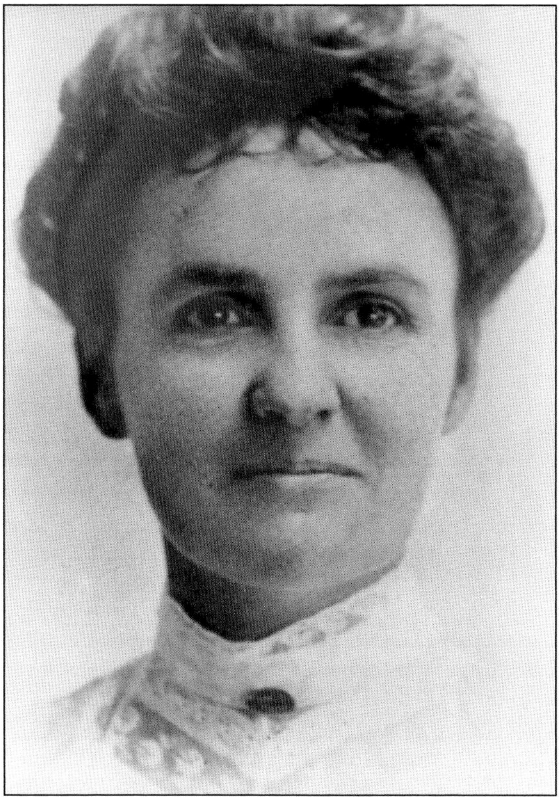

Jennie Moore, a native Tennessean, spent most of her adult life working for the Rocky Fork Community in the mountains of southern Unicoi County under the auspices of the Presbyterian Mission Board. Her mission school was a godsend to this remote mountain community, providing much needed education to local children, a church meetinghouse, a medical dispensary, and a library, as well as food and clothing for families in hard times. Two hundred sixty-three of "Miss Jennie's" pupils went on to college, with 43 of them becoming teachers. Frank Gentry Sr., who later served as the superintendent of Unicoi County Schools, became the first of Miss Jennie's Rocky Fork students to receive a college degree. Moore died in Birmingham, Alabama, on December 14, 1950, where she had retired to live with her sister. The old mission is now called the Jennie Moore Memorial Church in her honor. (Both images courtesy of the Unicoi County Historical Society.)

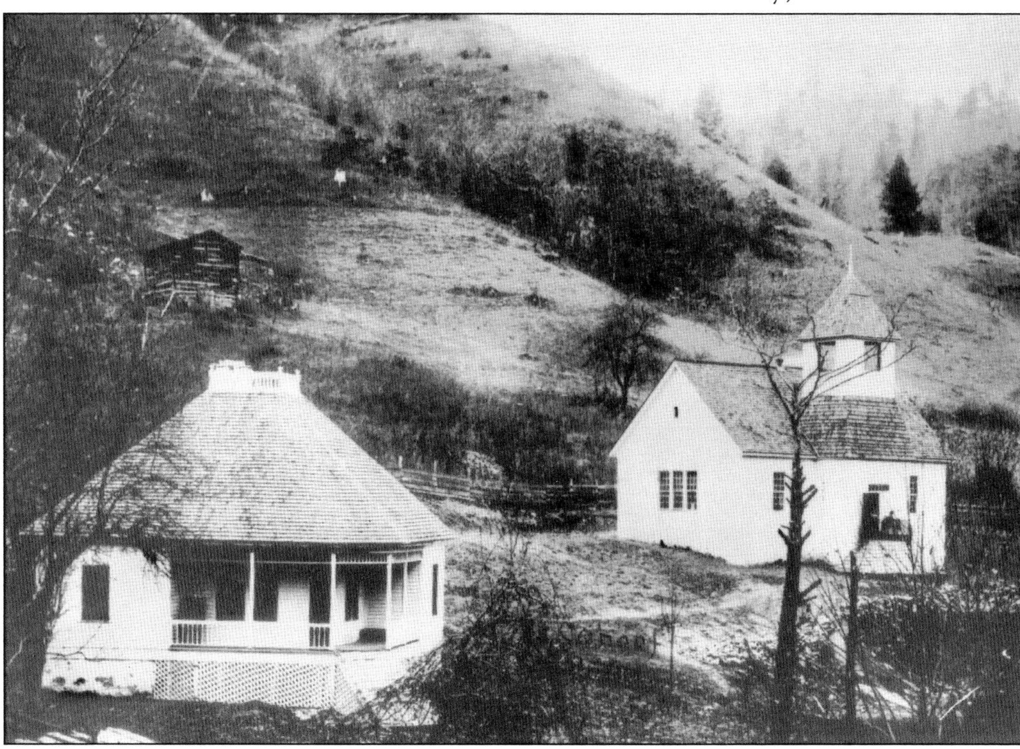

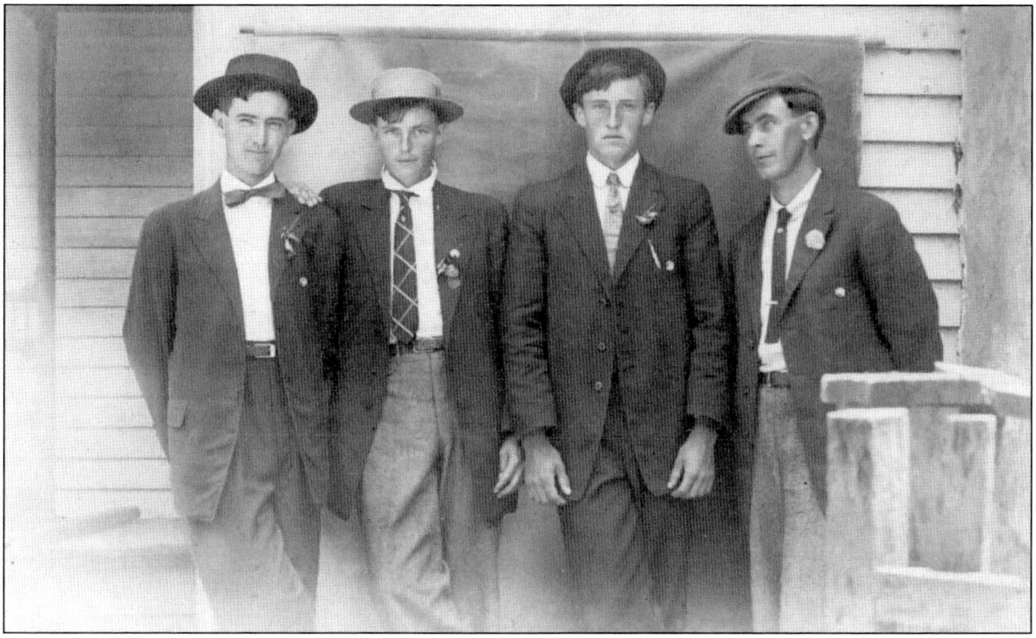

Decked out in their "courting best," these dapper Unicoi County youths pause for a brief moment in their young lives to have their picture snapped around 1915. Pictured from left to right are Bill Clouse, Berry Runion, Carl Metcalf, and Arlee Runion. (Courtesy of Christine Christy Tipton.)

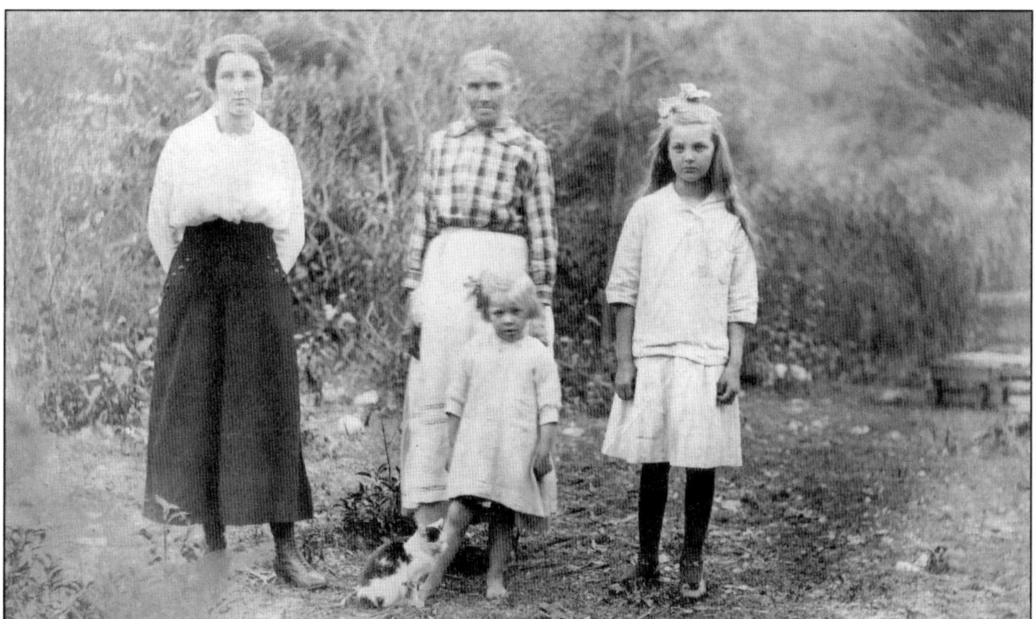

Mollie Crosswhite Banner, center, and her husband, Matt Banner, took in thier son Isaac's children when his wife, Julia, died in 1914. Shown about 1917, from left to right are Olga, the eldest; Charlotte, the youngest; and Mamie. Their brothers were Kelly, Orville, Ralph, and Harry. (Courtesy of Lucille Hensley Booth.)

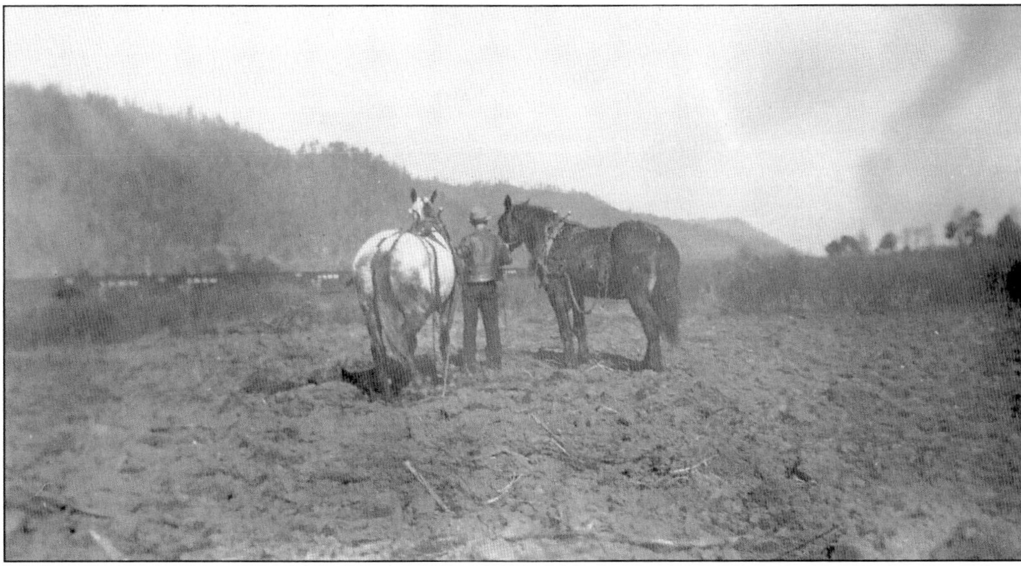

Bob Davis stands with his back to the camera about 1915, reining in his brace of workhorses in the farm fields his family owned between Main Street and the Clinchfield Railroad tracks. Just out of sight, to Davis's left, the bustling town of Erwin was making fast progress toward his Second Street home. In the background, a Clinchfield train can be seen making its way home to the train yard. (Courtesy of Juacquetta Davis Edwards.)

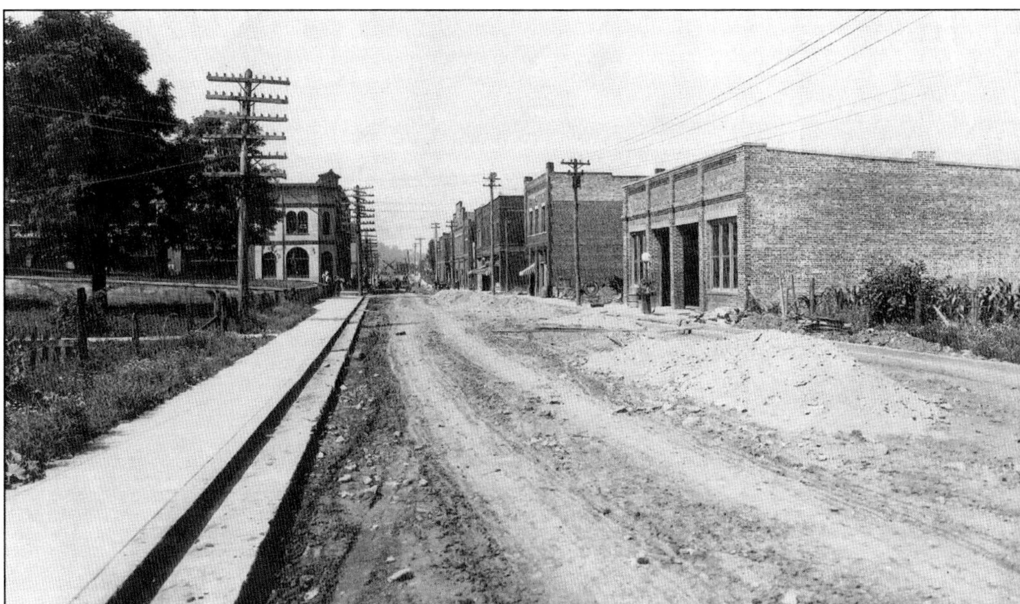

In this view from about 1917, the only gas pump available to the few existent Unicoi County automobiles can be seen in front of the brick motor garage located on the still-unpaved Main Street of downtown Erwin. Fortunately, that same year, the always dusty—and occasionally muddy—ankle-deep ruts were finally paved over. The concrete sidewalks were already in place. (Courtesy of James A. Goforth.)

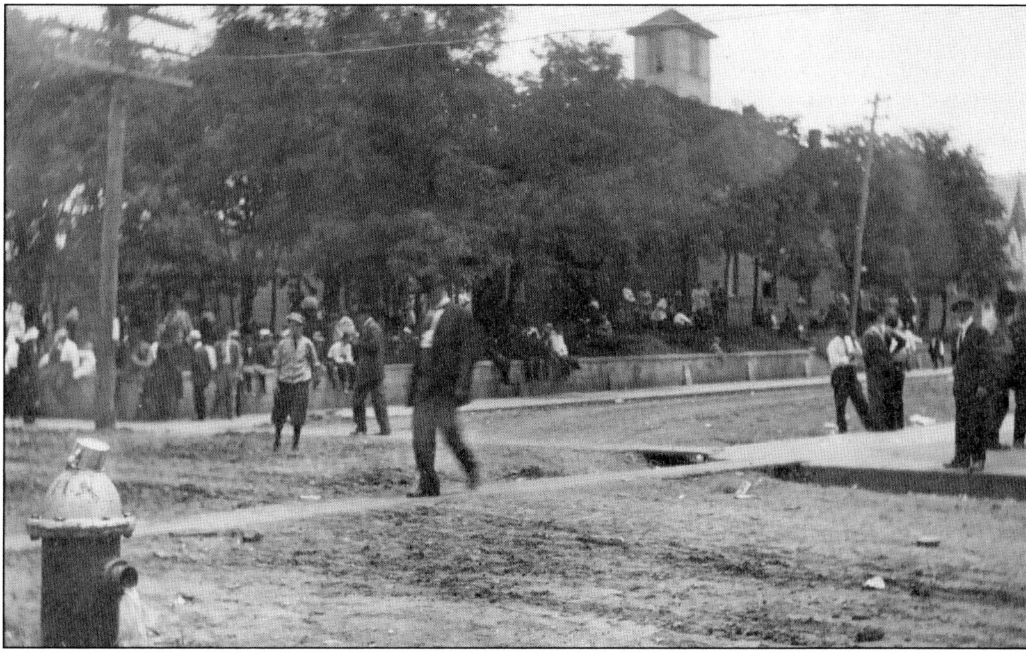

In this downtown view, the free-flowing hydrant shown in the foreground demonstrates the rapid progress making its way into the fast-growing town of Erwin during the first decade of the 20th century. Note the community cup on top of the water hydrant. Below is the source of that free-flowing water. Enterprising local businessman A. R. Brown saw the need for a reliable, centrally distributed system of clean drinking water in the town of Erwin. His solution was to harness the water from O'Brien Springs in the Hulen Hollow area just north of Gay Street. This photograph documents the "first ditch" dug for Brown's water company. A family anecdote recounts the time one of Erwin's matrons angrily confronted Brown with her bill for water, saying, "How can you charge people for what God gives you for free?" The always-diplomatic Brown replied that he was not charging her for the water, just the transportation. (Both images courtesyof Martha Brown Stromberg/A. R. Brown collection.)

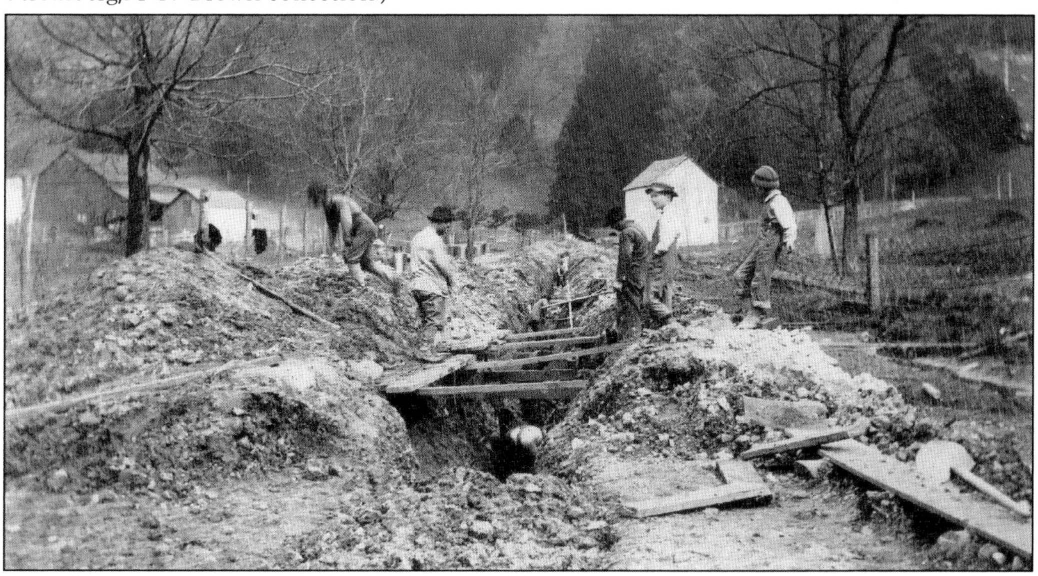

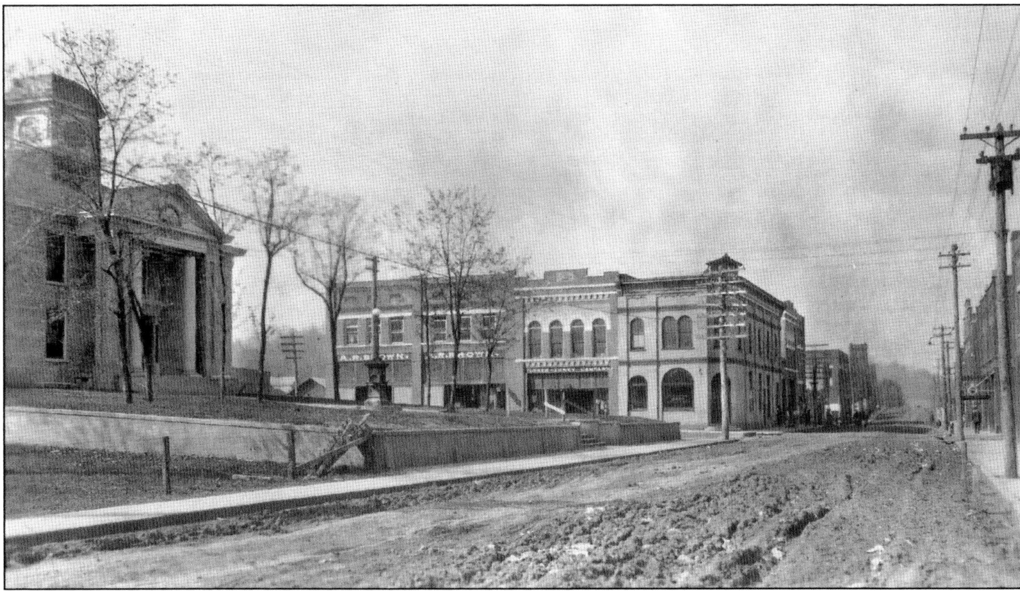

The A. R. Brown Department Store and the Tucker-Toney Mercantile, seen in the center of this pre-1917 photograph, were two of Erwin's most prominent and popular businesses. The building, which faces the corner of Main and Gay Streets, housed the First State Bank, which failed in the stock market crash of 1929. Today that building is home to the Unicoi County Chamber of Commerce. To the left stands the landmark Unicoi County Courthouse with its distinctive bun-shaped cupola. (Courtesy of Pat Lynch.)

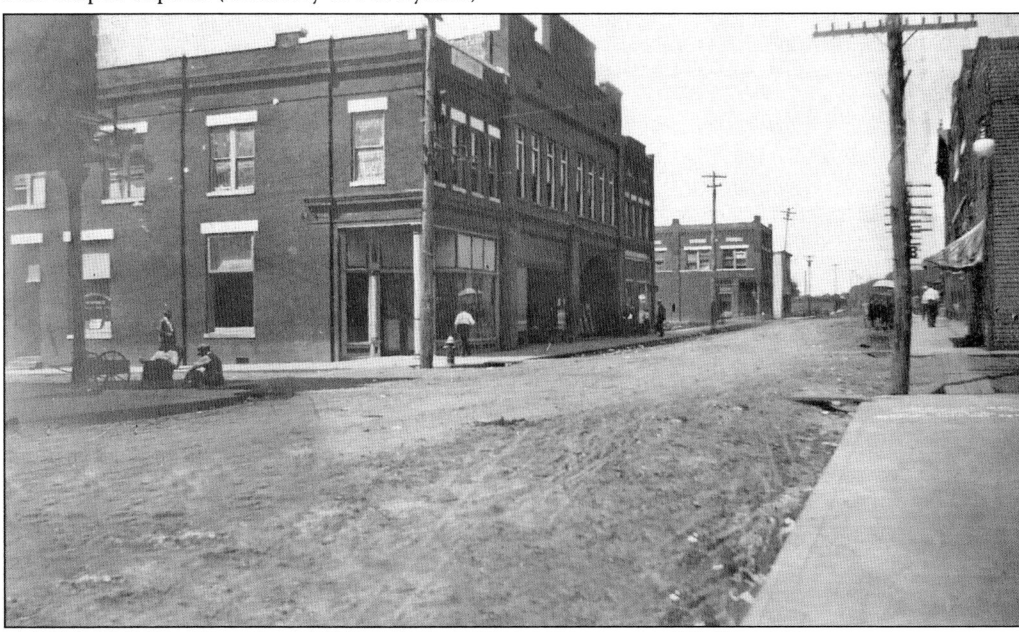

This c. 1900 view of downtown Erwin looks north on Main Street from the intersection of Main and Union Streets. The early Bank of Erwin can be seen in the center on the north corner. The building with the step-roof facade, which became Ewald's and later the Unaka Store, is adjacent to the bank. By 1910, new construction had filled the block to the next corner at Gay Street. (Courtesy of Martha Brown Stromberg/A. R. Brown collection.)

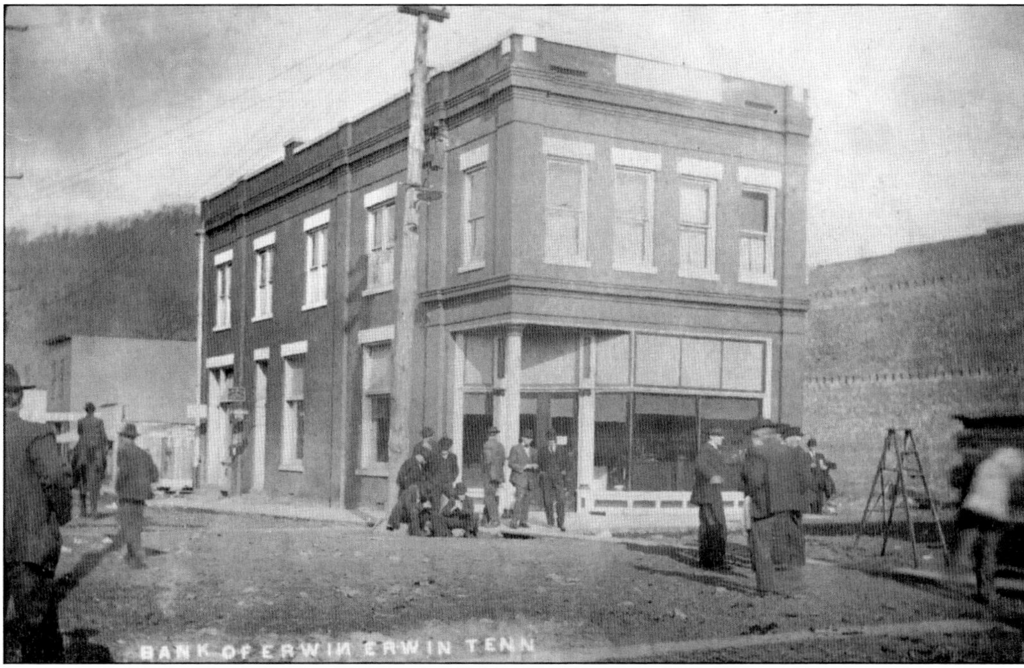

The Bank of Erwin was located on the north corner of Main and Union Streets in the early 1900s. Damaged by the 1927 fire at neighboring Ewald's Department Store, the bank was rebuilt on the same spot, renamed Erwin National Bank, and constructed on more fire-resistant limestone. Note the gentleman on horseback making his way down a very dusty, unpaved Union Street. (Courtesy of Martha Brown Stromberg/A. R. Brown collection.)

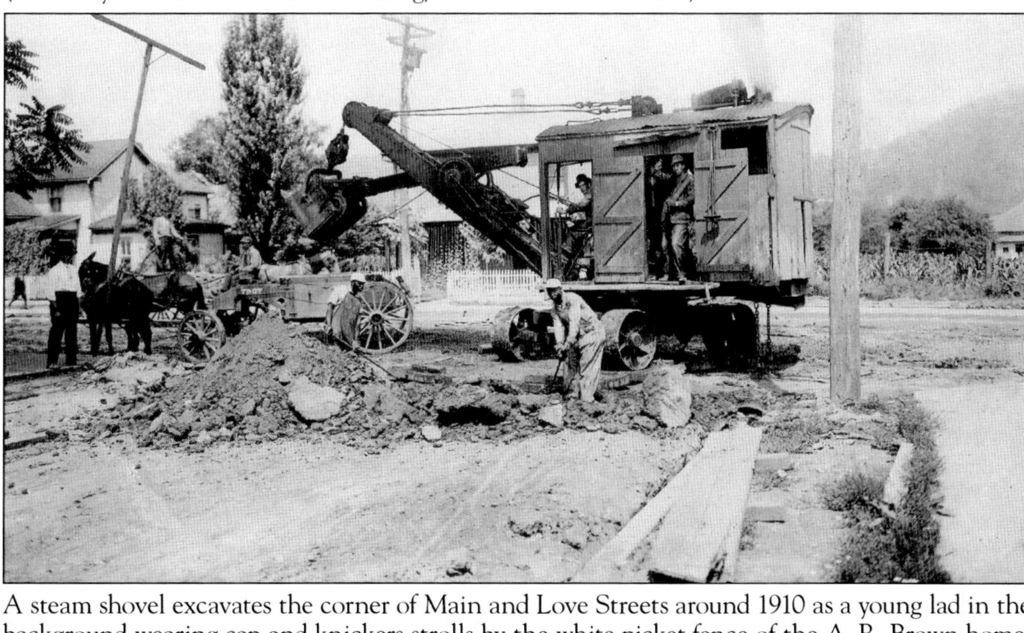

A steam shovel excavates the corner of Main and Love Streets around 1910 as a young lad in the background wearing cap and knickers strolls by the white picket fence of the A. R. Brown home. In addition to the new and often noisy vehicles of the day, Erwin's early dusty, unpaved streets still carried horse-drawn traffic as well. A livery stable was situated in downtown Erwin on the corner of Gay and Elm Streets as late as 1919. (Courtesy of the Unicoi County Historical Society.)

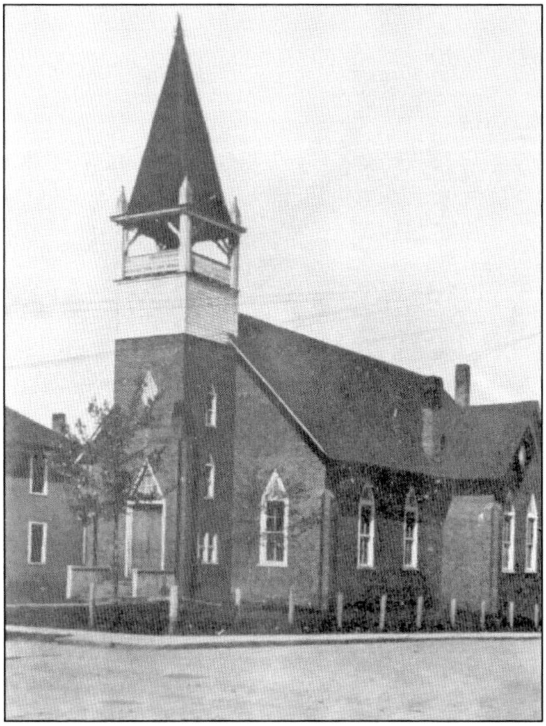

In 1888, the first house of worship for the members of the Christian Church in Unicoi County was a log building located near the Martin's Creek cemetery in the southern part of the county. Around 1893, the current church building was erected on South Main Street to house the growing congregation. The early, open-work design of the steeple, shown here about 1910, was later changed to a closed Colonial-style design when the church was refurbished in the 1950s. (Courtesy of the Arnold Williams family.)

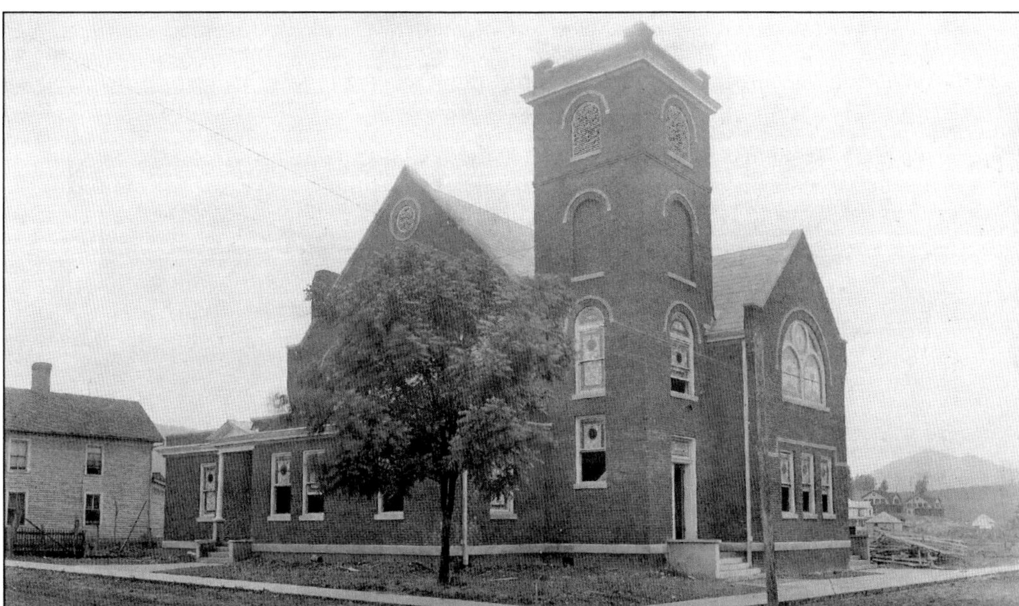

Chartered in 1822 as Indian Creek Baptist Church, the First Baptist Church in Erwin is the oldest in the county. The original log cabin church was used for the first county court session. By 1892, a frame church was built on the corner of Tucker and Church Streets. The current church, shown under construction in the early 1900s, is located on the corner of Main and Love Streets. A. R. Brown offered this lot to the Baptists in exchange for theirs on Church Street. (Courtesy of James A. Goforth.)

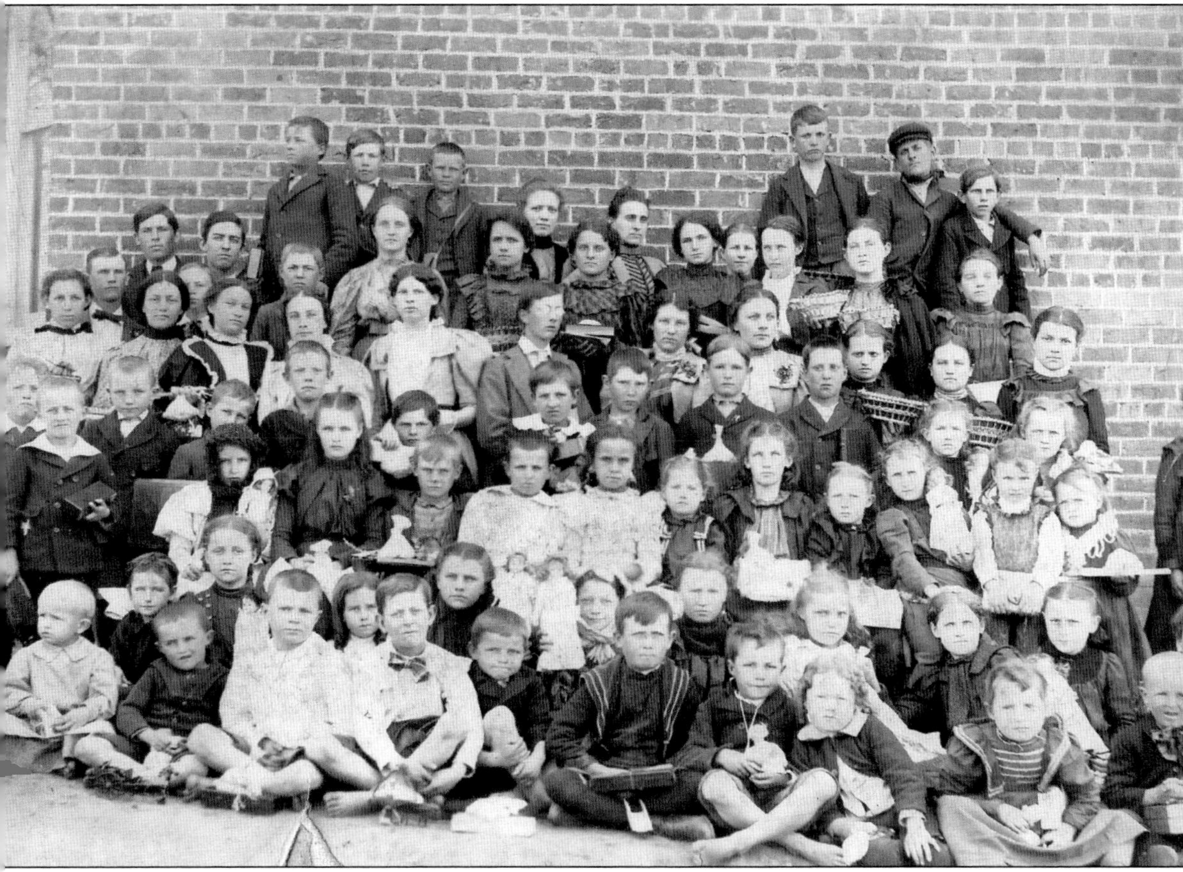

The reason for this healthy assemblage of young people outside the First Baptist Church on Main and Love Streets in the early 1900s is unknown. However, it must be a special day because each child is displaying a treasured toy. Some of the children in attendance were Walter Brown, Jake Burleson, Ben Bogart, Gertrude Tucker, Allie Huskins, Nita Erwin, Glennie Davis, Effie Ray, Pendleton Ray, Etta Ray, Salla Davis, Jesse Toney, Bell Erwin, Annie Capps, Lummie Davis, Bessie White, Ella Brown, Flecha Pippin, Herman Erwin, Neta Norris, Walter Ryburn, Cora Marklin, Ibbie Pope, Zella Davis, Fannie White, and Lynn Toney. Notice the barefoot boys. (Courtesy of Martha Brown Stromberg/A. R. Brown collection.)

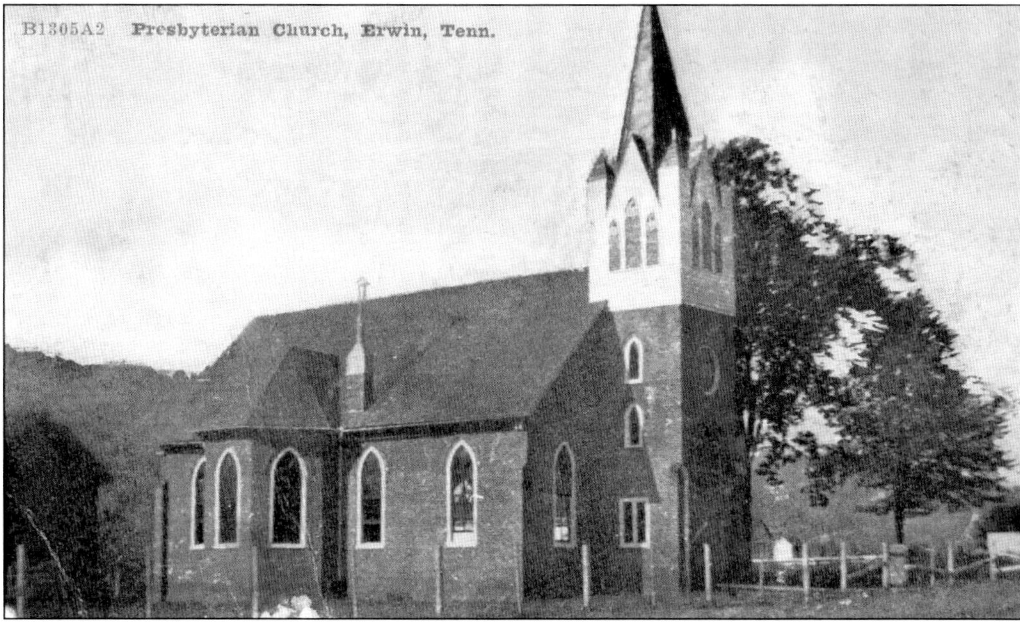

Tusculum College student Oliver G. Jones, under the direction of the Presbyterian Mission Board, was instrumental in the organization of the very first Presbyterian church in Erwin in 1891. The handsome brick edifice, with its distinctive, gabled steeple, was built in 1894 on Elm Street, just a block from downtown Erwin and was taken down in 1927 to make way for the current, magnificent Erwin Presbyterian Church, shown on page 83. (Courtesy of Martha Brown Stromberg/A. R. Brown collection.)

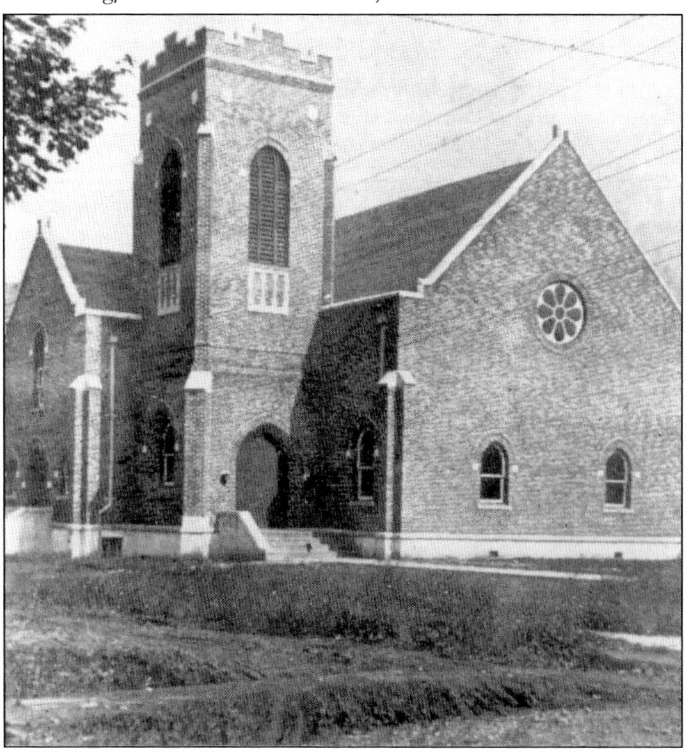

Circuit-riding ministers were visiting faithful Methodists in what became Unicoi County as early as 1858. Around 1885, Rev. J. W. Perry was assigned by the Holston Conference to a post in Erwin, and a more organized Methodist congregation then began holding services in the Masonic lodge behind the courthouse. After the initial frame church building on Tucker Street could no longer accommodate the growing congregation, a more refined brick sanctuary was built in 1920 on Elm Street. (Courtesy of the Arnold Williams family.)

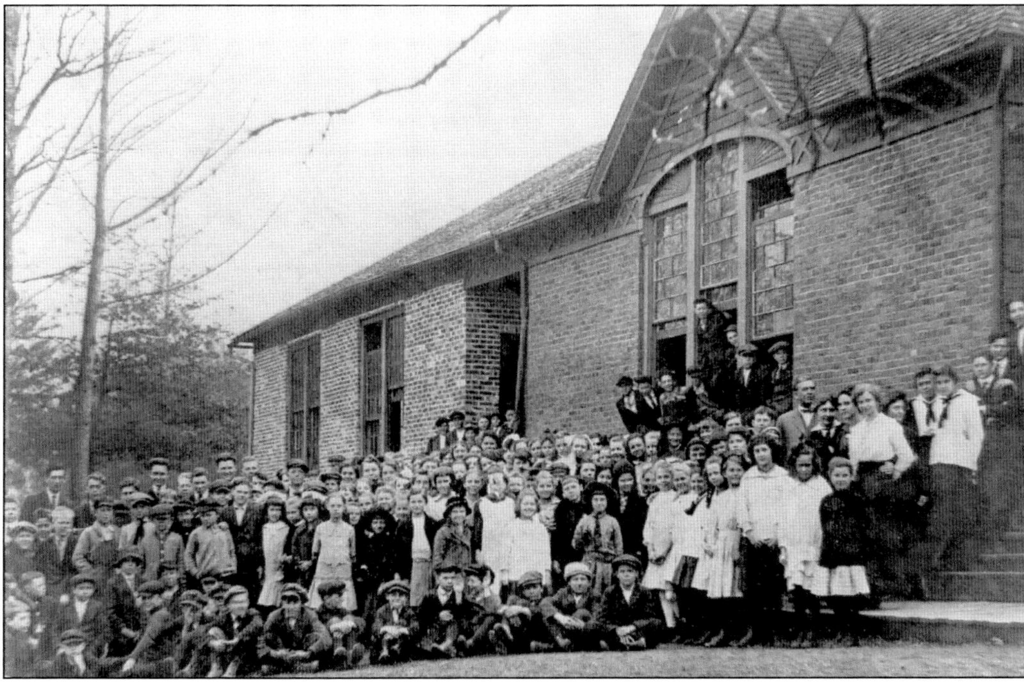

The Dwight Institute, situated on the hilltop at the end of Willow Street, was one of the earliest of the public day schools of Unicoi County in the early 1900s. A principal and a faculty of three teachers orchestrated the higher education of the children of Erwin's ever-expanding middle class. (Courtesy of the Unicoi County Historical Society.)

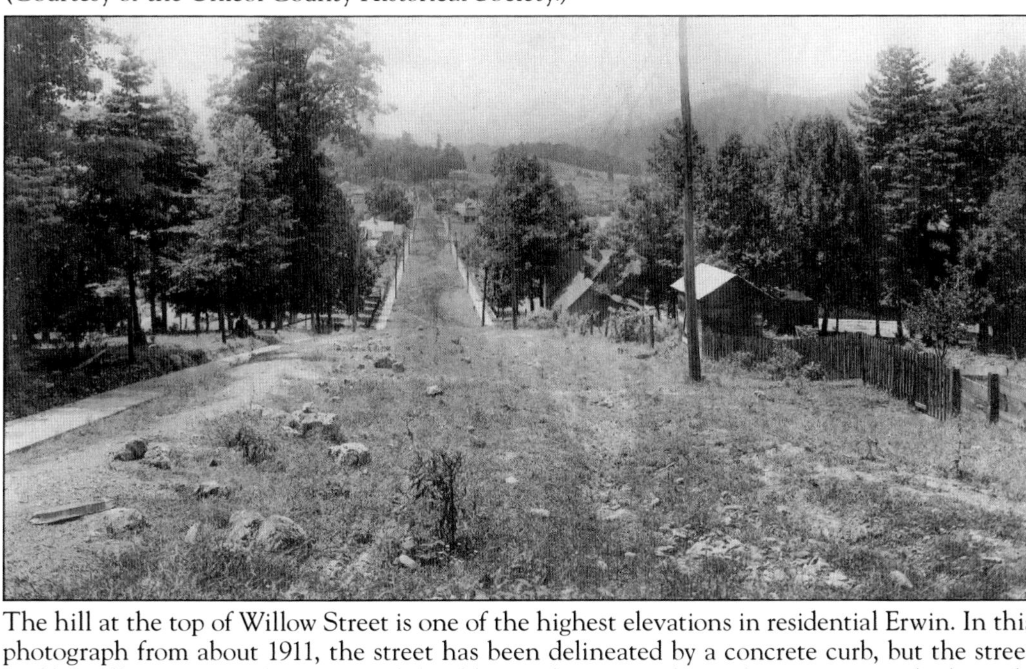

The hill at the top of Willow Street is one of the highest elevations in residential Erwin. In this photograph from about 1911, the street has been delineated by a concrete curb, but the street itself is still a grassy track strewn with boulders and stumps. This is the same view, which would have been familiar to the students of the Dwight Institute situated at the top of Willow Hill. (Courtesy of the Unicoi County Historical Society.)

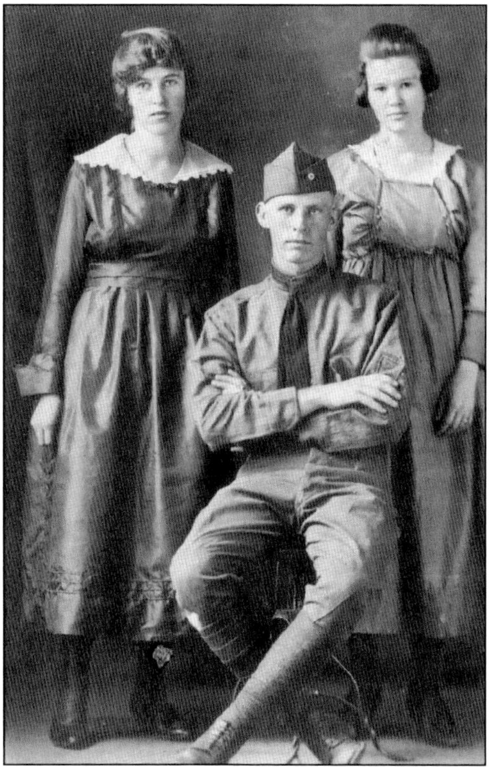

Lifelong friends and second cousins Lydia Tinker (left) and Sara Coffie flank Manasia Presnell, seated in the center of this c. 1915 studio portrait. Lydia and Manasia became engaged, but the union was not to be. Manasia went away to college and eventually moved from Erwin. Lydia, however, met and married Jim Christy, who had come to town with his parents from Ohio when Southern Potteries was established in Erwin in 1916. (Courtesy of Christine Christy Tipton.)

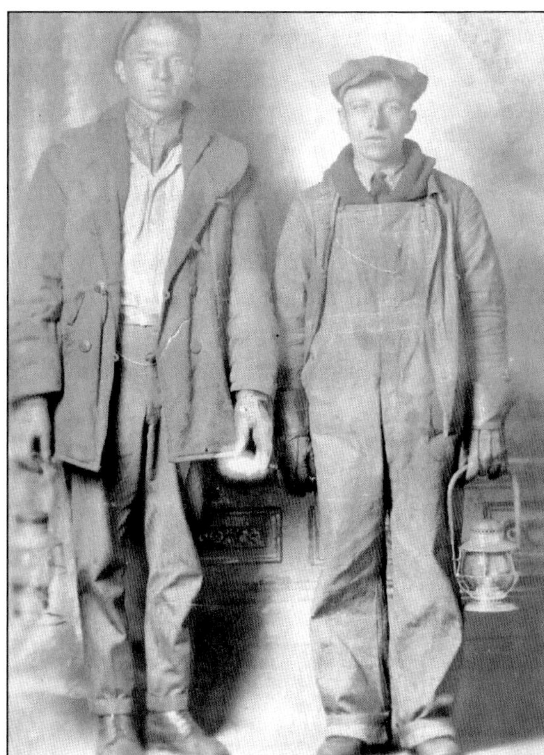

Harry Franklin, at left, and his friend Fred Britt, carrying the railroad lantern, were photographed about 1920 in their railroad work clothes. These young men were typical of the scores of eager workers who flocked to Erwin and Unicoi County once Erwin became the headquarters for the Carolina, Clinchfield, and Ohio Railway. The county's population skyrocketed during the period from 1909–1914, so much so that, for a time, a tent city sprang up near the railroad headquarters off Union Street. (Courtesy of Hilda Padgett.)

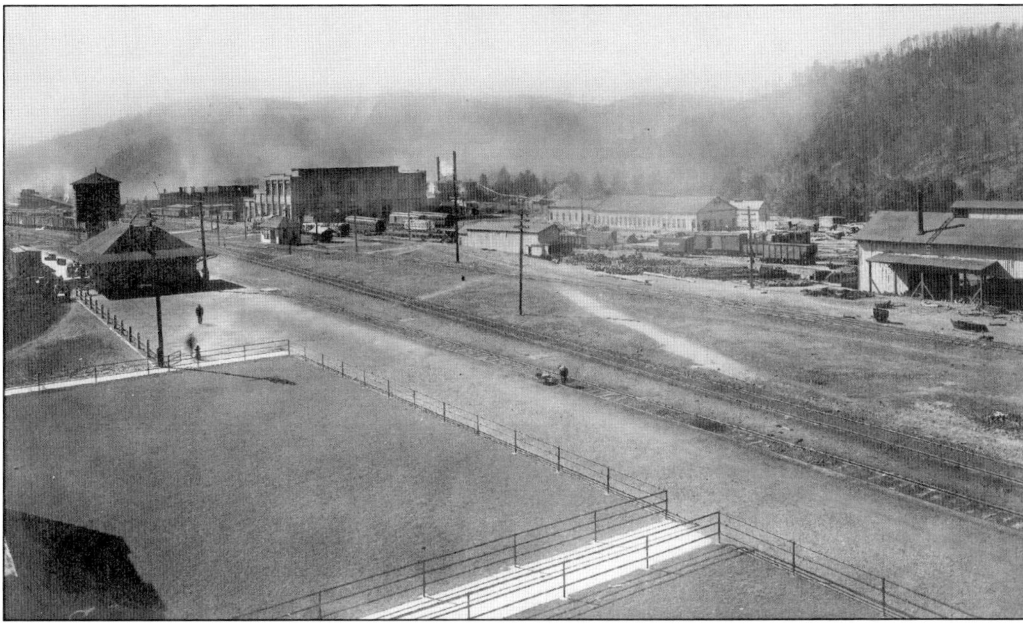

The Carolina, Clinchfield, and Ohio Railway shops building was constructed in 1923. By 1925, when the CC&O Railway changed its name officially to the Clinchfield Railroad, there was plenty of work to do on an inventory of some 8,000 freight cars, not to mention the big Mikado and Mallett locomotives also purchased during this period. (Courtesy of the Unicoi County Historical Society.)

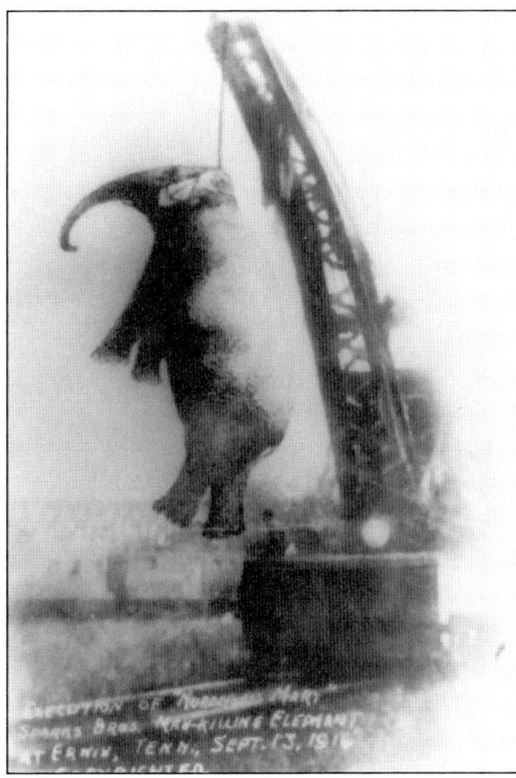

This grainy "doctored" photograph supposedly shows the hanging of Mary the Elephant, from the Sparks Brothers Circus. Since that unfortunate day in 1916, Erwin and the Clinchfield Railroad have become inadvertently linked to the destruction of the elephant. After Mary had killed her handler during a random fit of rage in a circus parade in Kingsport, the circus owners, feeling public pressure, asked the Clinchfield Railroad in Erwin for the use of their heavy-duty crane derrick to accomplish the deed. The five-ton elephant is buried in the train yard. (Courtesy of the Arnold Williams family.)

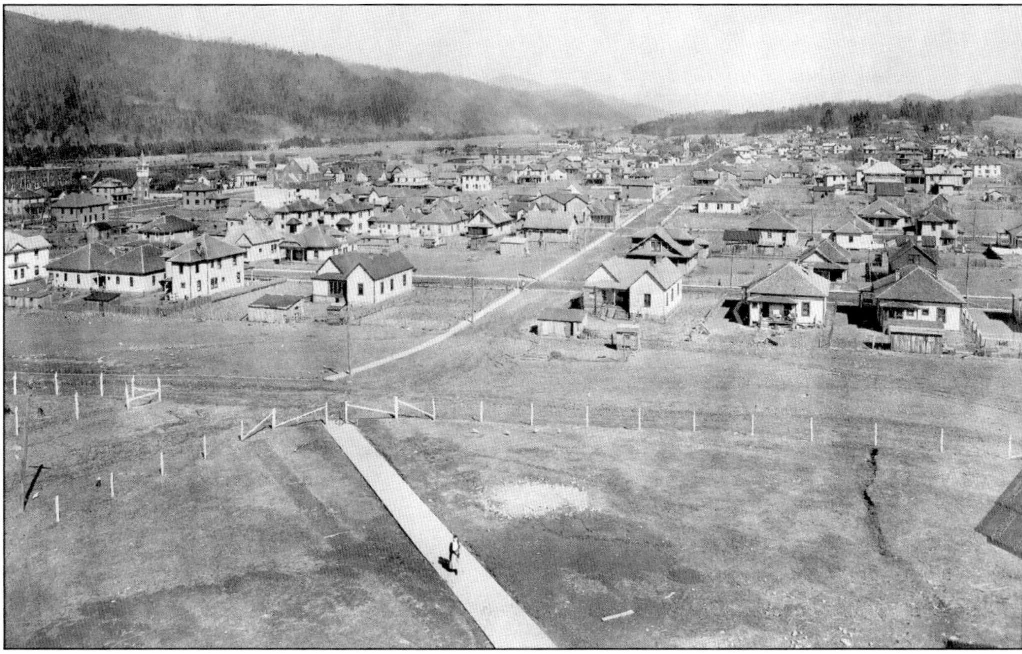

The top photograph, taken about 1917 from the promontory lawn of the old Unaka Academy, gives a wide perspective of the rapid surge of population in Erwin from 1909–1914. Looking north and left, the neighborhood south of Main Street, can be easily identified. The downtown business district stretches from the steeple of the first Christian Church to the courthouse. Just above the foreground is the dirt track that became Academy Street. Next are Opekiska Street, then Catawba Street, and then Love Street. Below, the view turns east, past the roof of the old Unaka Academy dormitory, seen at right. New construction can be seen under way on the eastern end of Opekiska and Catawba Streets. In the distance are Love Street, Union Street, and Gay Street, which is tucked under Elephant Back Mountain. Farther in the distance, horses graze in Fairview Field, with O'Brien Springs in the left center. (Both images courtesy of the Unicoi County Historical Society.)

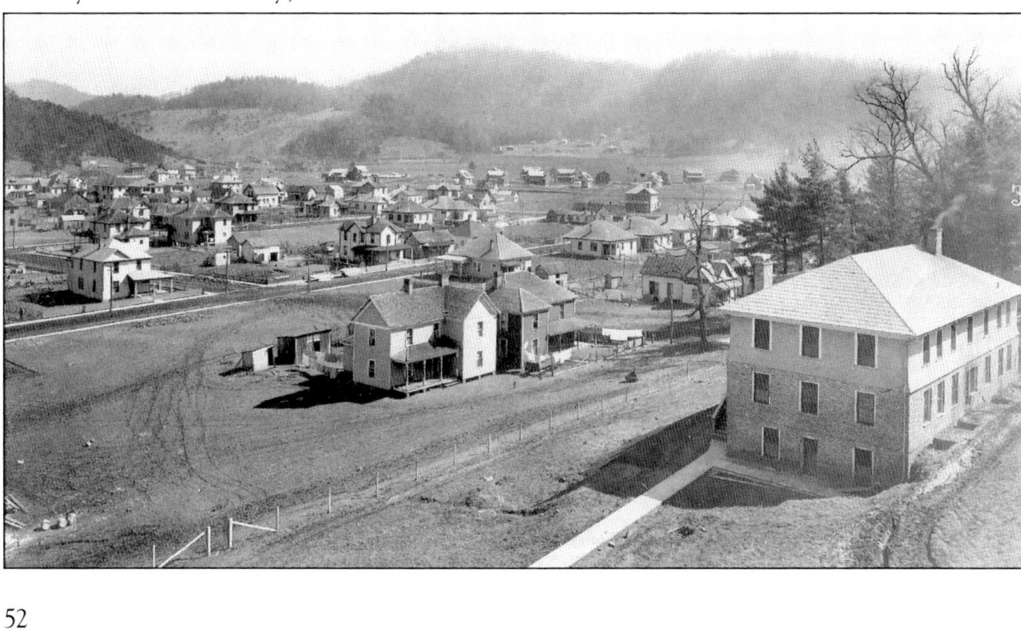

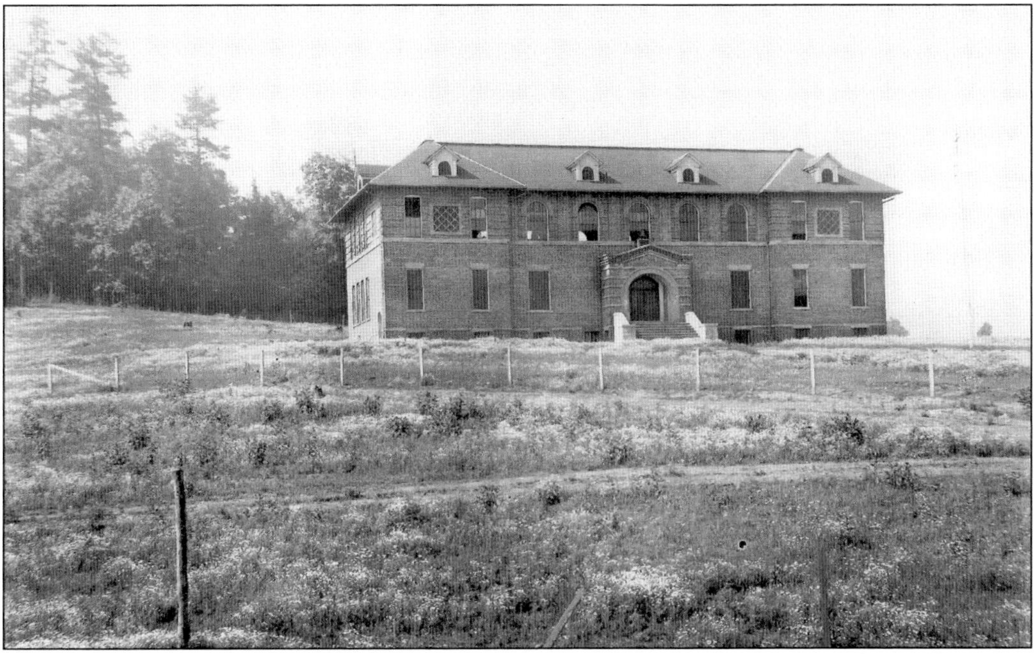

The First Baptist Church initiated the construction of the Unaka Academy as a day and boarding school. Situated on the hill near present-day Gentry Stadium, the private school offered grades 1–12 and a tuition that ranged from 75¢ per month for grades 1 and 2 to $2.50 per month for grades 11 and 12. A dormitory was available for boarding students at a rate of $1 to $1.25 per month. In 1916, the Baptist church sold the academy building to Unicoi County for use as a high school. When the brand-new 1929 Unicoi County High School was built, the old academy ceased to exist. People still remember the grand ballroom on the second floor used for community dances and special ceremonies. Around the late 1930s or early 1940s, the old Unaka Academy dormitory was converted to a county hospital. (Both images courtesy of the Unicoi County Historical Society.)

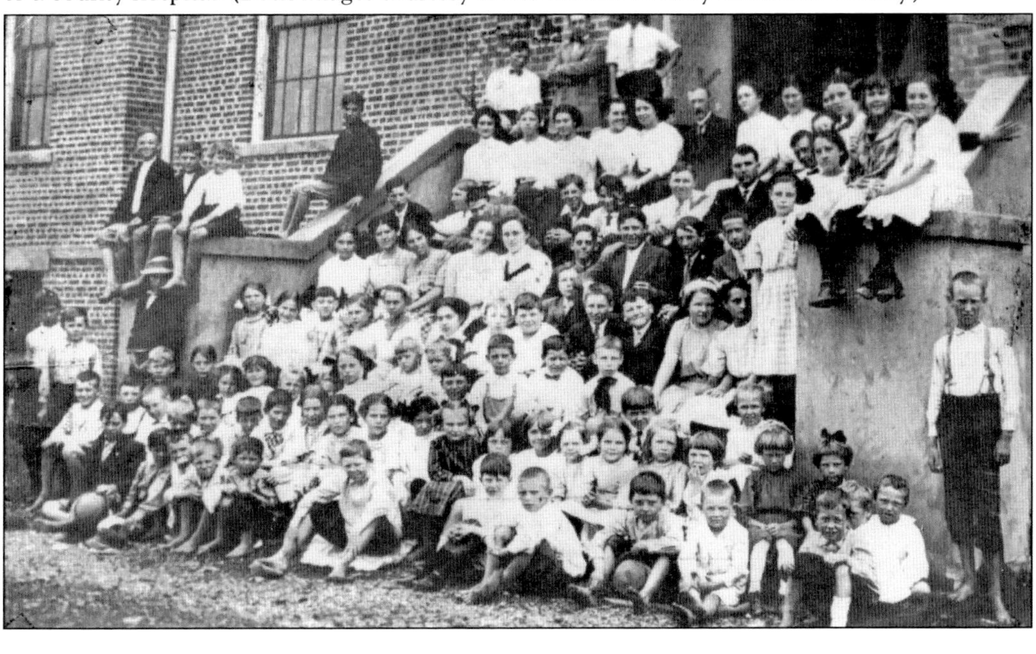

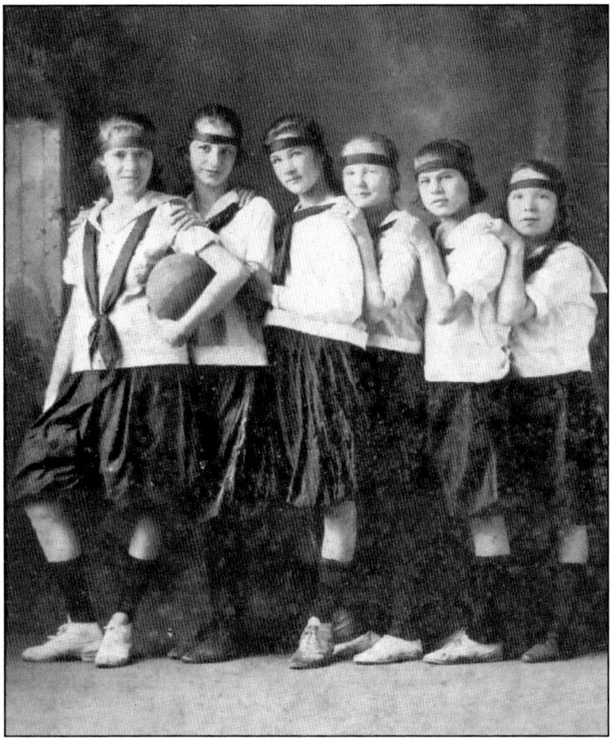

The students of the Unaka Academy enjoyed a healthy athletic environment open to both girls and boys. Shown is the Unaka Academy girls' basketball team of about 1920 in the requisite bloomer and middy blouse outfit of the day. Pictured from left to right are Opal Stallard, Agnes Tucker, Gertrude Love, Alberta Brown, Janice Stubblefield, and Margaret Bolton. (Courtesy of Martha Brown Stromberg/A. R. Brown collection.)

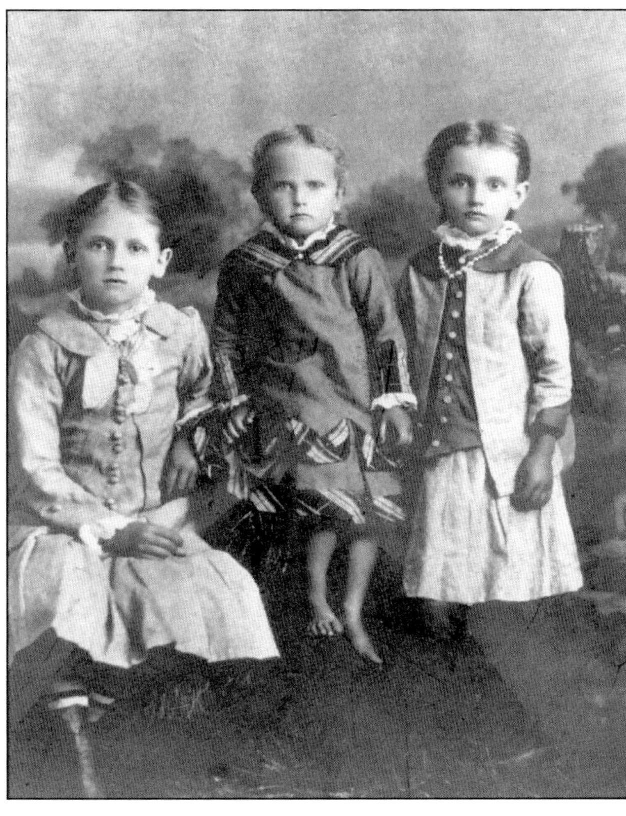

Myrtle, Doran, and Clarice Ingram sat for this portrait in the Charley Cargile Studio in Johnson City about 1914. Myrtle Ingram Taylor, at left, became an elementary school teacher and taught for many years at Elm Street School. Her little brother Doran, in the center, grew up to be publisher of the *Erwin Observer* newspaper in the late 1930s and early 1940s. Clarice Ingram Snider, at right, became a home economics teacher at Unicoi County High School. (Courtesy of Violet Kelley.)

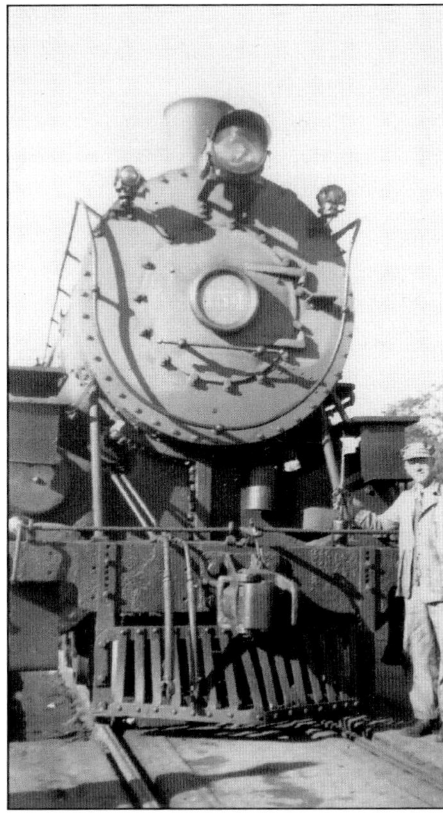

Engineer George Ingram stands beside a Clinchfield locomotive in the 1940s. Years before, he wrote on the back of the penny postcard photograph below saying, "This is a picture of our house in Erwin. I am running a Mallet Compound Engine No. 555 between Erwin, TN and Bostic, N.C. This leaves all well." George Ingram's four children (from left to right) were Doran, Myrtle, Clarice, and little Billy (in the carriage). Billy died before he reached adulthood. The wrought iron fence still encloses the old Ingram house at 423 Love Street, now owned by the Kelley family—direct relatives of George Ingram. (Both images courtesy of Violet Kelley.)

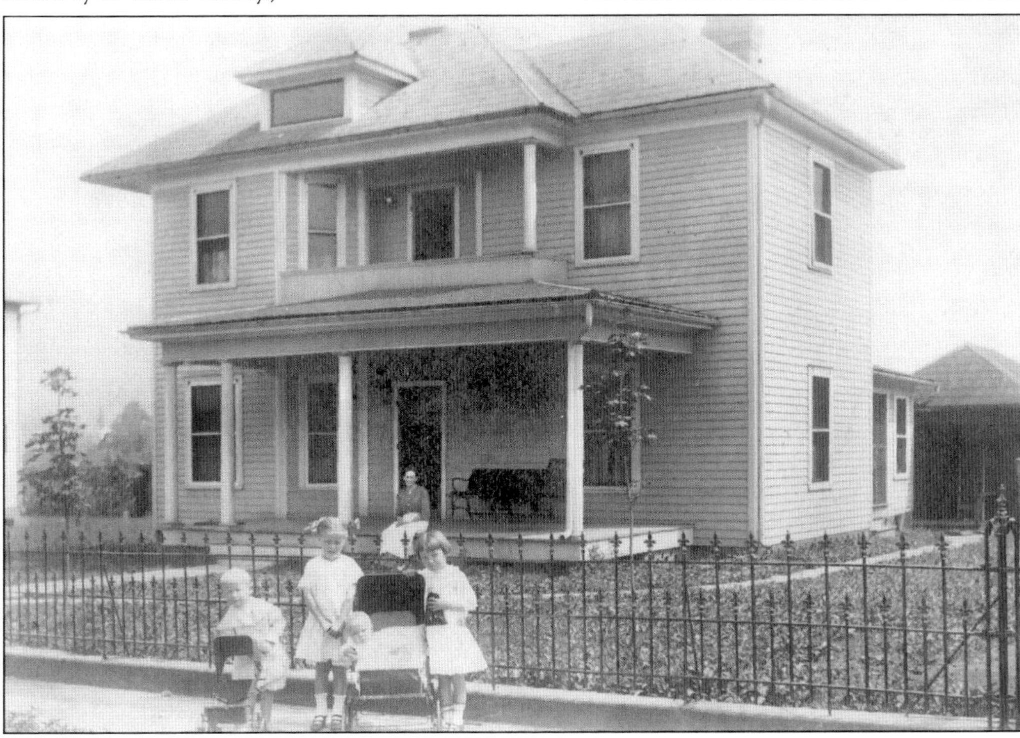

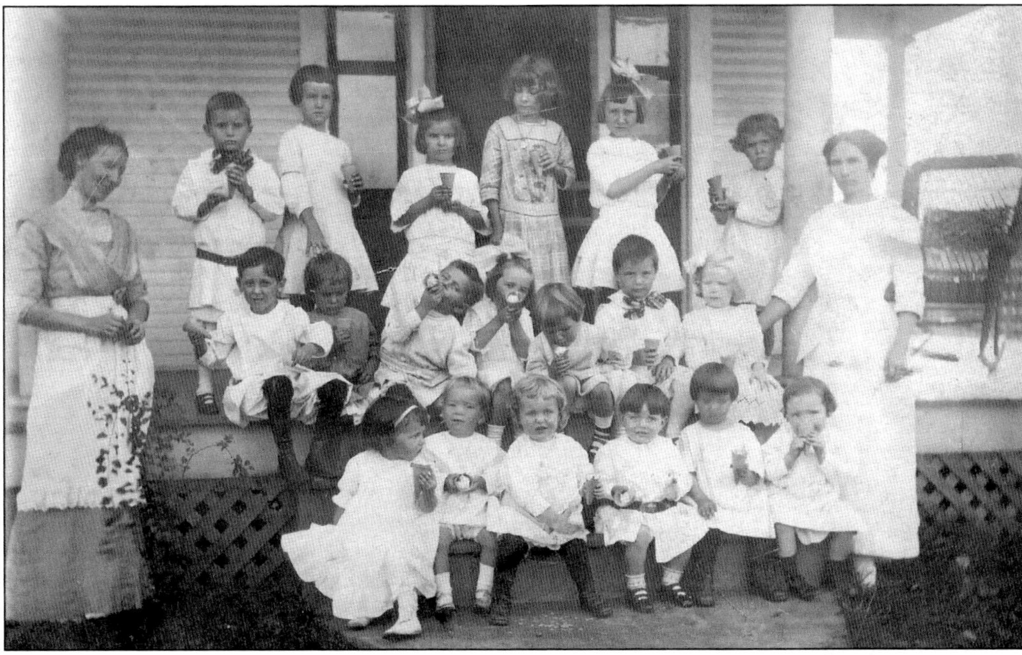

Elizabeth Harrington celebrated her birthday about 1912 with a party at her home on Love Street. Her mother, Mrs. Fred Harrington, at left, invited all the neighborhood children, shown enjoying a treat of quickly melting ice cream. Among Elizabeth's 15 guests were Nelle Wohlford, Ollie Tucker, Myrtle Ingram, Shirley Peters, Alberta Brown, Junior Hale, Robert Woodward, and Lucille Peters. Elizabeth Harrington is the little blonde girl, third from left, on the bottom step. (Courtesy of Martha Brown Stromberg/A. R. Brown collection.)

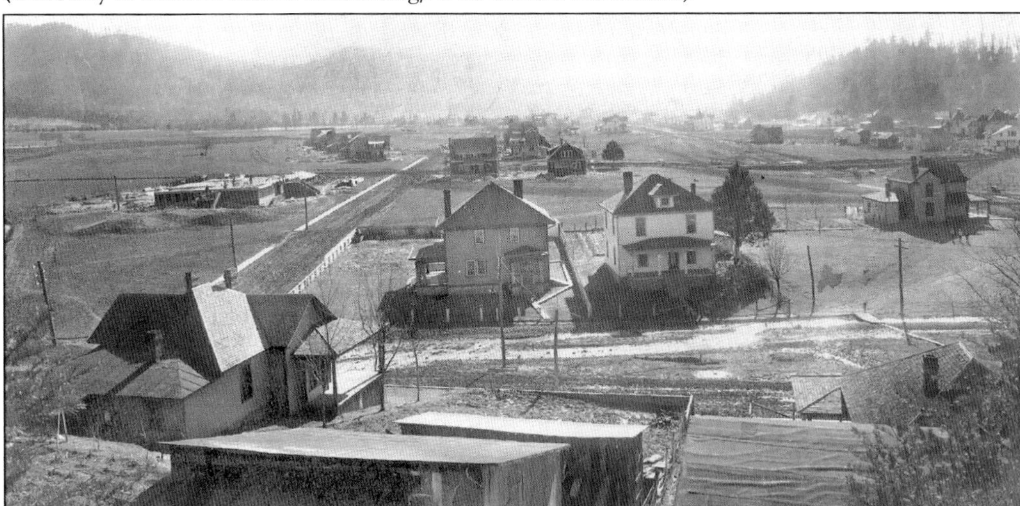

The foundation of Love Street School is underway, upper left, in this view from about 1916. This was Erwin's first new public school, built at a cost of $20,000. In January 1926, a fire destroyed the core structure of the building, but the 1924 addition was saved. Love Street School continued operation until consolidation of county schools, and advanced age sent the old school the way of the wrecking ball in 1972. Today the new YMCA complex occupies the site. (Courtesy of the Unicoi County Historical Society.)

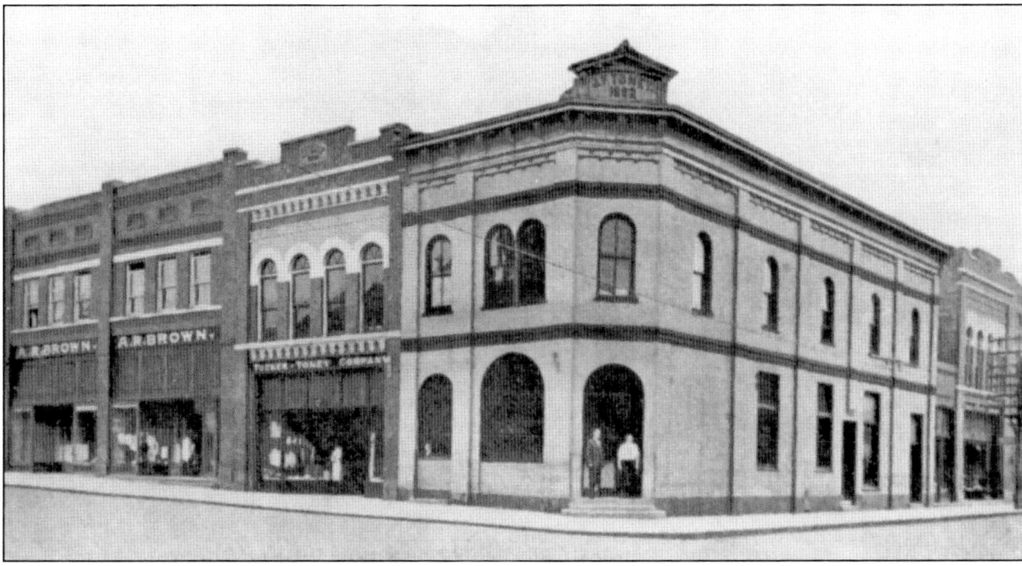

This photograph from about 1927 displays the pristine nature of the paved streets of downtown Erwin. By this time, the business district had solidified into several city blocks of locally owned enterprises—two banks, several mercantile establishments, a newspaper, a bakery, theaters, a telephone company, a water company, law offices, medical practices, and numerous other shops. (Courtesy of the Arnold Williams family.)

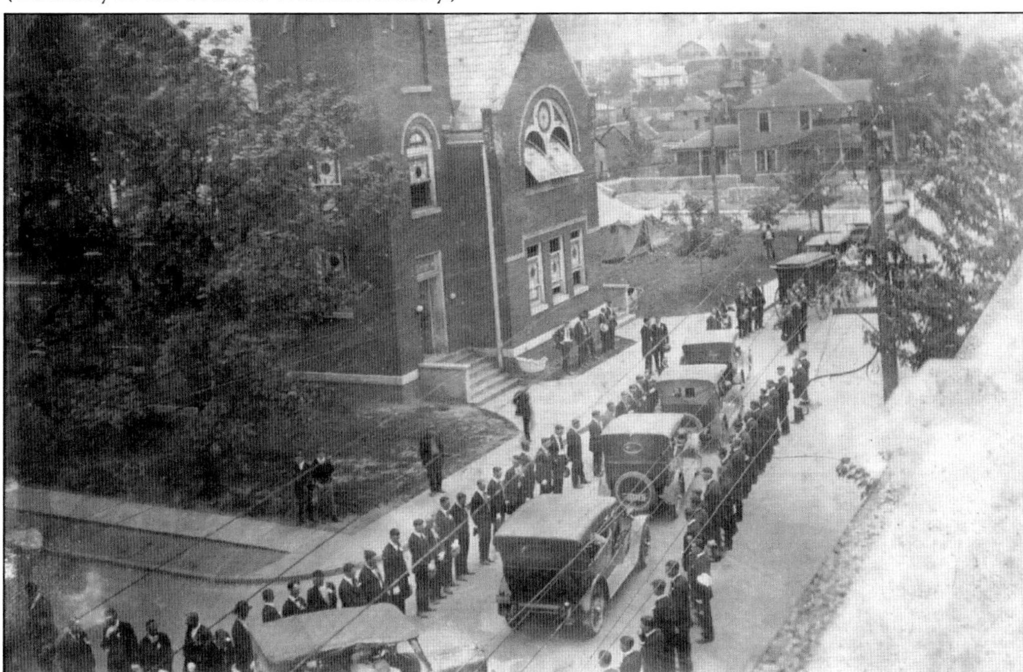

A lengthy funeral procession snakes its way through South Main Street in front of the First Baptist Church in the mid-1920s. The deceased is unknown, but his cause of death, apparently, was by electrocution—a new danger in the increasingly electrified world of 1920s America. Judging from the bird's-eye perspective, the photograph must have been taken from the roof of the Hotel Erwin on Main Street. (Courtesy of Debbie Tittle.)

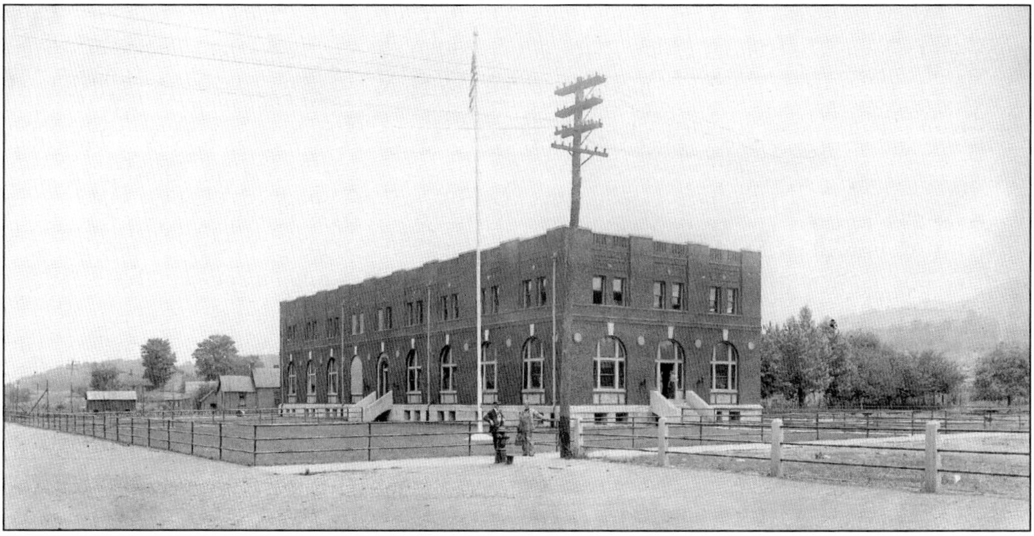

Southwest Virginia coal baron George L. Carter, who had acquired various mid-Atlantic rail lines in an effort to move his coal to southern seaport markets, organized the Carolina, Clinchfield, and Ohio Railway in 1908. After a failed attempt to establish headquarters in Johnson City, Carter put his general offices in Erwin in 1909. This efficient office building, always referred to as "the Big Office," was constructed in 1915. By 1925, with the addition of a third story, this building housed the entire operations department of the Clinchfield line. (Courtesy of the Unicoi County Historical Society.)

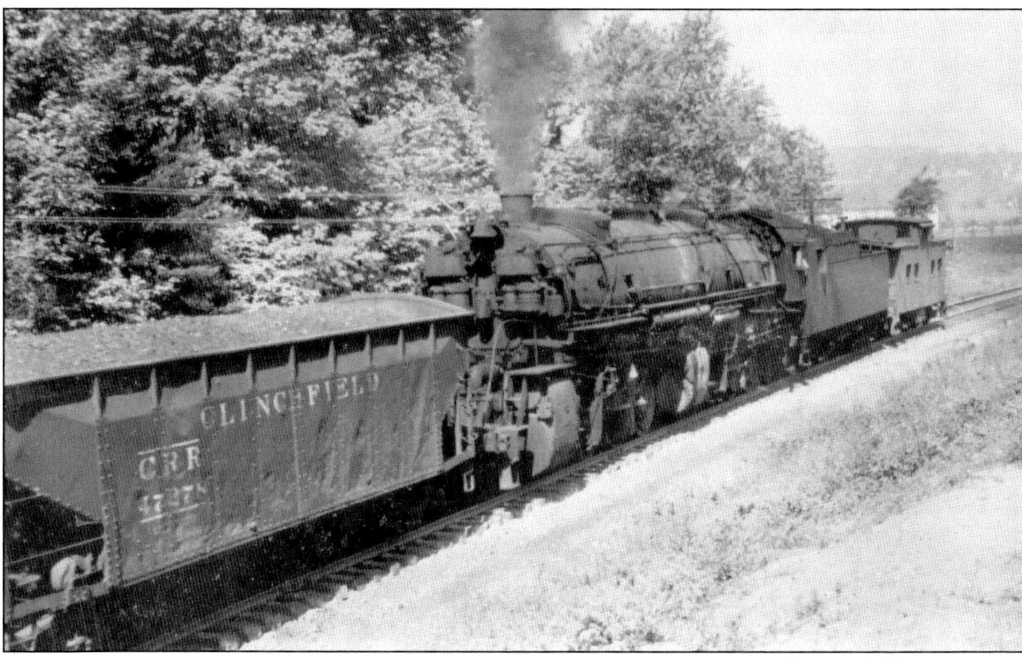

Pusher engines were the workhorses of the Clinchfield line, called on to get behind the increased tonnage created by the transport of 150 to 200 loads of coals from Erwin up into the Blue Ridge Mountains. The unheralded pushers, traveling at an excruciating 8 to 10 miles an hour at the end of the load, made sure the coal cars made it safely over the top and on into the markets of South Carolina. (Courtesy of Bob Sams.)

Charlie Davis pauses in his workday in the doorway of the Clinchfield Railroad shops building about 1920. Away from his day job at the railroad, Charlie was a sporty dresser with a unique flair. He died at the age of 39. A cowcatcher from a locomotive engine can be seen just behind Charlie inside the shops building. (Courtesy of Juacquetta Davis Edwards.)

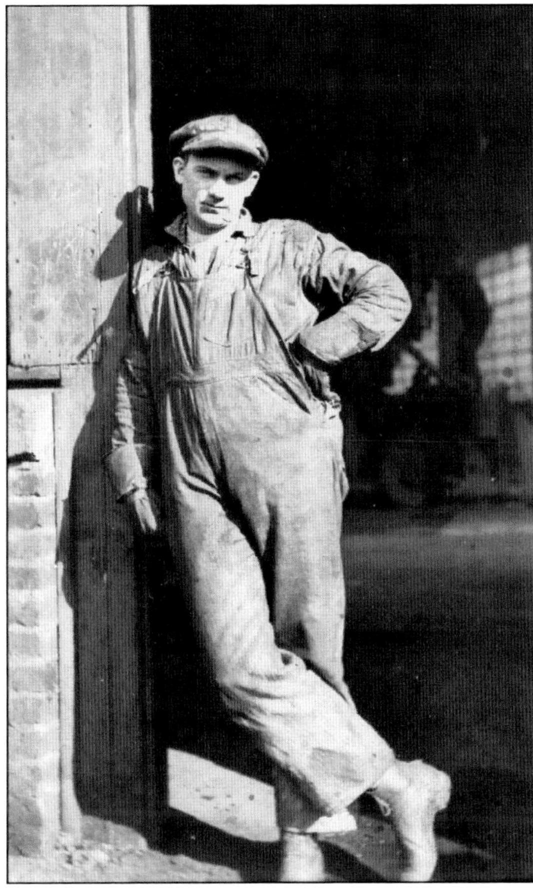

In the days before the town of Erwin instituted a community-wide electric utility system, the Clinchfield Railroad Powerhouse independently maintained all the electric power necessary to satisfy the needs of the railroad. Electric power was noisily generated by compressed air and steam heat, which rose from the massive smokestack. A town-wide fire alarm also originated from the powerhouse—two blows meant a fire to the south, three meant north. (Courtesy of the Unicoi County Historical Society.)

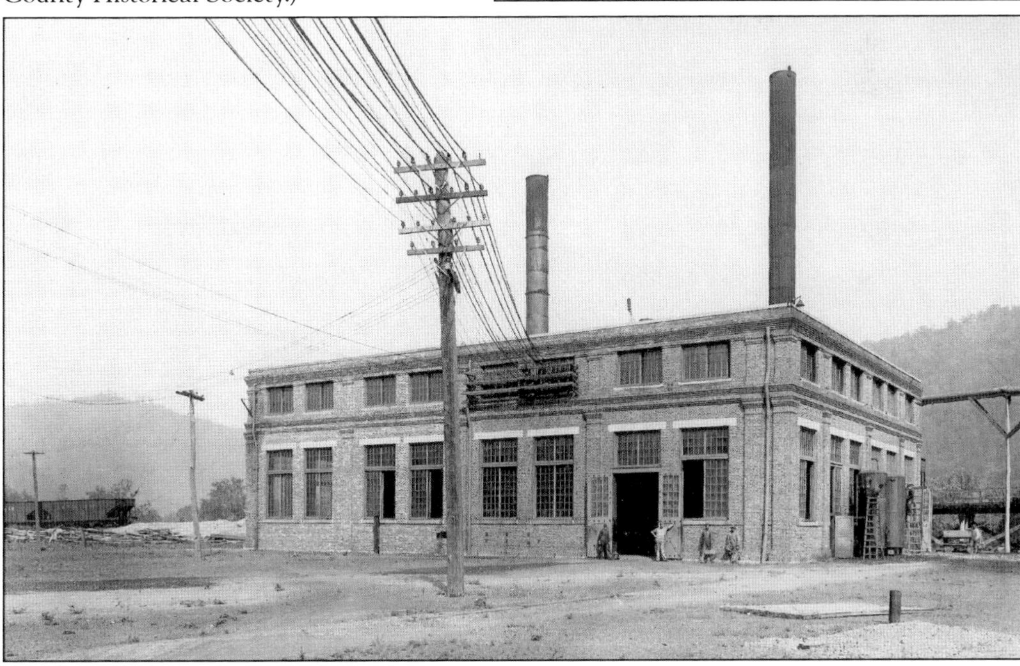

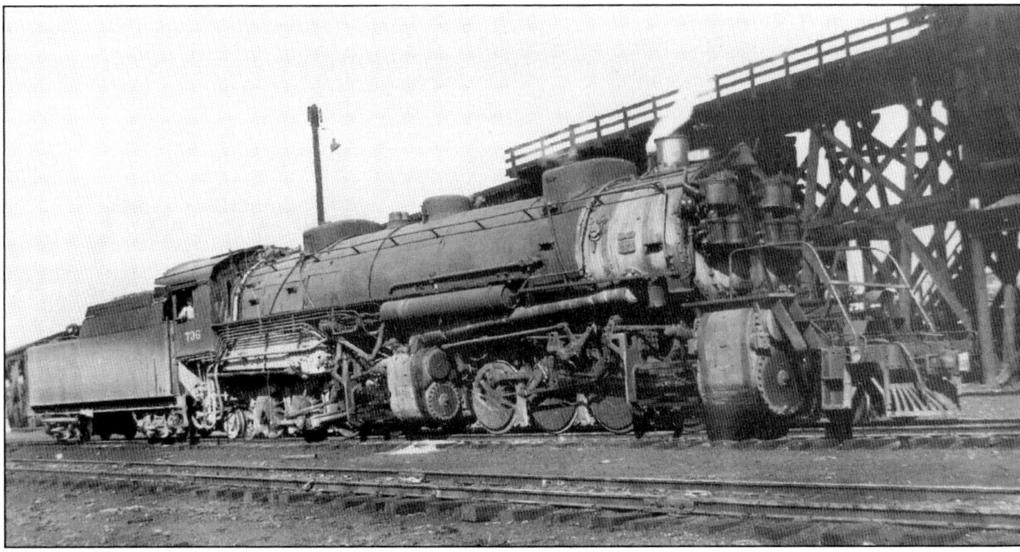

The steam-snorting mechanical monster above was a compound Mallet locomotive. Ten were purchased in 1923 by the Clinchfield Railroad. The impressive Mallet was 110 feet long, weighed 375 pounds, and could pull a 100-car coal train. Below is the Mikado locomotive, 1 of 10 also purchased in 1923 as the Clinchfield Railroad increased its presence and superiority as an efficient freight-hauling corporation. According to James A. Goforth in his book, *Building the Clinchfield*, the Mikes were multiple service locomotives, used for fast and slow freight, coal drags, yard switching, and passenger runs. A utilitarian coal tipple can be seen above the Mikado. (Both images courtesy James A. Goforth.)

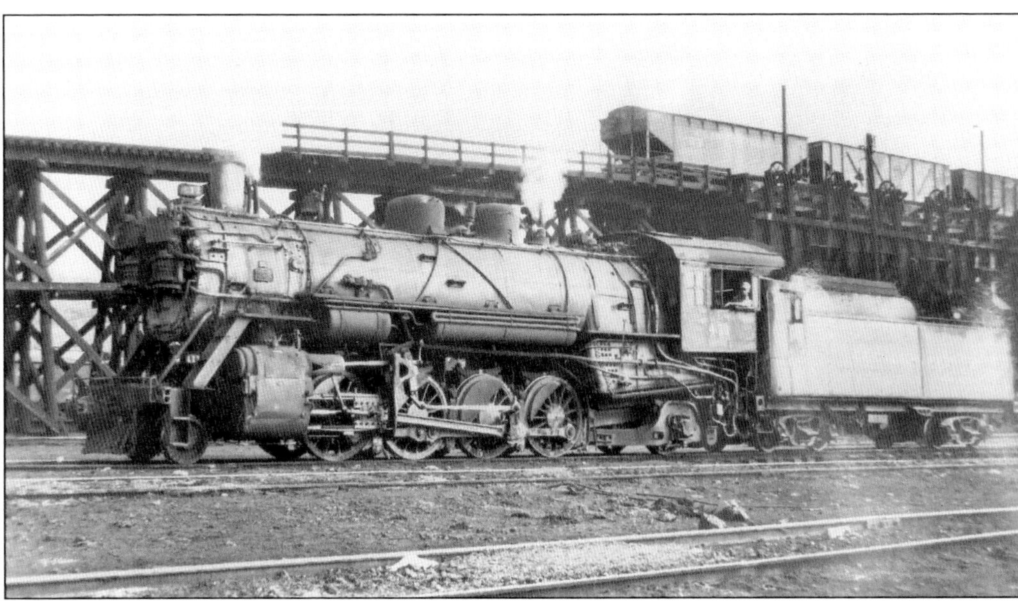

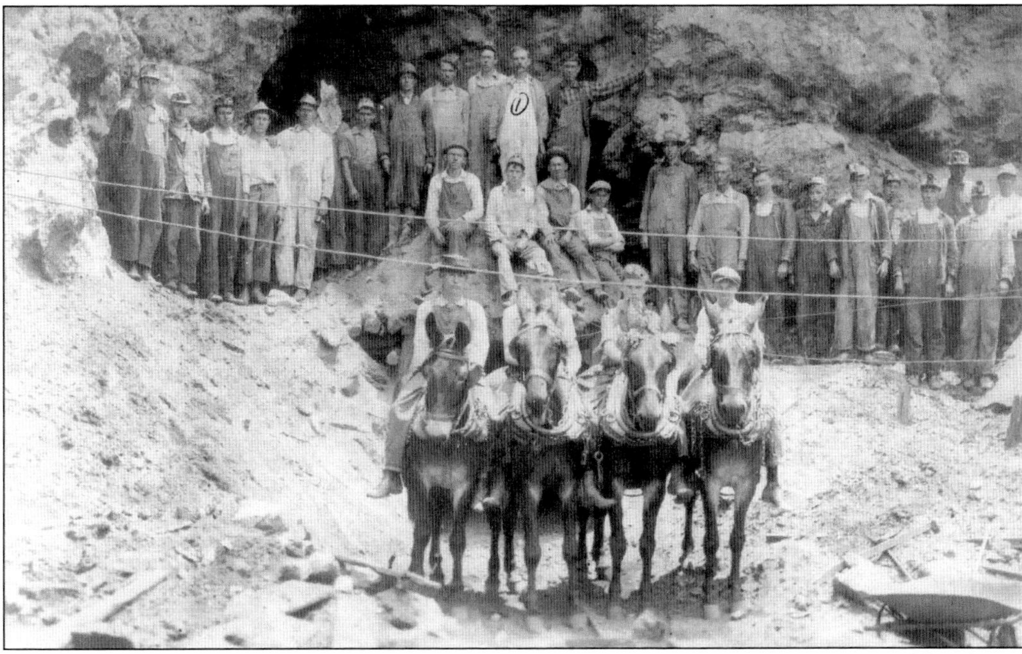

The Bumpass Cove Mines, situated on the western edge of Unicoi County and bordering Washington County, were so named because their potentially slippery slopes could often land a fellow on his backside. Pictured in 1920 are the workers at the Fowler Mine. (Courtesy of the Unicoi County Historical Society.)

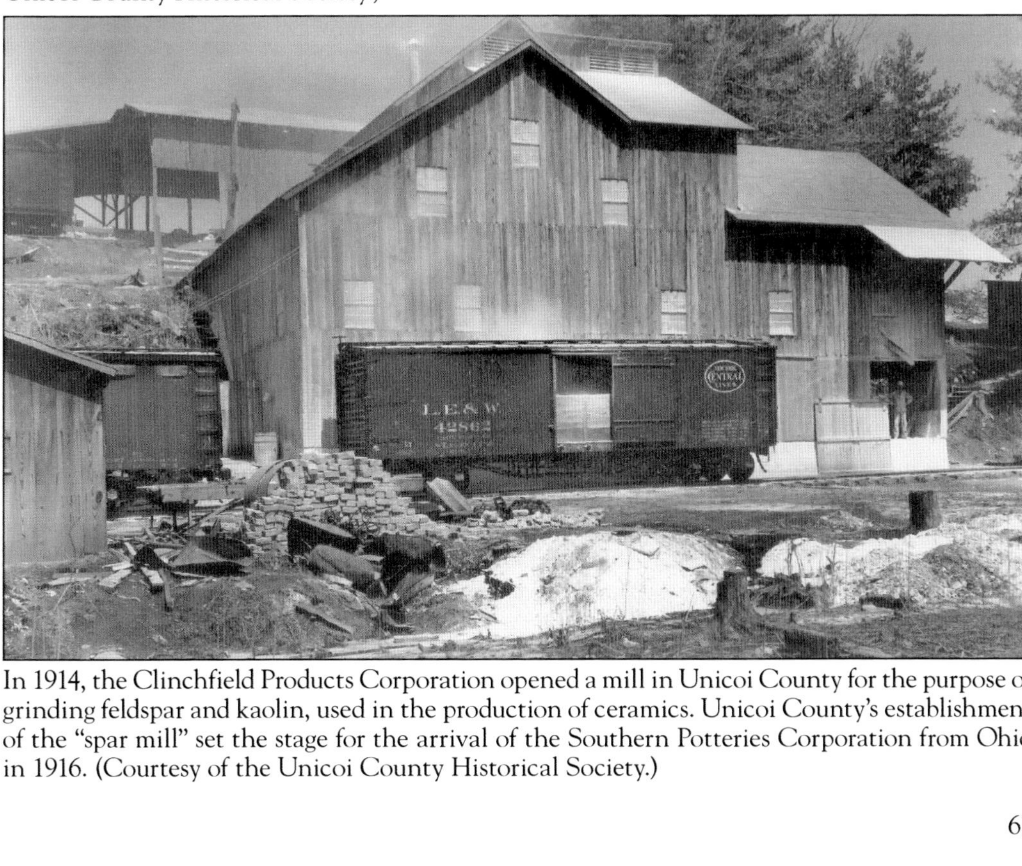

In 1914, the Clinchfield Products Corporation opened a mill in Unicoi County for the purpose of grinding feldspar and kaolin, used in the production of ceramics. Unicoi County's establishment of the "spar mill" set the stage for the arrival of the Southern Potteries Corporation from Ohio in 1916. (Courtesy of the Unicoi County Historical Society.)

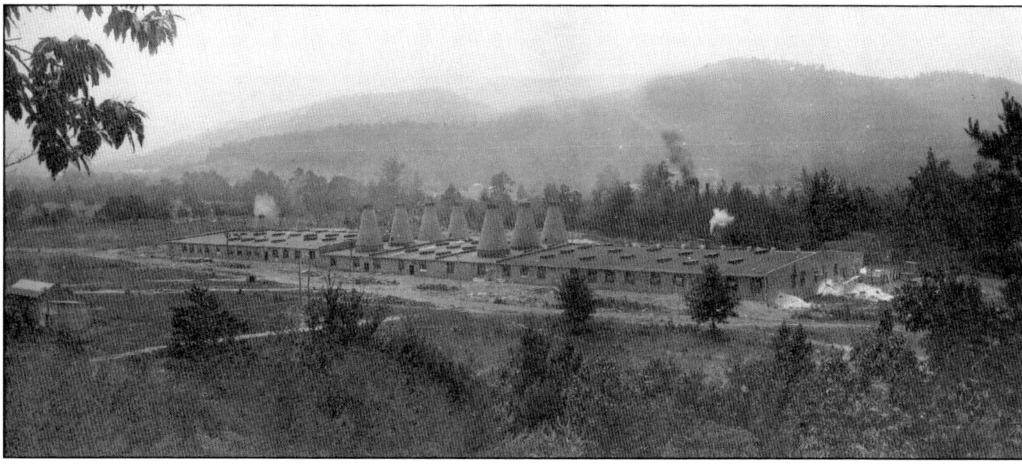

In 1916, representatives from the pottery production centers of Zanesville and Sebring, Ohio, chose Unicoi County as a prime location for the making of ceramic pottery. Southern Potteries, with its beehive kilns, turned out nationally popular Blue Ridge hand-painted dinnerware until the facility closed in 1957. (Courtesy of James A. Goforth.)

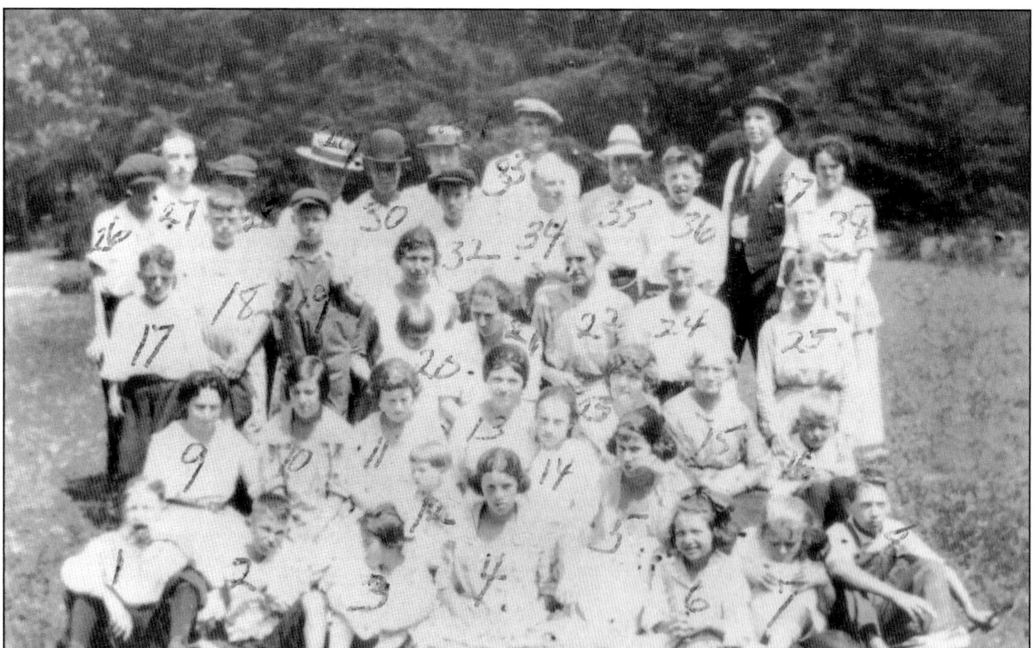

Pottery workers assemble at "the Fishery" (the federal fish hatchery) in Erwin about 1920 for the company outing, which came to be known as the annual Potters Picnic. At its height, the pottery was the second largest employer in Unicoi County, second only to the railroad. Many Unicoi County residents today take great pride in the heirloom pieces of now-collectible Blue Ridge Pottery once painted by their own relatives. (Courtesy of Hilda Padgett.)

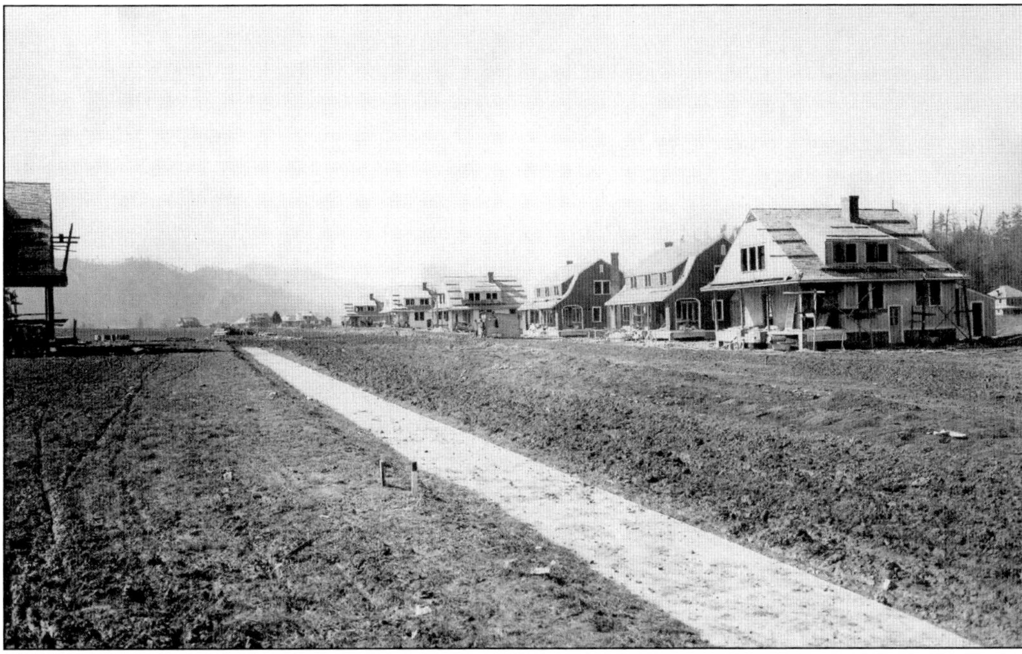

Above, a wide-angle perspective draws the eye down the length of Ohio Avenue as it stretches toward Love Street in this photograph from the 1920s. New York architect Grosvenor Atterbury received the commission in 1916 from the Clinchfield Railroad's Holston Corporation to plan a new residential development. Although it originally called for 135 acres, the pottery addition today incorporates the immediate neighborhoods along Ohio Avenue north to Love Street, including the short spur of adjacent Unaka Way. The arts-and-crafts–inspired "Pottery Houses," built initially for workers of the Southern Potteries, were designed from three primary plans. Below is a 1920 view of Holston Place, the "horseshoe" street off Ohio Avenue. The basic, one-story plan sold for $1,000 in 1916. (Above courtesy of the Unicoi County Historical Society; below courtesy of Hilda Padgett.)

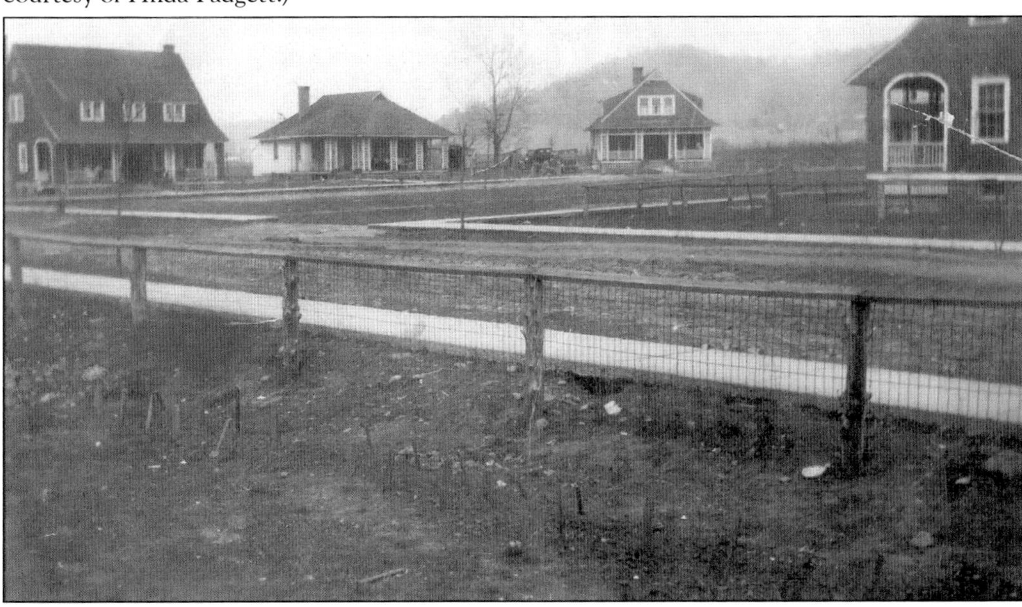

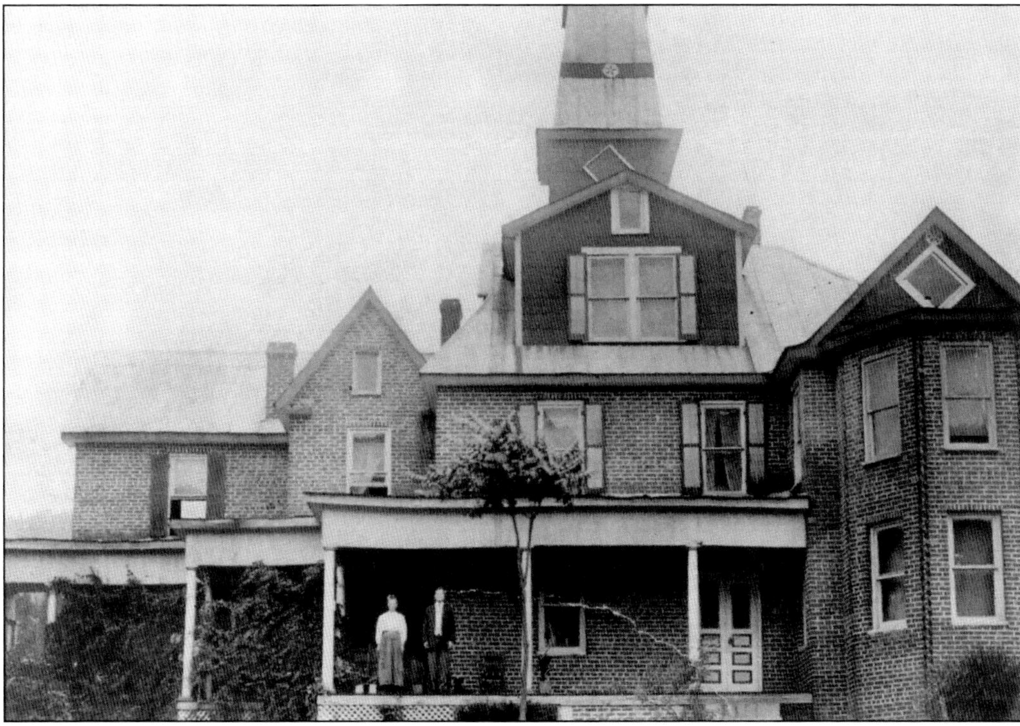

A lawyer and educator, Robert William Henry Gilbert was well-known throughout Unicoi County for his honesty, integrity, and legal expertise, as well as his wisdom and intellect. Gilbert rode across the county on horseback as a teacher and principal, and served as school superintendent. This spectacular, 20-room home, which he and his wife, Serena Banner, built in the rural Martin's Creek community around 1900, contained four fireplaces, a well-stocked library, and a grand piano. The expansive lawn was used for community gatherings. (Courtesy of Bob Gilbert.)

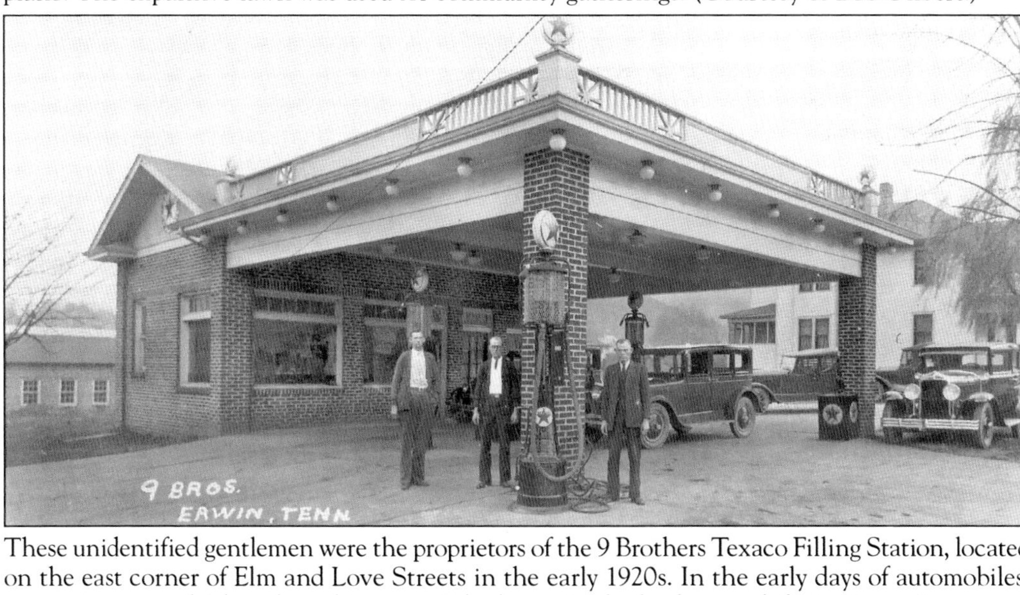

These unidentified gentlemen were the proprietors of the 9 Brothers Texaco Filling Station, located on the east corner of Elm and Love Streets in the early 1920s. In the early days of automobiles, gas stations were high-style architecture. The home in the background, facing Love Street, was later owned by Myrtle Ingram Taylor. (Courtesy of Violet Kelley.)

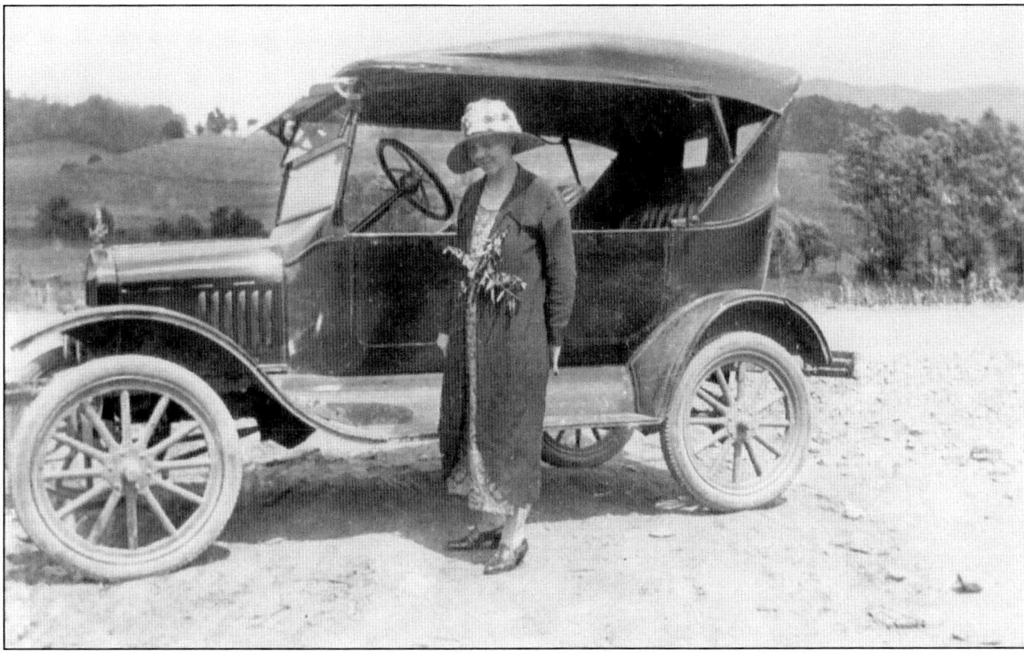

Lottie Tapp stands proudly beside her 1920s-era Ford, which she purchased with her own earnings from a job at the telephone company in Erwin. She was typical of the changing face of a new generation of women in the 1920s. Tapp went to business school in nearby Johnson City and learned accounting and then returned to Erwin in 1919 to become one of the first two telephone operators in Unicoi County. She and her friend Ida McInturff worked the first switchboard, located in the home of Sheriff Tom Tapp. Below, the Unicoi County telephone operators of the mid-1920s display their new-fangled technology during a Main Street parade. "Hello Central," was the familiar phrase for those lucky enough to own a telephone and place a call to the central switchboard located on the corner of Willow and Union Streets. (Both images courtesyof F. B. White.)

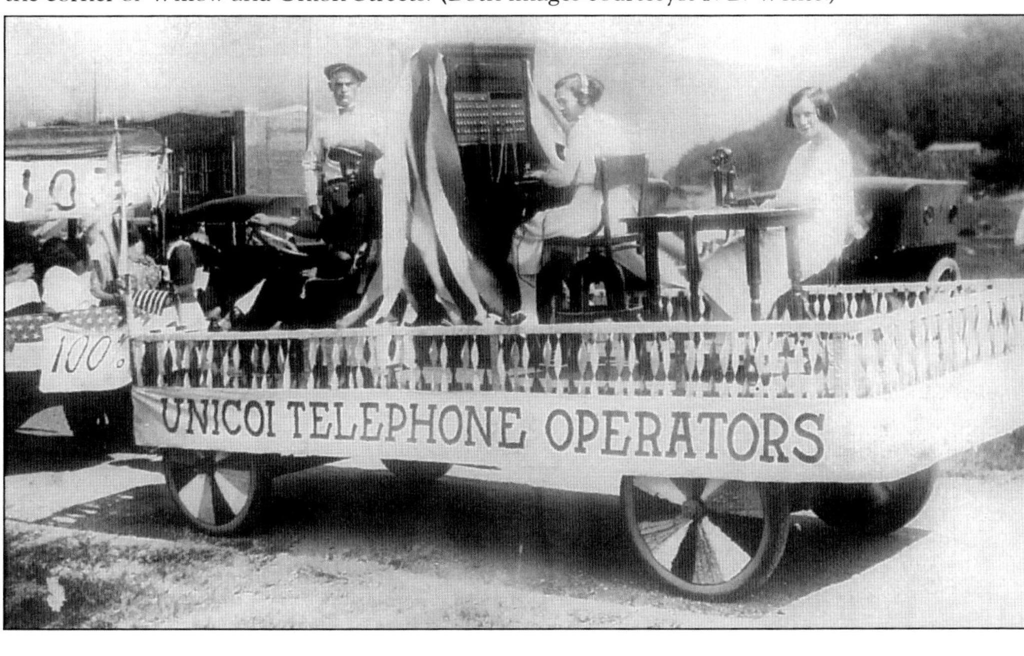

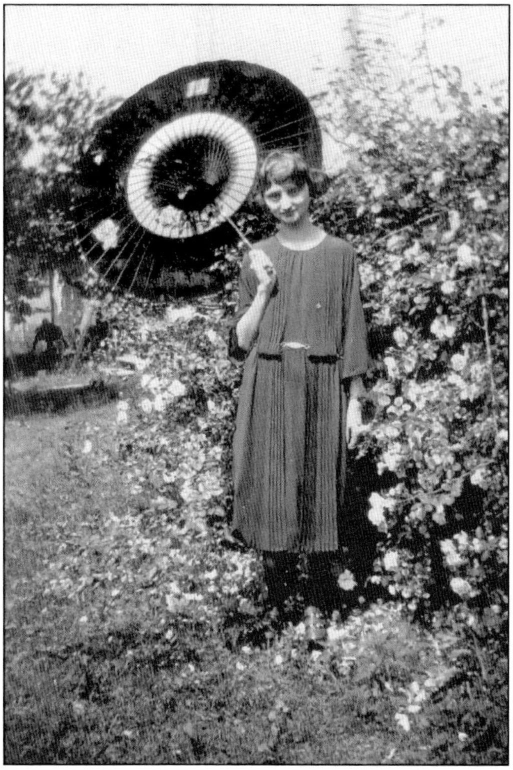

An oriental parasol and a blooming rose bush in an Erwin side yard make an aesthetically pleasing background for this c. 1925 photograph of Edith McLaughlin. McLaughlin's hairstyle, with its "mouse," or earmuff arrangement, and her drop-waist frock are characteristic of the period. (Courtesy of Juacquetta Davis Edwards.)

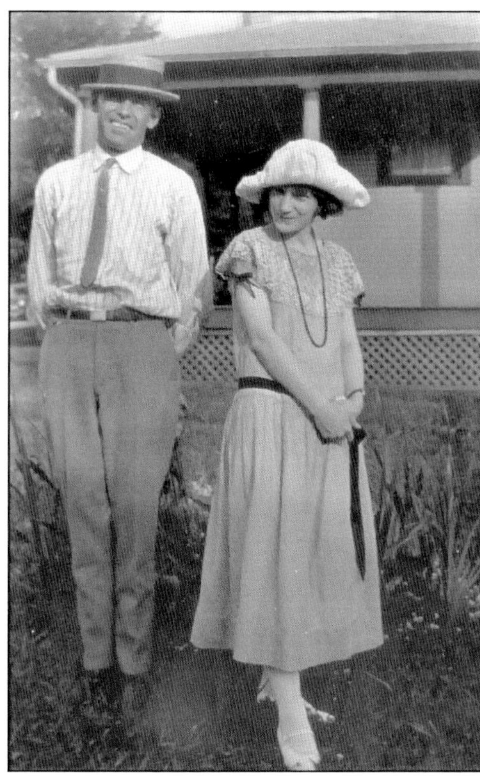

Etta Davis and Dillon Kinsland were married in the mid-1920s and were typical of the generation affected by World War I. Dill had served in France, was a lifelong member of the American Legion, and was instrumental in gaining a courthouse memorial to Unicoi County's World War I servicemen and women. In her teens, Etta took a job as an accountant in the Big Office at the railroad and stayed there well into her 70s. (Courtesy of Juacquetta Davis Edwards.)

These young sports from the mid-1920s, with watch fobs, jaunty headgear, and cigars are, from left to right, the following: (first row) Ernest Henson, J. Q. Brown, and Charles Pugh; (second row) Clyde Slagle and unidentified. (Courtesy of Juacquetta Davis Edwards.)

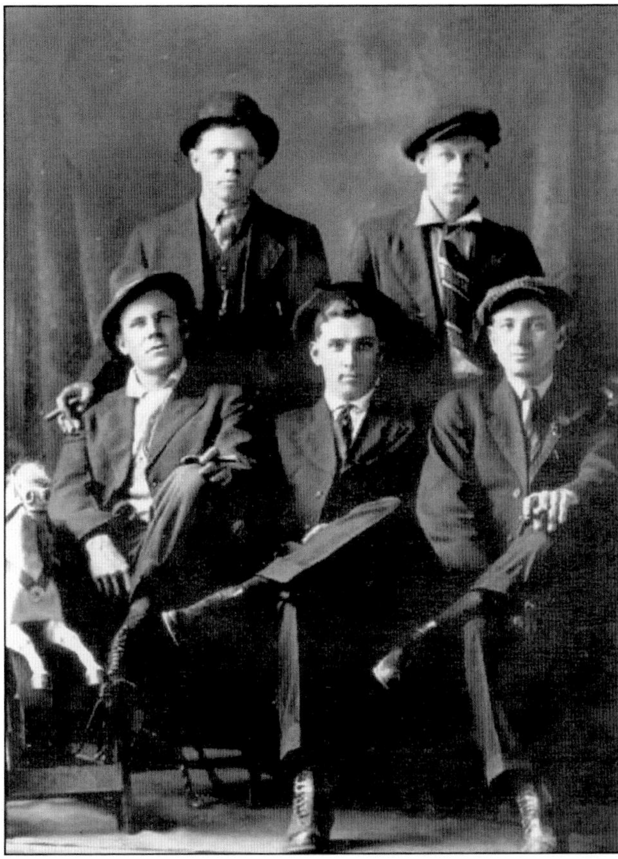

In the 1920s, before the repeal of Prohibition in 1933, the illegal manufacture of alcoholic spirits was rampant in the hills and hollows of Unicoi County. The operation of a still offered easy money in hard times. But law enforcement was hot on the trail, particularly Sheriff S. W. Shelton, shown here in 1924 posing happily in the midst of a vigorous display of his successful destruction of a moon shiner's livelihood. (Courtesy of Myra Anne Sellars Murray.)

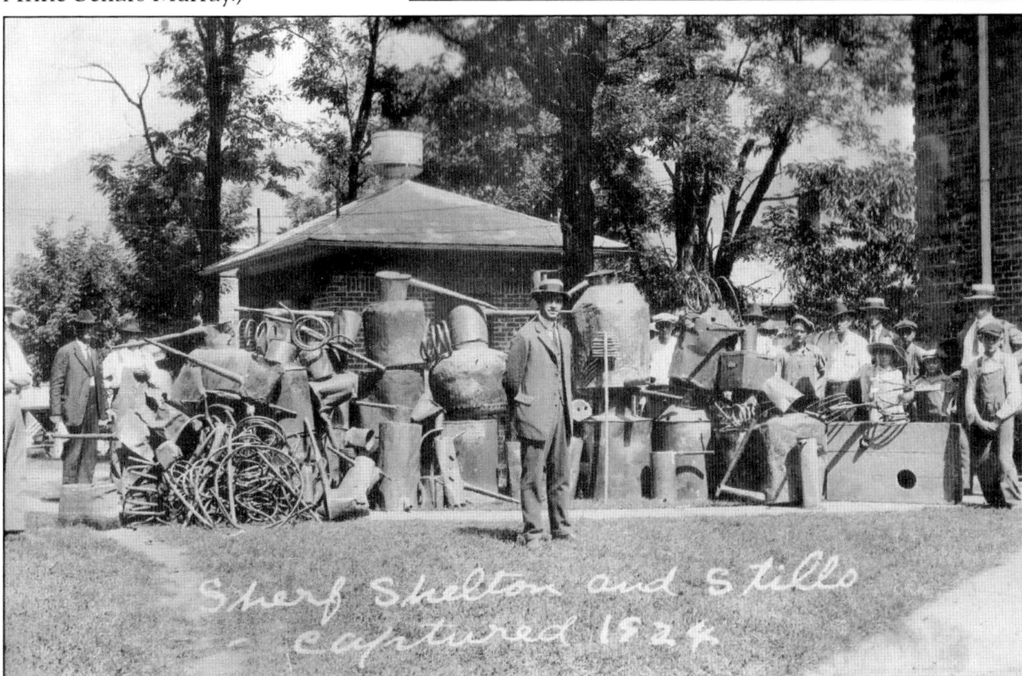

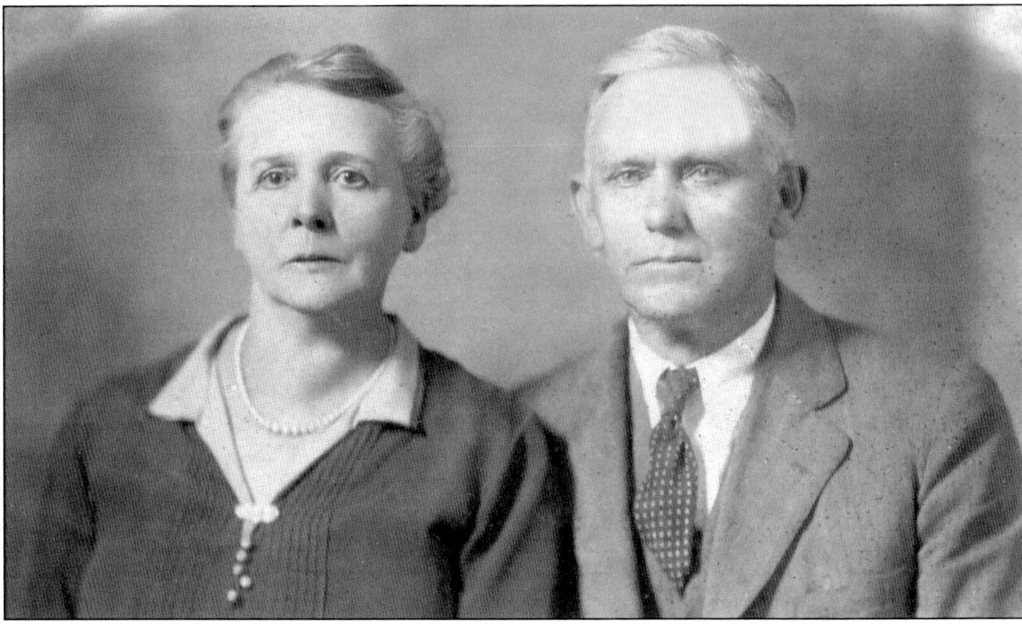

Dosser Buchanan and his wife, Martha Anne Street Buchanan, were prominent citizens of the village of Unicoi. Dosser Buchanan was the first postmaster of the village of Unicoi, accomplishing his mail delivery on horseback. As Unicoi County grew, Buchanan became a merchant, was active in politics, and was elected county judge in 1938. He also generously donated land for the Union Baptist Church in Limestone Cove and the Freewill Baptist Church in Unicoi. (Courtesy of Martha Erwin.)

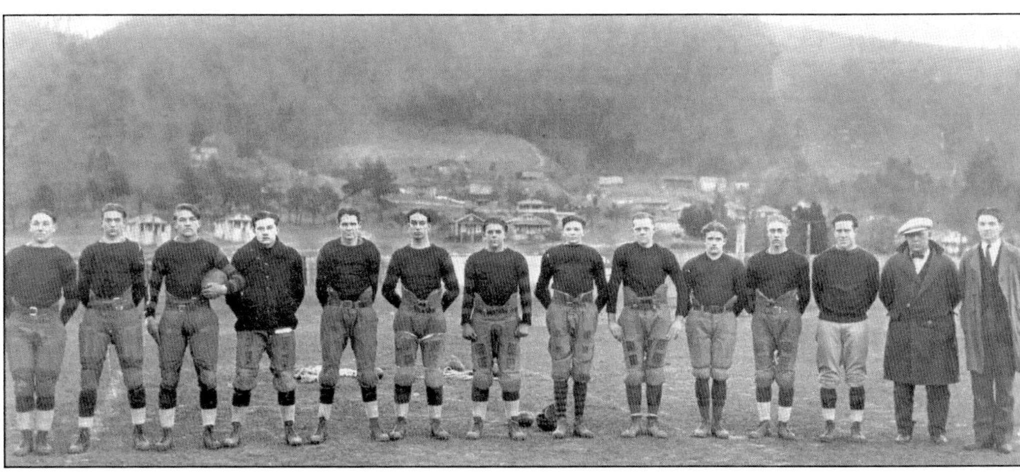

Coach Red Higgins's Erwin High Yellow Jackets football team, with a record of only one loss, played Knoxville Central in 1924 for the state championship, defeating the Bobcats in a 14-0 upset. Coming into the championship game on the strength of two forfeits by other teams, the Erwin team was praised by the *Knoxville Sentinel* as "The Big Boys," whose prowess was worthy of a college team. August Babel and Harry Shull made the winning touchdowns. (Courtesy of the Arnold Williams family.)

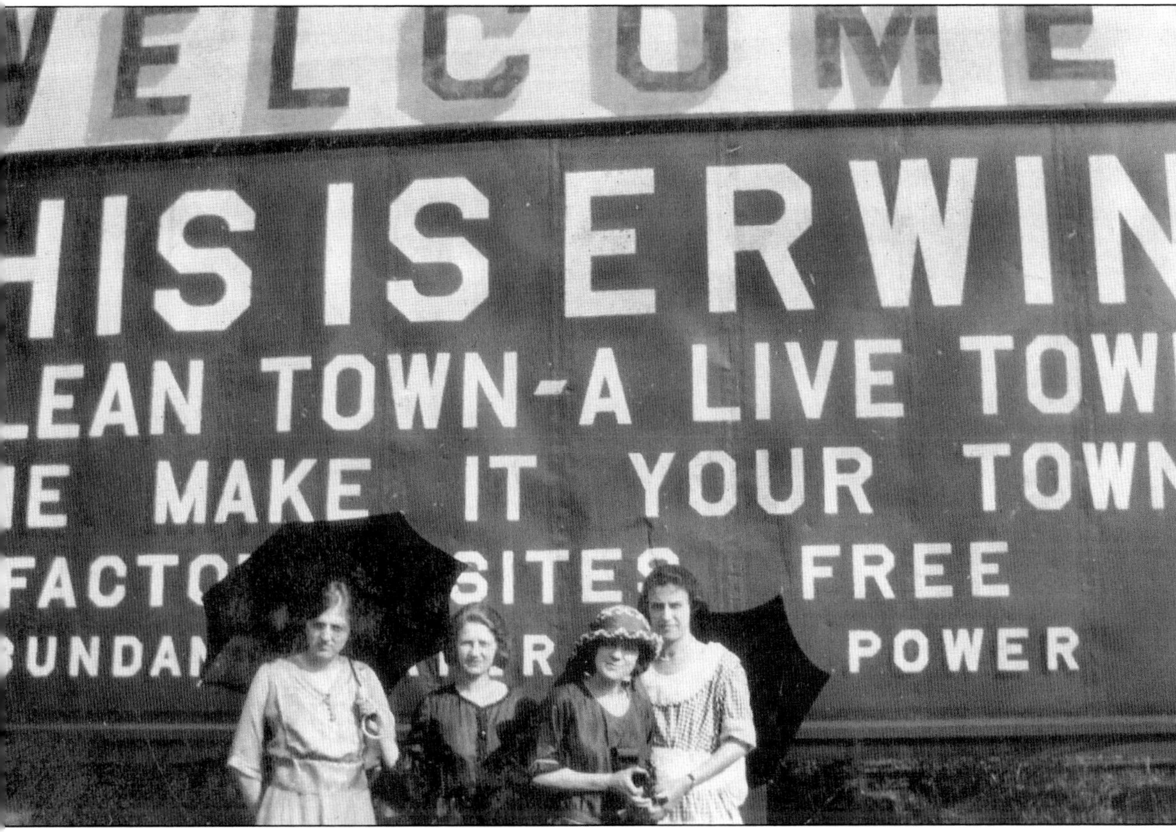

These female members of the "young set" in 1920s Erwin found the town welcome sign the perfect place for a snapshot for their scrapbooks. "This Is Erwin," the oversize sign declared, "A Clean Town—A Live Town, Come Make It Your Town." Business leaders had formed the Commercial Club of Erwin (a forerunner to the chamber of commerce) about this time in an effort to lure new industry and new families to this up-and-coming town. (Courtesy of Juacquetta Davis Edwards.)

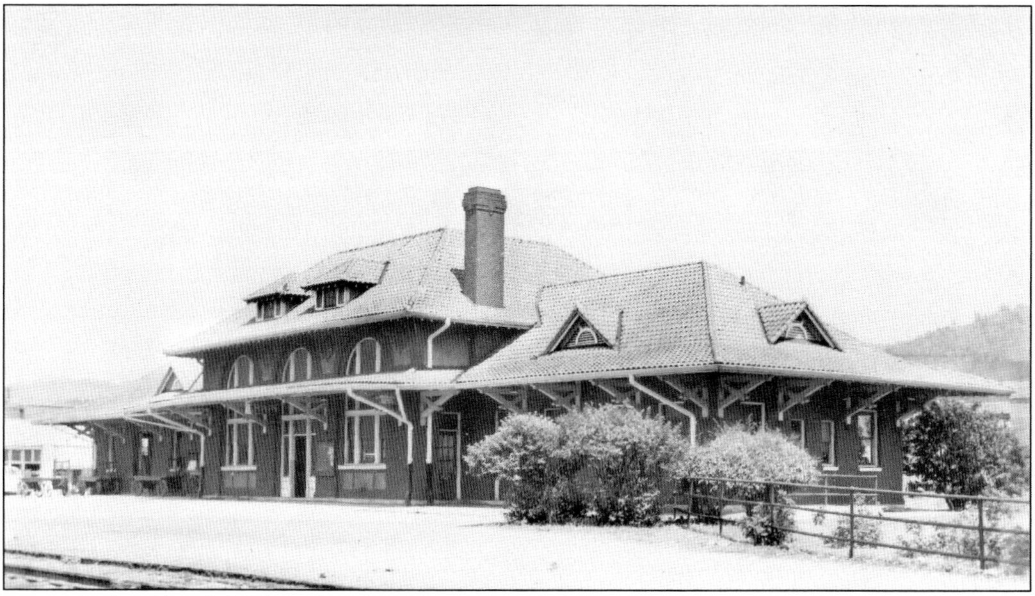

In 1925, the Clinchfield Railroad was enjoying a dizzying prosperity that seemed to have no end. The railroad in Unicoi County employed some 500 workers, and more improvements were promised. One of the most noteworthy was the 1925 construction of this modern and stylish depot on Nolichucky Avenue, designed entirely by the engineering department of the Clinchfield Railroad. Today the old depot has been renovated and is home to Unicoi County's Col. J. F. Toney Memorial Library. (Courtesy of James A. Goforth.)

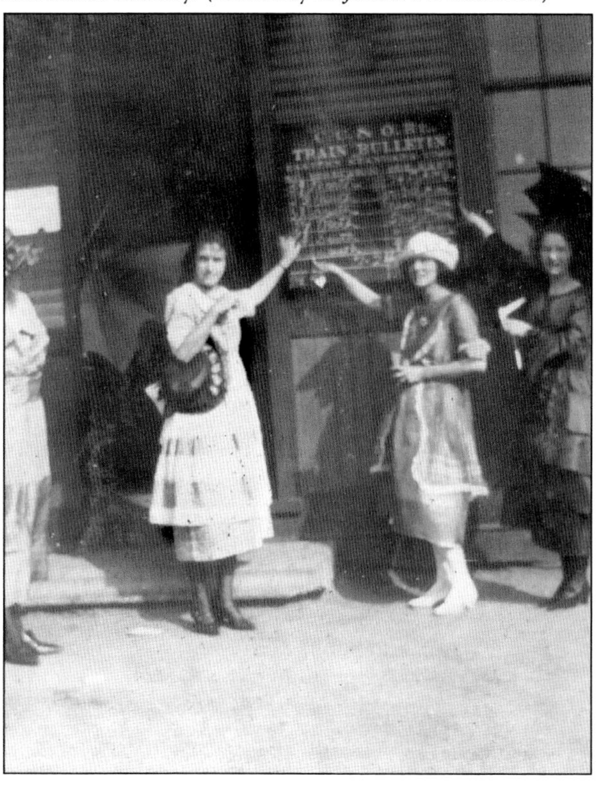

The same young ladies who paid a visit to the town welcome sign on page 69 also visited the new Clinchfield Depot the same day in 1925. The girls emphatically point to the busy Clinchfield passenger train schedule. The chalkboard schedule kept track of the fact that there were as many as six passenger runs a day to and from Erwin to Johnson City—the nearest "big city." (Courtesy of Juacquetta Davis Edwards.)

Toddler Hilda Hope Britt clutches the rail of this ornate settee as she sits, rather precariously, for this studio portrait about 1928. The bright-eyed child grew up to become Hilda Padgett, a local historian and the author of *The Erwin Nine,* the incredible account of nine Unicoi County servicemen who amazingly found themselves in the same POW camp in Germany during World War II. (Courtesy of Hilda Britt Padgett.)

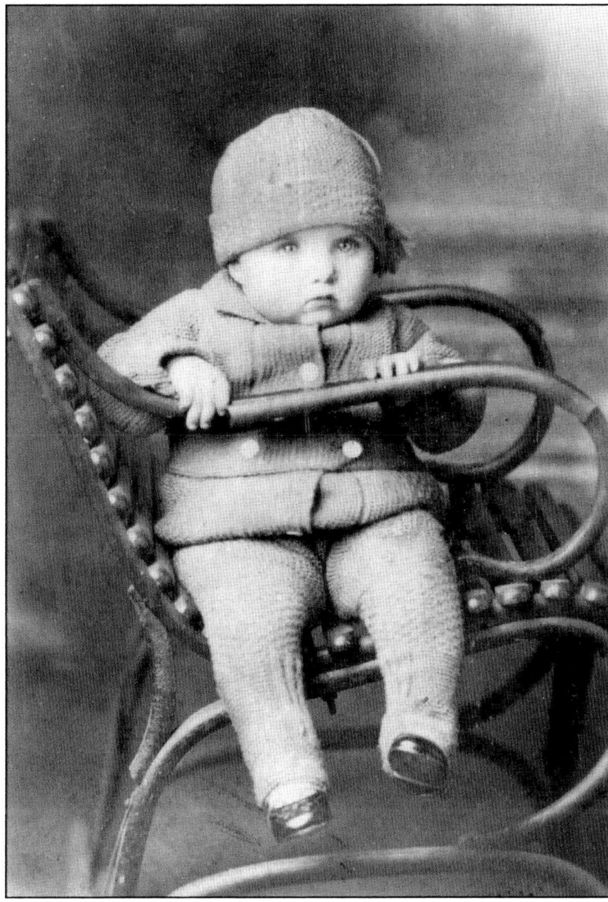

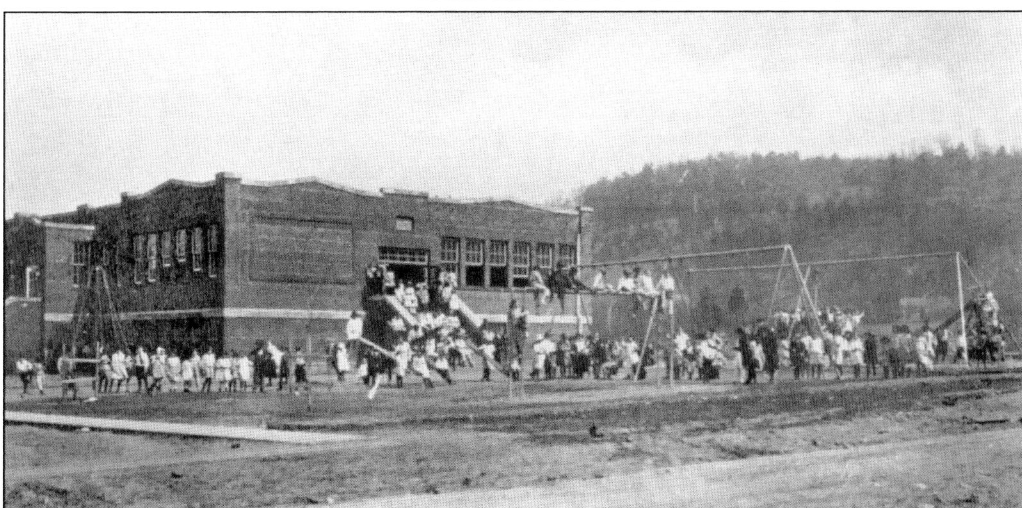

In this photograph from the mid-1920s, the students of Love Street School take full advantage of recess as they run, swing, climb and generally have fun in the open air and sunshine of the playground. The current Unicoi County YMCA and a community soccer field occupy the former site of swings, slides, monkey bars, and teeter-totters. (Courtesy of the Arnold Williams family.)

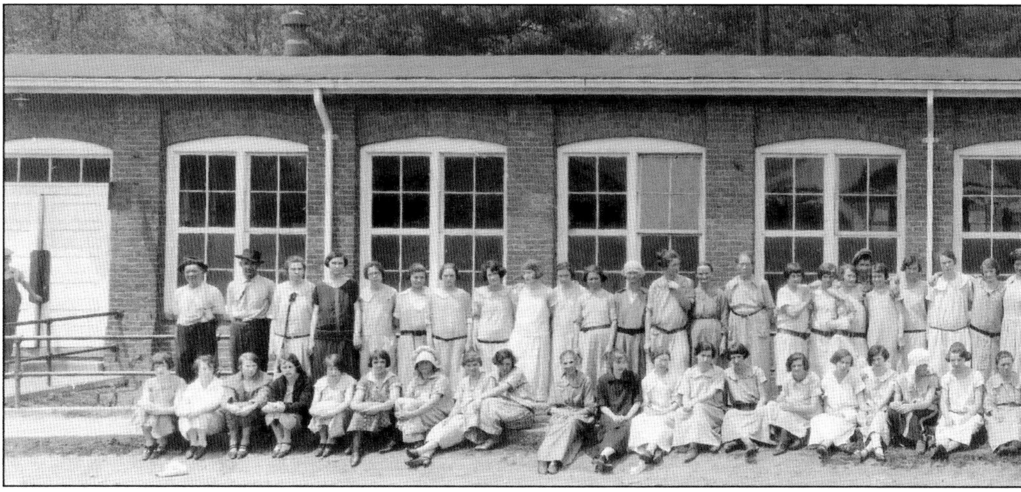

The Silk Mill, located at the south end of Carolina Avenue, was one of the first factory operations in Unicoi County. This panorama photograph, taken in 1927, shows a largely female workforce, reflecting the shift after World War I for women to be able to work outside the home and supplement the family income. The Industrial Garment Company later occupied the site in the 1950s. (Courtesy of the Unicoi County Historical Society.)

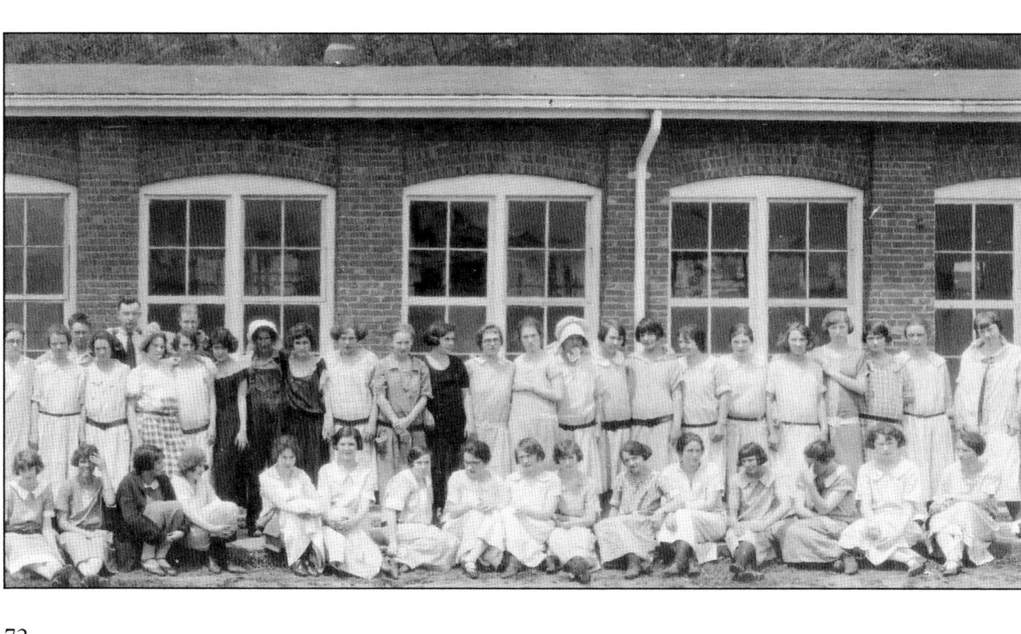

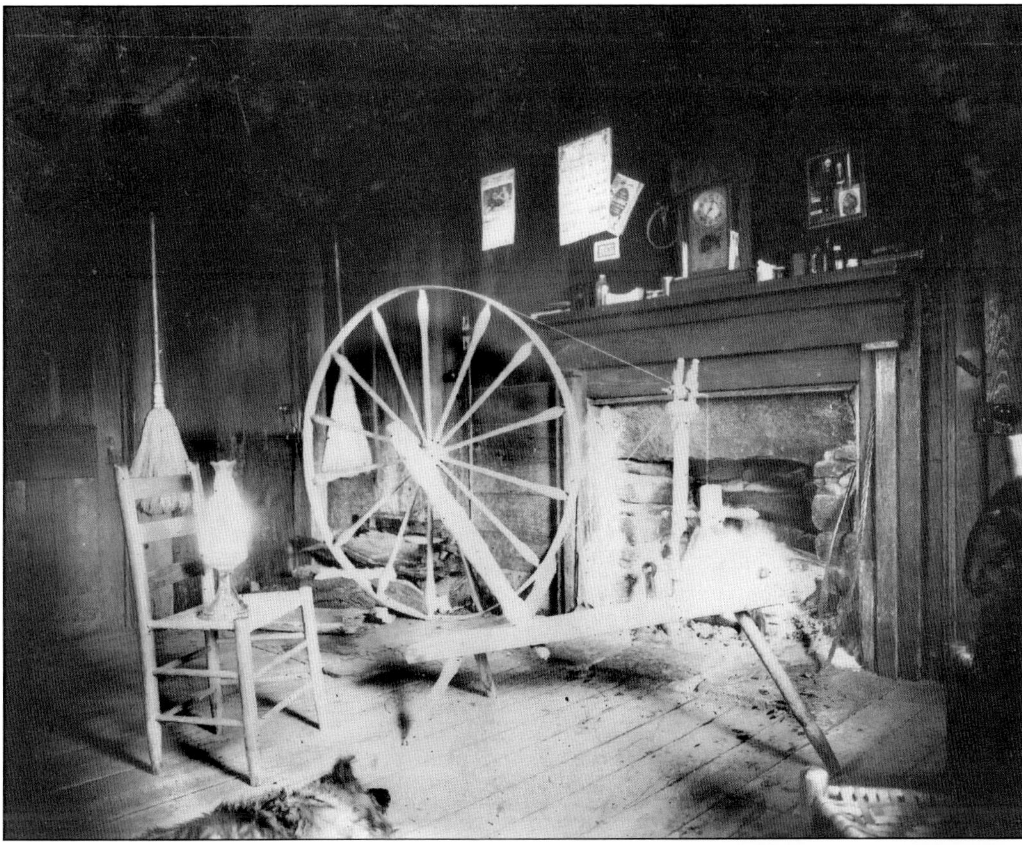

The natural light of a wide-open door and the warm glow of an oil lamp illuminate the interior of the cabin home place of Rev. Jacob Stewart Farnor and his wife, Rebecca, in the late 1920s or early 1930s. An ancient spinning wheel forms the rustic centerpiece of this view of a family hearth typical of early Unicoi County pioneers. The simple serenity of the lifestyle is marked by the handmade chair that holds a lamp, family mementos that decorate the mantelshelf, and a treasured photograph of the cabin's elderly inhabitants, which takes prominence on the wall above the fireplace. That same photograph is seen to the right. Reverend Farnor, born about 1854 in Greene County, was also an educator, serving schools around his Clear Branch community. Rebecca Hardin Farnor, born about 1852, bore five children, Jacob H., John B., Horace H., Clara C., and Laura Lily Abigail. Reverend Farnor died in 1934 and Rebecca in 1939. They are buried in the Clear Branch Cemetery. (Both images courtesy of Dennis and Lillian Foster/ Jakie Farnor collection.)

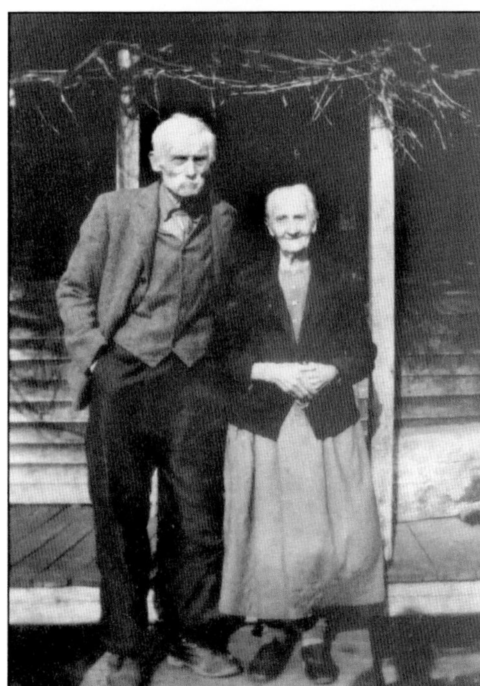

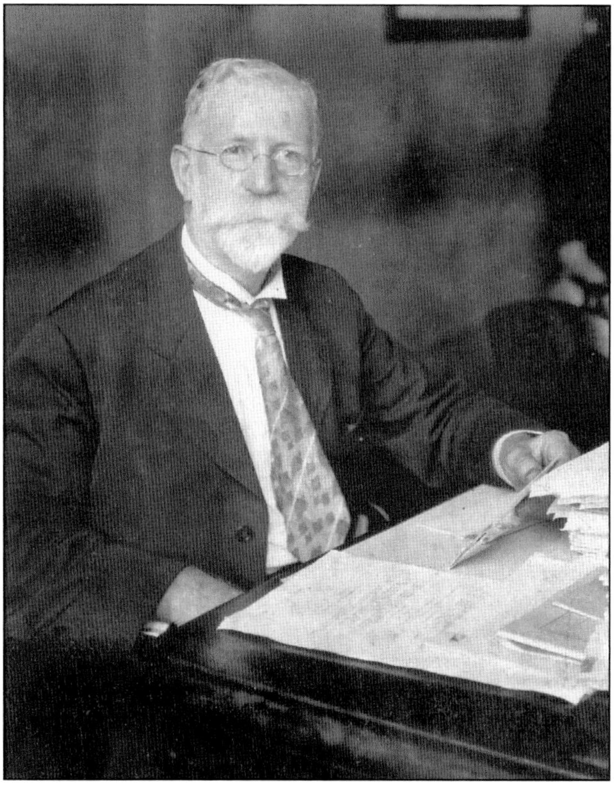

When A. R. Brown died in a tragic automobile accident in 1937 while returning from his son Hayne's graduation at Mars Hill College, it was shock to the whole county. In addition to his own family, A. R. Brown always seemed to include the people of Unicoi County as a sort of extended family. At his death, he left a bequest to benefit those in the county of diminished circumstances. (Courtesy of Martha Brown Stromberg/A. R. Brown collection.)

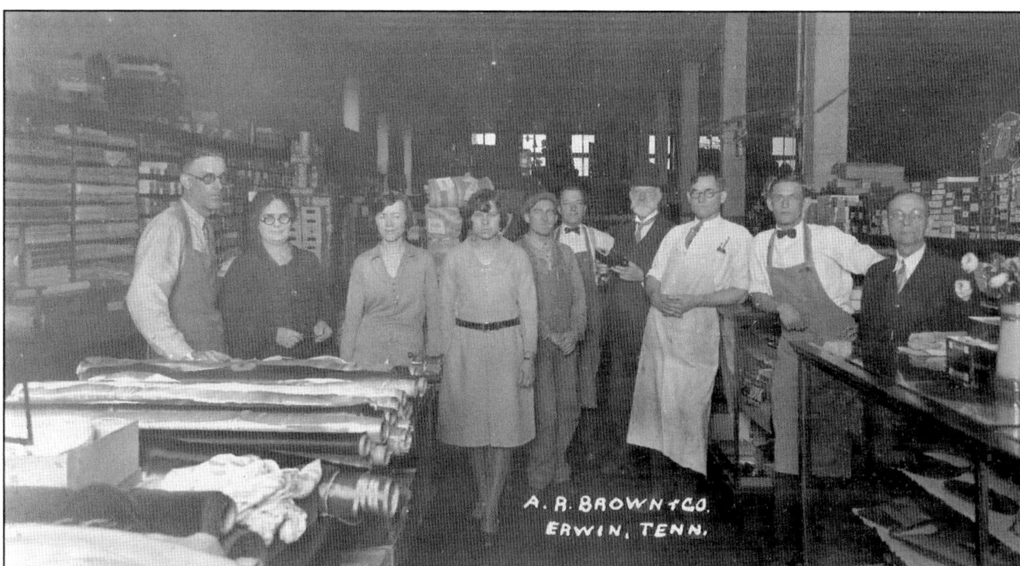

A. R. Brown, the gentleman with the white beard, is seen in the 1920s surrounded by his employees in the dry goods and notions section of his Erwin department store. The store carried not only dry goods and notions, but also family clothing, shoes, and hardware; it also featured a butcher shop and a grocery. In the 1920s and 1930s, a beauty shop operated from the mezzanine. In the 1940s and 1950s, the mezzanine served as a teen music shop and listening room. (Courtesy of Martha Brown Stromberg/A. R. Brown collection.)

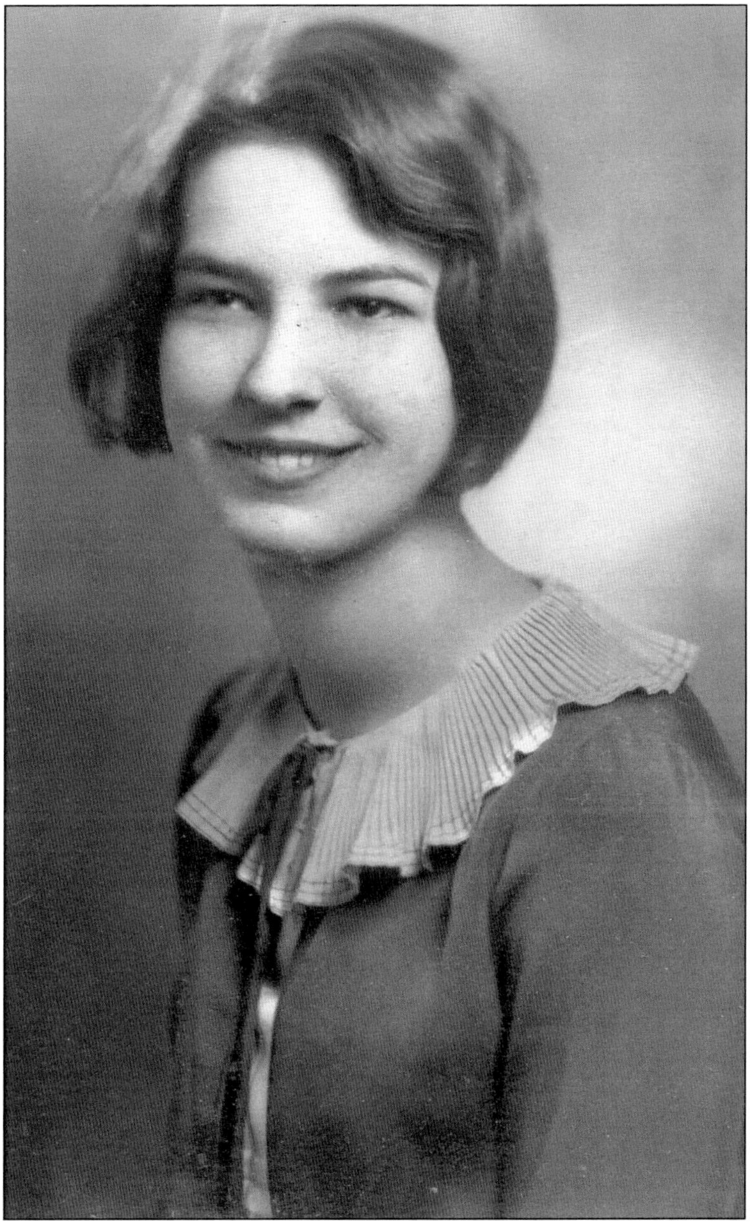

Jodie Brown was the youngest daughter of A. R. and Tuppy Burleson Brown of Erwin. "Miss Jodie," as she was always known, graduated from Carson-Newman College about 1931. She was an archer, an enthusiastic hiker, and an amateur photographer of great skill. When college friends came to visit, Miss Jodie would round everyone up for an energetic hike to "The Pinnacle," the fire tower constructed on Buffalo Mountain in 1931. Beloved by her many friends, she was a devoted daughter to her family. After her father's tragic death in an automobile accident in 1937, Miss Jodie poured all her energies into the family business—A. R. Brown Department Store—often putting her own financial interests aside in favor of customers suffering from hard times. She was known many times to pay out of her own pocket for a child's school shoes or warm winter coat. The much-loved Miss Jodie died in the fall of 2006. (Courtesy of Martha Brown Stromberg/A. R. Brown collection.)

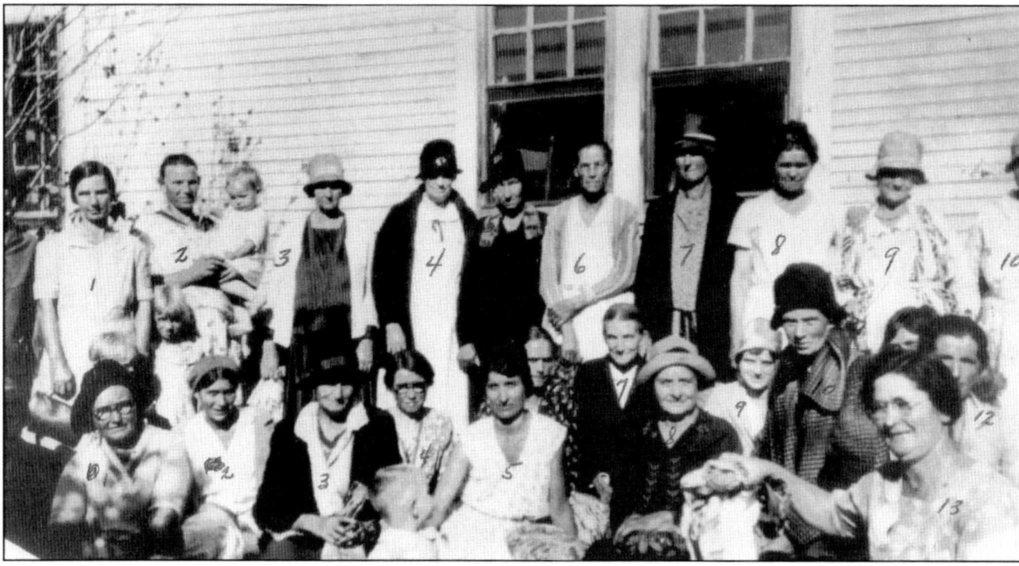

The Rocky Fork community in the mountains of southern Unicoi County has always been prized for the natural beauty of its forest setting. And that very same rugged nature and remote access naturally encouraged folks to turn to each other for social communion. This group of ladies represents the Rocky Fork Ladies Sewing Circle from the 1930s. (Courtesy of the Unicoi County Historical Society.)

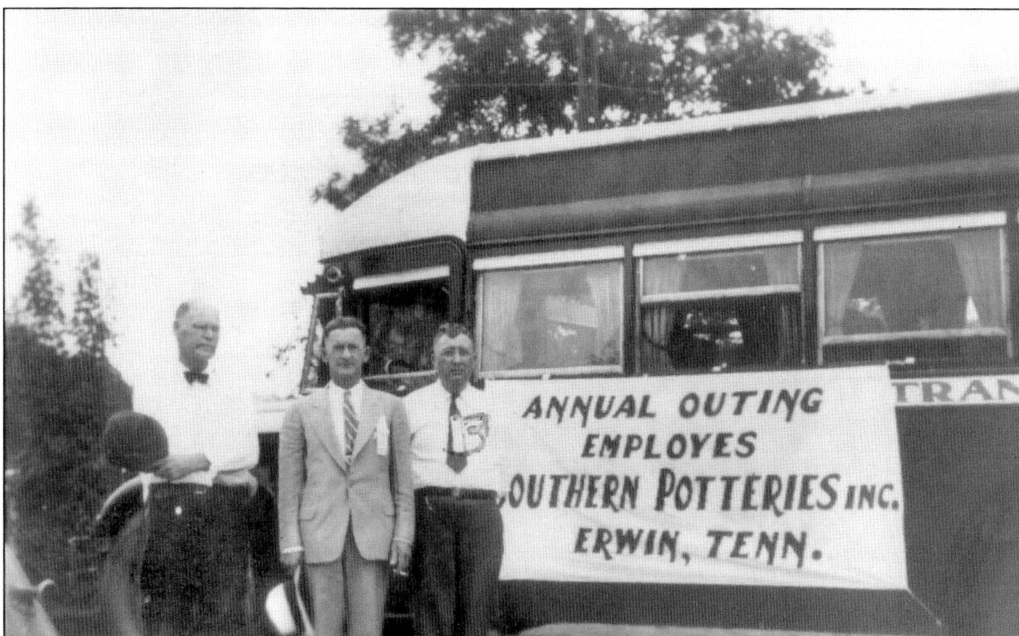

These formally attired gentlemen from the mid-1930s are ready to step aboard the waiting motorbus set to transport workers to the annual Potters Picnic. Erwin's Southern Potteries provided this opportunity for family recreation to its employees as long as it was in operation. The Potters Picnics were first held at the old Fish Hatchery grounds and later as far away as the popular Recreation Park in Asheville, North Carolina, offering fun, games, contests, and lots of wholesome, homemade food. (Courtesy of Hilda Padgett.)

Three

Hard Times and Wartime

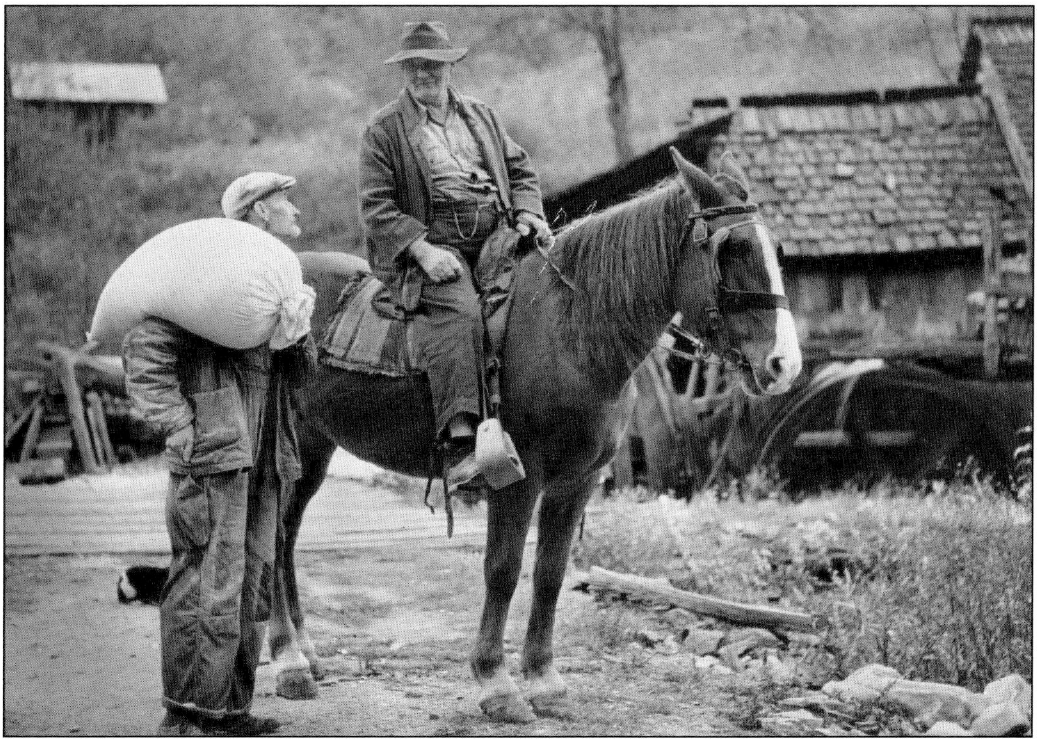

George Frank Tilson and a neighbor on horseback trade a few words near Tilson's gristmill in the Flag Pond community about 1935. Situated in the shadow of big Bald Mountain, the old overshot, water-powered gristmill was one of the last of its kind in the United States. According to the late Pat Alderman, in his book *Tilson Grist Mill*, George Frank Tilson was a self-taught millwright whose natural mechanical ingenuity enabled him to fashion the wooden gears and cogs that operated the grinding stones of his old mill. Customers were neighbors who paid Tilson an eighth of a bushel of ground corn for his services and lived by the "first come, first served" rule. No one minded the wait when there was opportunity to swap news and a few tall tales in the meantime. George Frank and his wife, Matilda, had nine children. George Frank Tilson's descendants have donated the Tilson Grist Mill in total to the Tennessee State Museum in Nashville. (Courtesy of Dennis and Lillian Foster/Jakie Farnor collection.)

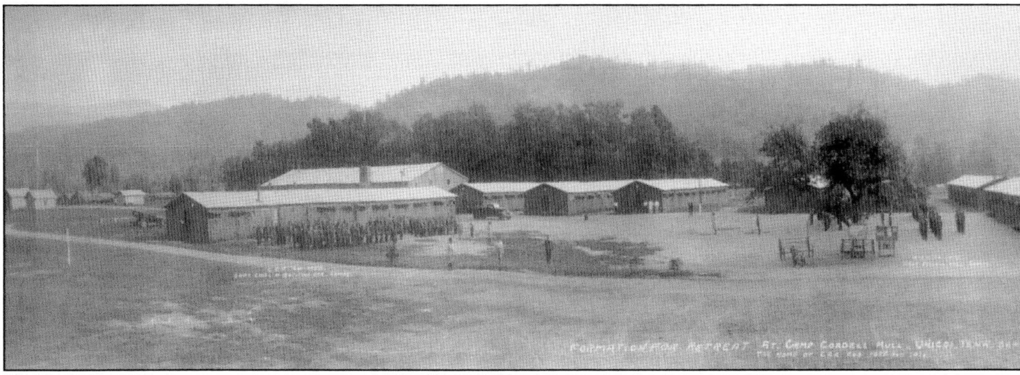

Camp Cordell Hull was Unicoi County's Civilian Conservation Corps (CCC) facility, established on May 27, 1933. The military barracks–style camp, situated off present-day Highway 107 in Limestone Cove, just one mile east of the Town of Unicoi, was home to Companies 1455 and 1472. Working an eight-hour day, the CCC boys earned a wage of $30 a month, $25 of which had to be sent home. They built roads and other projects, such as the Rock Creek Park recreational facility. Below, at right, CCC enlistee Ted Lynch, with an unidentified friend, pauses at the back of an army-issue CCC truck. These trucks ferried the boys to work and back and often to Erwin and Johnson City for some welcome R&R. F. B. White remembers, as a boy, that all the local kids would line Rock Creek Road at day's end to wave to the long parade of CCC trucks as they made their way back to camp. Many of the marriageable young girls of Rock Creek also did the same. (Above courtesy of Guy Street/Cherokee National Forest District Fire District Management; below courtesy of the Ted Lynch family.)

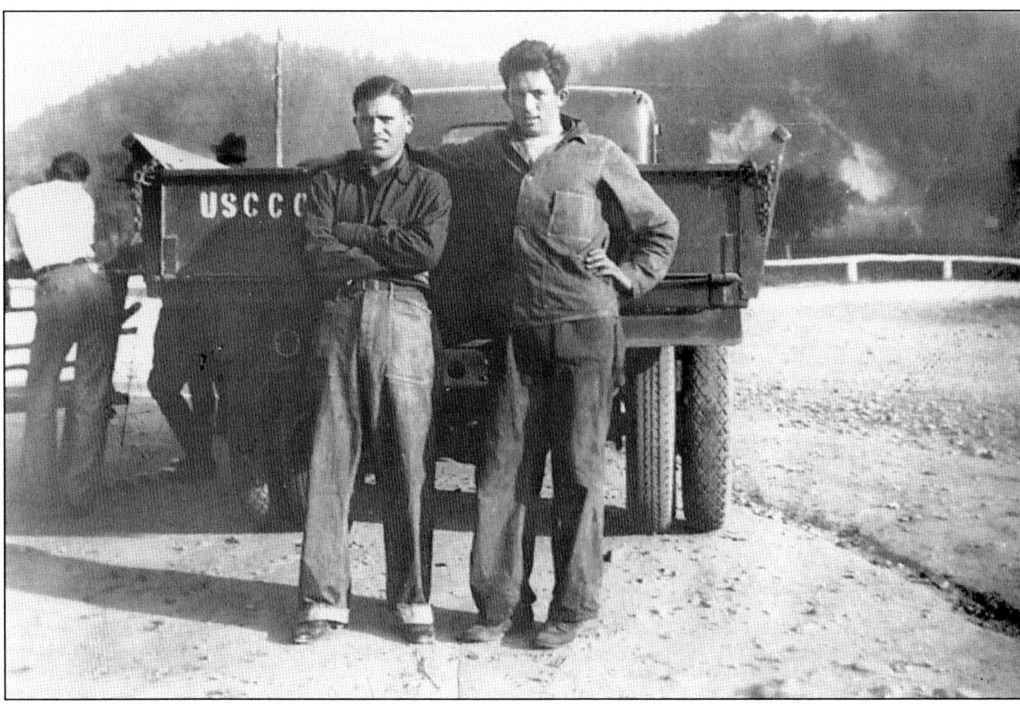

The Oscar E. Bergendahl family of 422 Love Street congregates in a warm family portrait in the side yard of their Victorian home around 1936. Bergendahl, an official at the railroad, and his little son Mick were surrounded by a house of loving females, which included, from left to right, (seated) Mary Frances, Cora, and Catherine. In the second row standing beside their father are Thelma, Ellen, and Theda. Jack, the family dog, is at Mick's feet. The Bergendahl family has lived at 422 Love Street since 1923. (Courtesy of the O. E. Bergendahl family.)

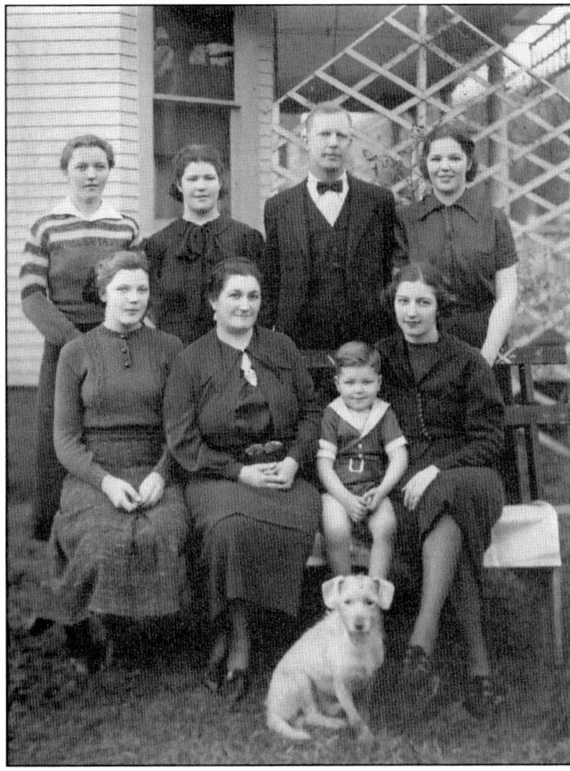

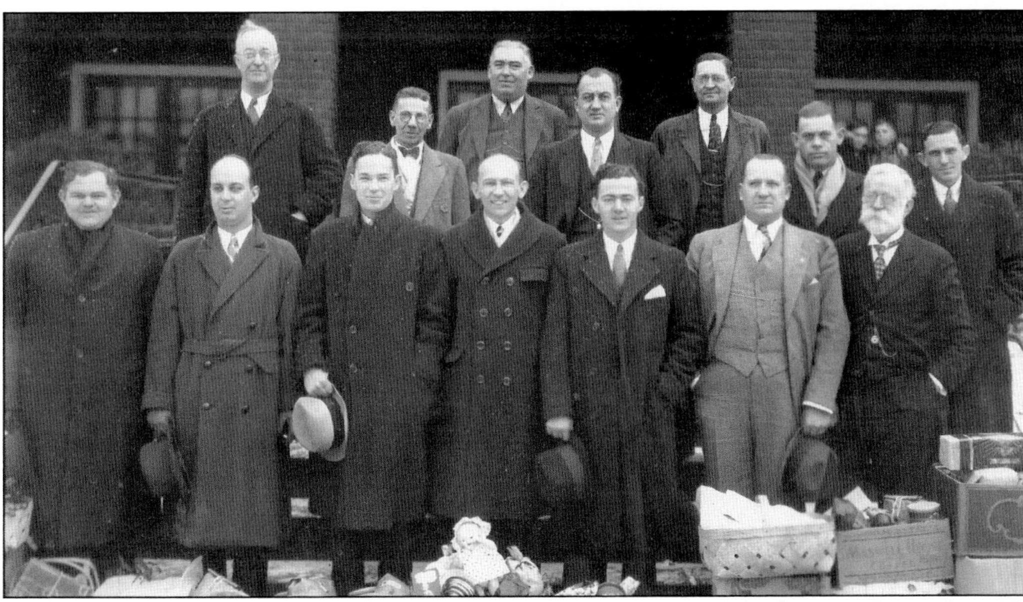

These prominent gentlemen are all members of the Erwin Kiwanis Club. Shown in December 1935 on the steps of the old Main Street YMCA, are, from left to right, the following: (first row) Dr. Harmon Monroe, Dennis Erwin, Jack DeArmond, Carl Miller, Clifford Rule, Fred Booth, and A. R. Brown; (second row) Bill Erwin, J. H. Chapman, Frank Gentry, coach Bob Snyder, unidentified, Guy Robbins, and Ben Husband. Organizations such as the Kiwanis helped Depression-weary citizens cope with the times. (Courtesy of Martha Brown Stromberg/A. R. Brown collection.)

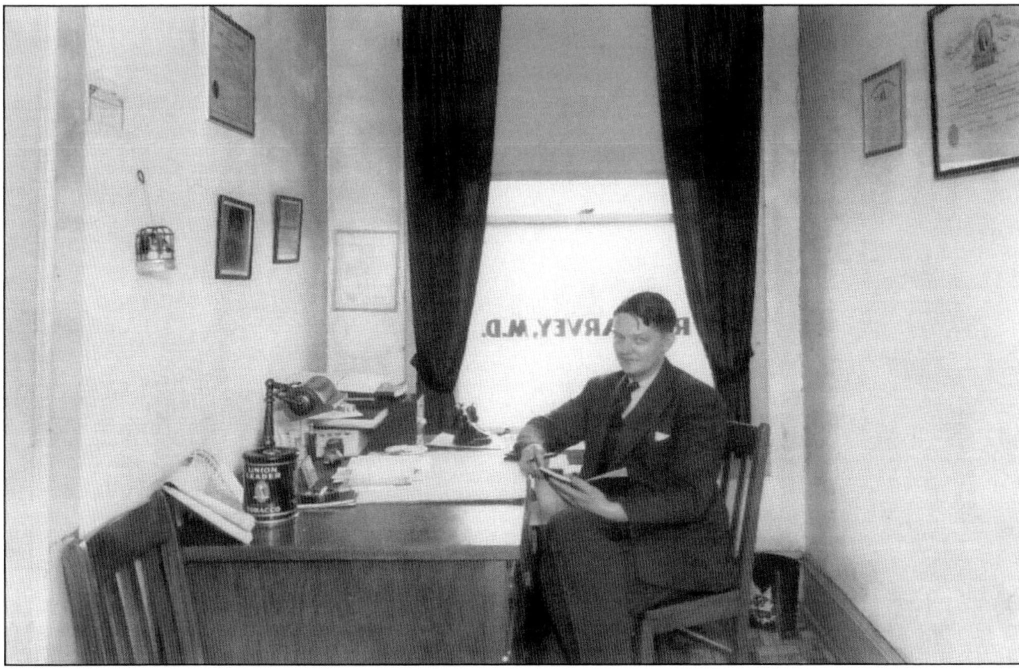

Dr. Robert Harvey's office was situated on Gay Street, upstairs from the old Erwin's clothiers. Graduating from Vanderbilt University, Dr. Harvey came to Erwin in 1936 following a medical residency that stipulated that he practice initially in areas of greatest need. He delivered many Unicoi County babies in his long career, including the author. (Courtesy of Becky Harvey Love.)

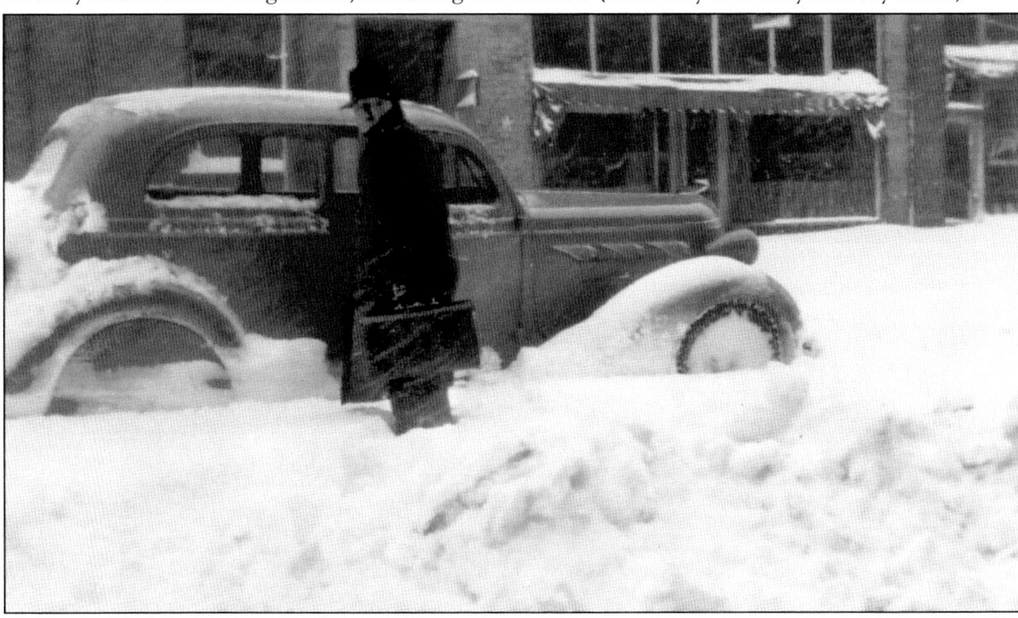

Overwhelming the area with almost 4 feet of snow, the Big Snow of 1936 is the stuff of legend in Unicoi County. In those Depression-era days of limited communication and transportation, most everything came to a standstill but the railroad. Dr. Harmon Monroe is seen here attempting a house call. That day he had to abandon his automobile and walk knee-deep in snow to a home in Banner Hill to deliver a baby. (Courtesy of Carole Monroe Tilson.)

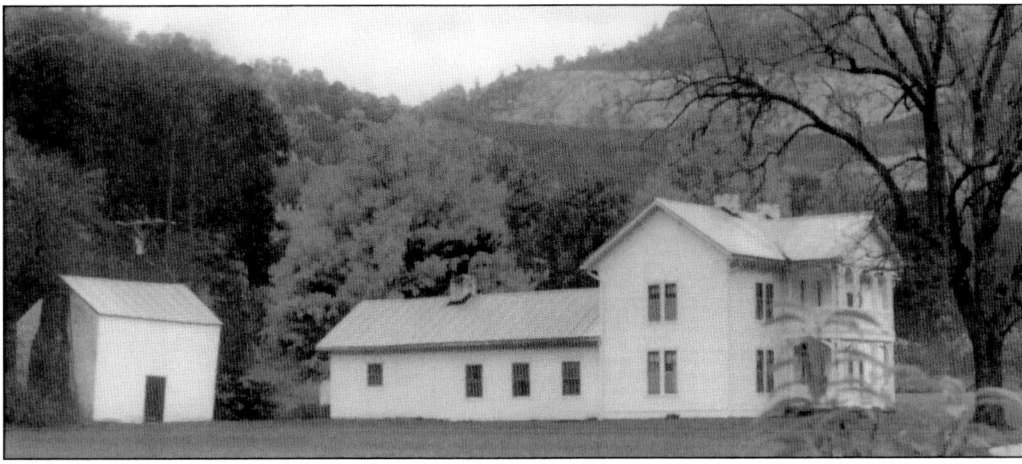

Josiah B. Sams and his wife, Rebecca Murray, raised eight children in this elegant home in the fertile valley in Flag Pond known as "Sams Gap," which is near the North Carolina border. According to family history, Josiah's father, James Brown Sams, from North Carolina, first settled in this area after his wagon broke down on top of the mountain at the border with North Carolina. The original James B. Sams cabin is situated behind the larger home and was later used as a summer kitchen. Below, the children of Josiah B. Sams gathered for a family reunion at the homestead in 1937. Pictured from left to right are the following: (first row) J. E. Sams, W. T. Sams, Lee W. Sams, and J. P. Sams; (second row) John B. Sams, Mathilda Sams Webster, Lucinda Sams Bailey, and Mary Elizabeth Sams Phillips. (Both images courtesy of Bob Sams.)

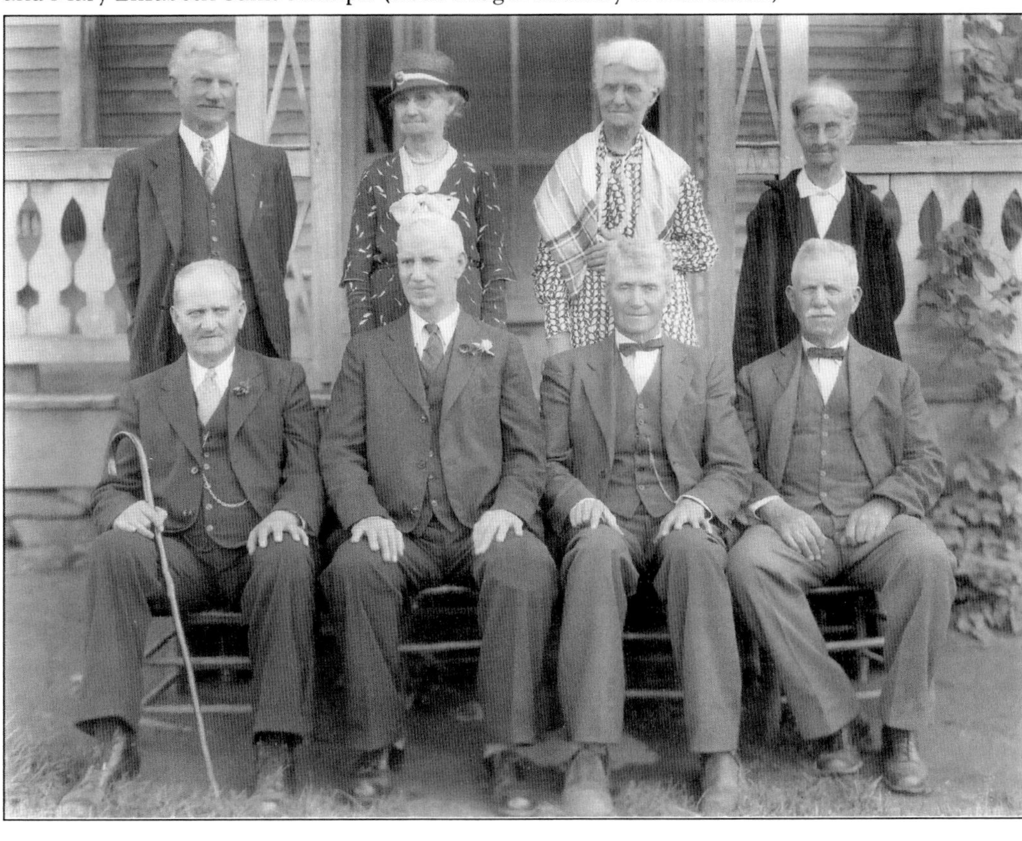

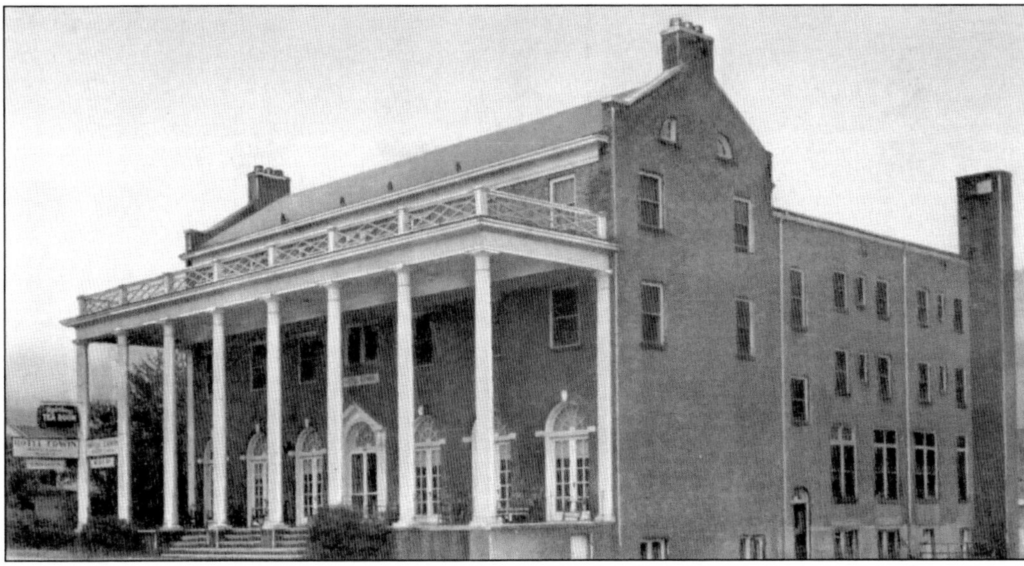

For many years, the Hotel Erwin was a prime destination for hospitality, dining, and important community gatherings in Unicoi County. Constructed in 1922 at a cost of $100,000, all rooms boasted private baths and in-room telephones. A lavish dining room could accommodate almost 200. Known as "the Town House Hotel" after a refurbishment in 1957, a special congratulatory edition of the *Erwin Record* documented the grand reopening event. (Courtesy of Lewis Thornberry.)

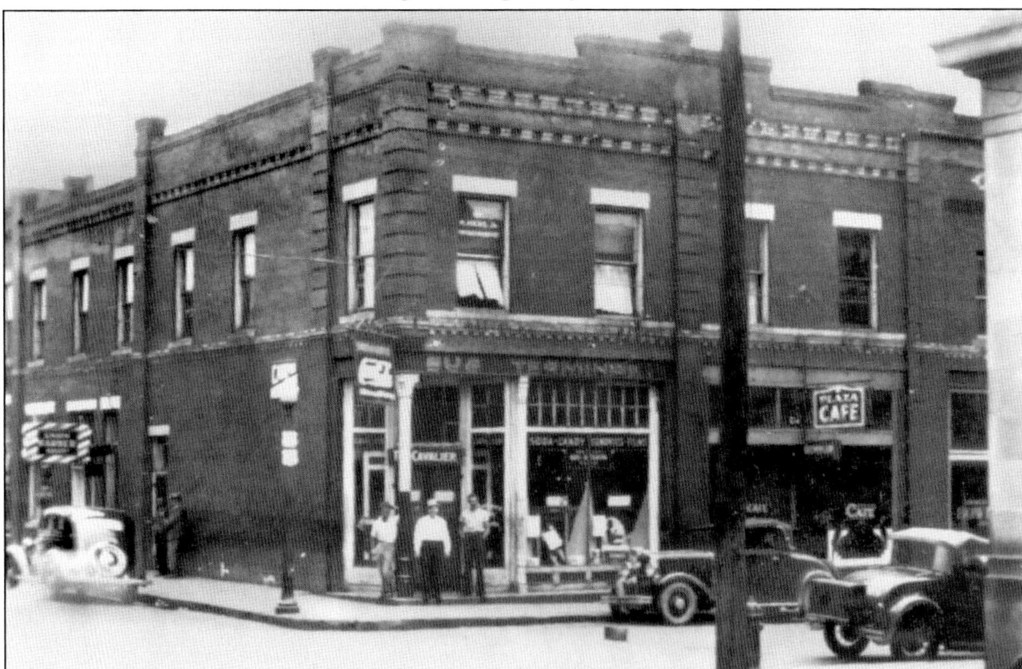

This view of the south corner of Main and Union Streets is unrecognizable today. In the 1930s, it was home to the Palace Confectionery, reputedly the source of the best nickel ice cream cone in town. The building served as a bus terminal as well. To the right is the Plaza Café and just out of sight was the old city newsstand and smoke shop. A 1930s-era coupe is parked just outside the 1928 Erwin National Bank. (Courtesy of the Arnold Williams family.)

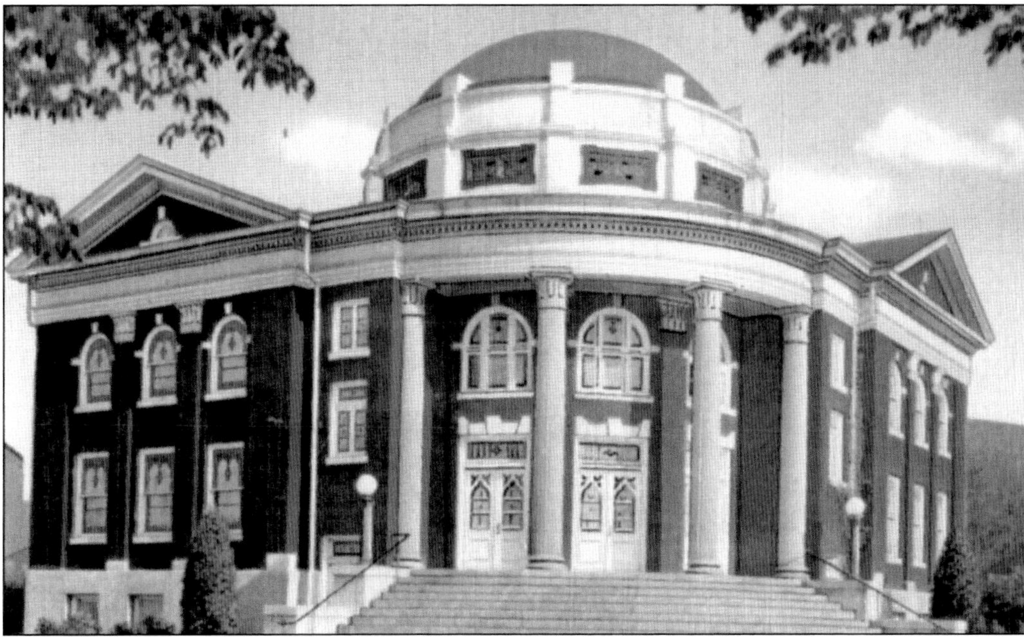

The classic architecture of the Erwin Presbyterian Church on Elm Avenue, with its beautiful central dome, fluted columns, and Palladian windows is featured in this postcard from the 1930s. This distinctive church building, completed in 1927, replaced the earlier, more traditional Presbyterian church that had been originally constructed on the site. (Courtesy of Lewis Thornberry.)

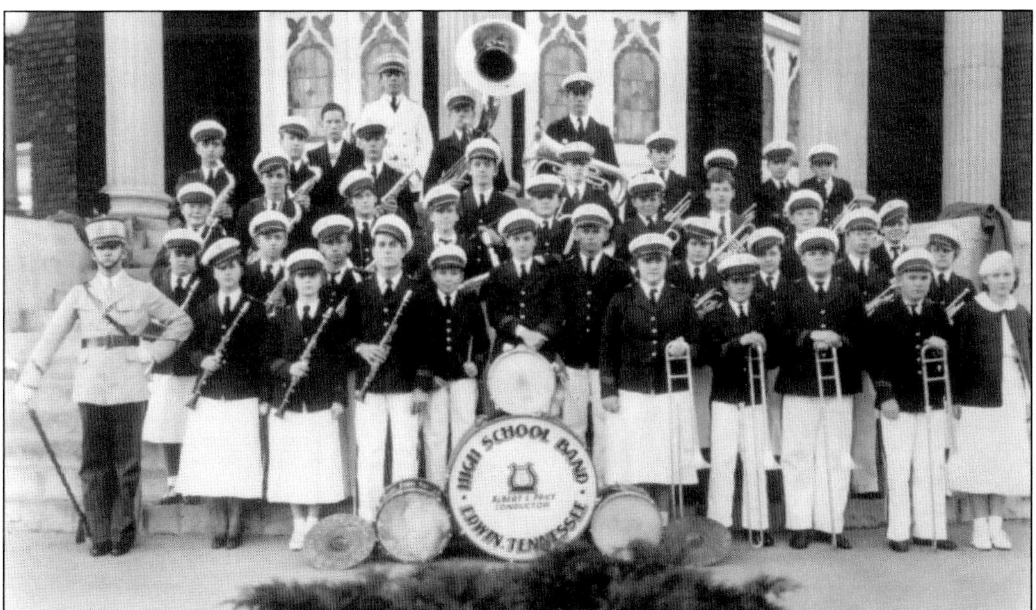

The Erwin High School Band came into being in 1931 under the direction of Prof. Albert L. Price and proved its marching prowess at a halftime field show during a 1933 home game between Erwin and Jonesborough. The drill team formed the letter "E" while the band played. Posed on the steps of the Erwin Presbyterian Church is the 1938 Erwin High School Band in full parade regalia. (Courtesy of Lewis Thornberry.)

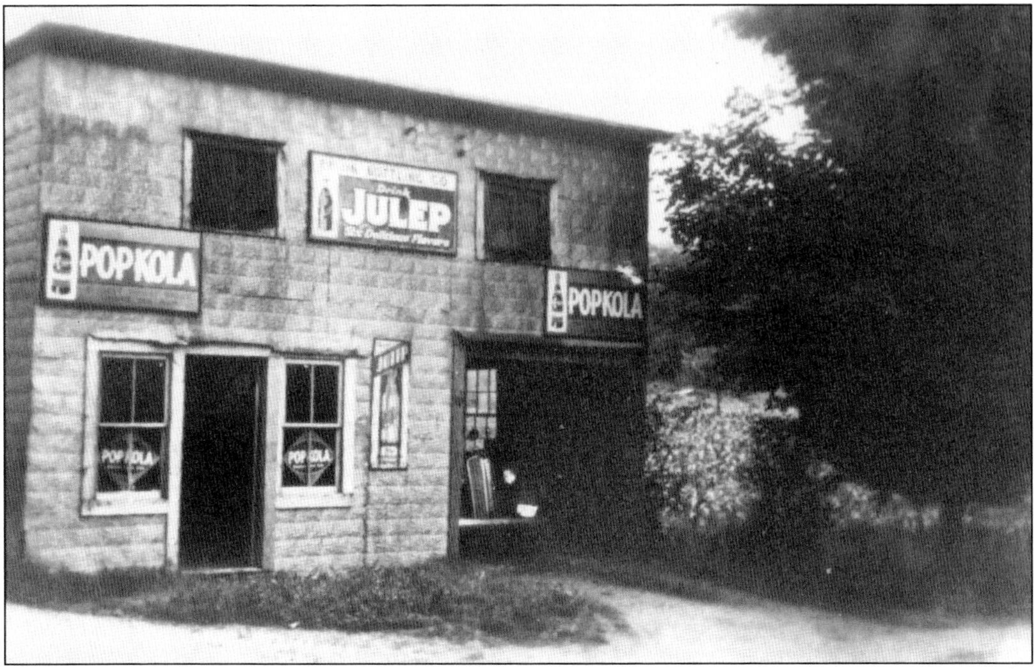

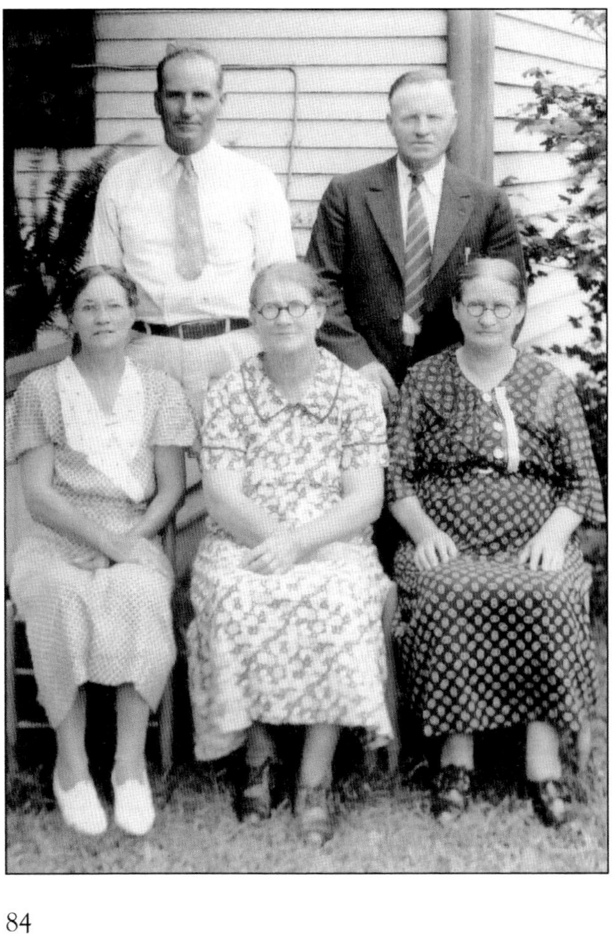

The Charlie Brummett family bottled POP KOLA and JoJo Chocolate locally. This cinder block building on North Elm Avenue was the headquarters, factory, and distribution site for these two regional soft drink favorites from 1924 to the late 1950s. POP KOLA was offered in an array of fruit flavors with root beer and ginger ale variations as well. Heated bottles of JoJo Chocolate were favorites available at nighttime Blue Devil football games at Gentry Stadium. (Courtesy of Sam Keesecker.)

The five McInturff siblings gathered for a family photograph in the late 1930s. Shown from left to right are the following: (first row) Sally McInturff Huskins, who married Jim Huskins; Margaret McInturff Booth, who married William Henry Booth; and Molly McInturff Tapp, who married Tom Tapp (an early sheriff); (second row) Charlie and Alfred McInturff. (Courtesy of Bill Booth.)

Madison Love Banner was born in 1853. Matt's grandfather Benjamin came to Tennessee with his brother Ephraim from North Carolina. His father, Lewis, a respected gunsmith, settled at Indian Grave Gap near the Beauty Spot. Matt, who lived at Martin's Creek, operated one of the chief sawmills in Unicoi County, providing a significant supply of lumber during the county's population boom. When he died in 1937, Matt was buried in a cherrywood casket of his own design. (Courtesy of Lucille Hensley Booth.)

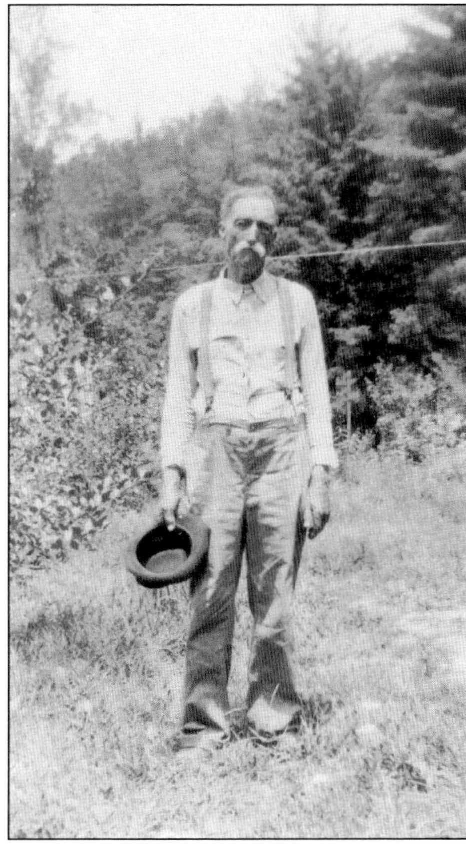

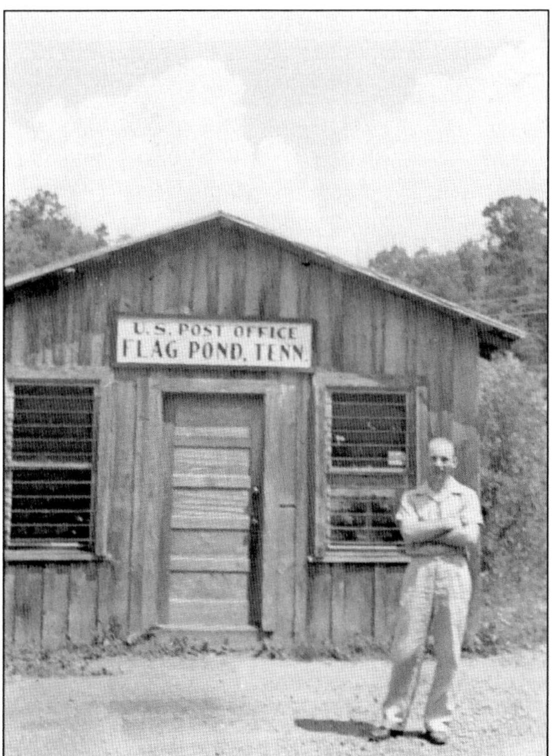

The proud postmaster of Flag Pond, in Unicoi County's southern mountains, poses in front of his place of business sometime in the 1930s or 1940s. The mail was important to the rural communities in the coves and hollows surrounding Erwin, where travel was often difficult at best. (Courtesy of Dennis and Lillian Foster/Jakie Foster collection.)

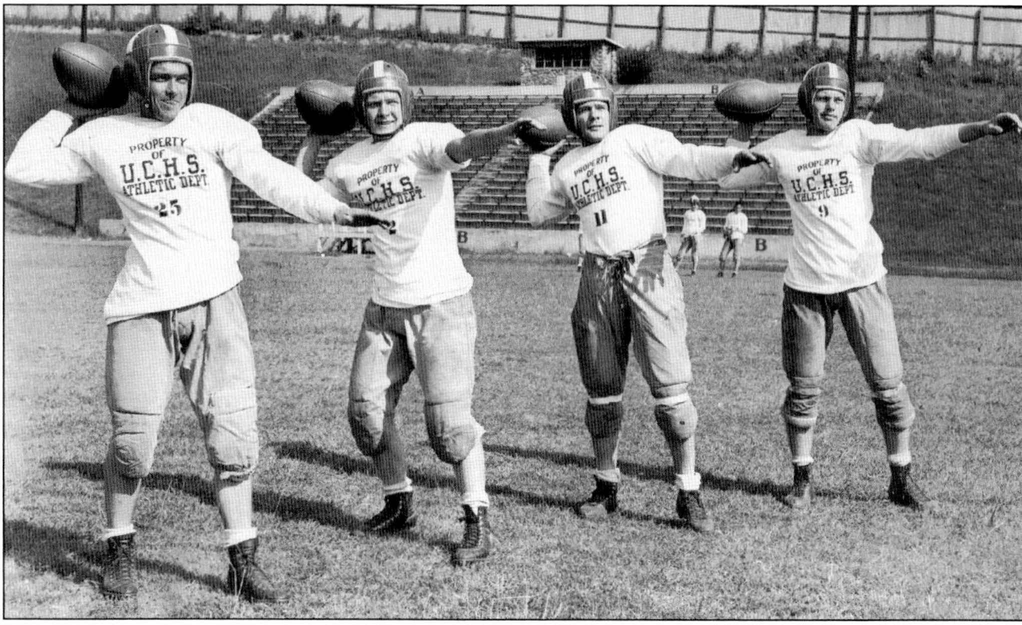

From left to right, Clyde Doan, Howard Bailey, Jack Heilman, and Jake Pope demonstrate the form of the Unicoi County High School football offensive line in this photograph, taken at Gentry Stadium in 1940. Football helmets had no face guards in those days, and padding was at a minimum. Gentry Stadium, a Works Progress Administration (WPA) project, was built in 1935 and named for school superintendent Frank Gentry Sr. (Courtesy of Bert Thompson.)

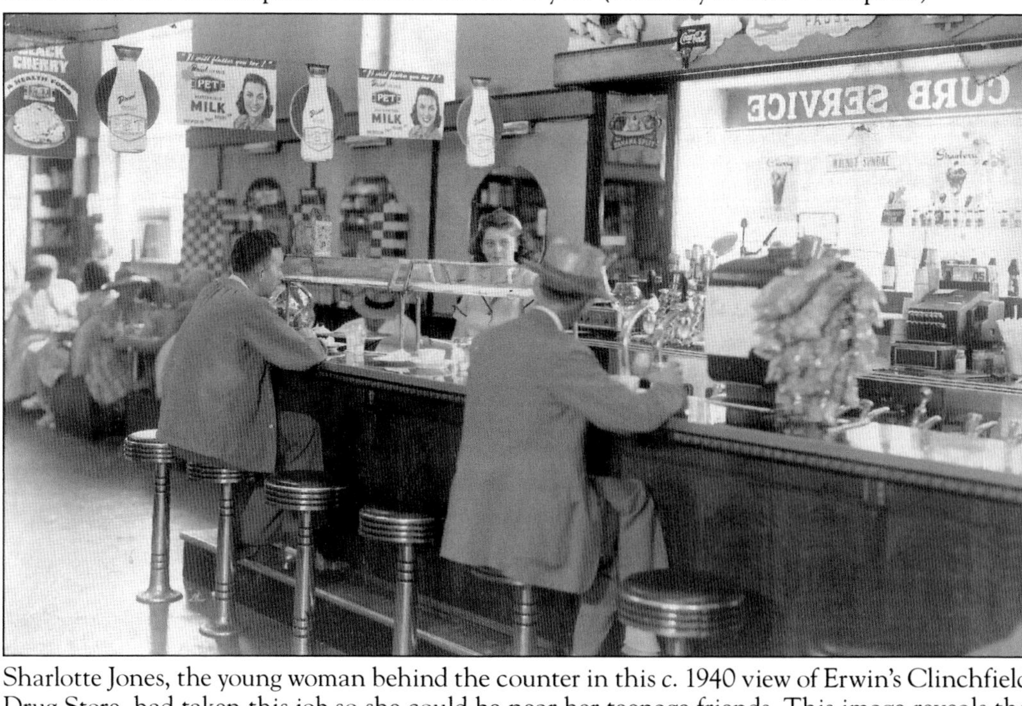

Sharlotte Jones, the young woman behind the counter in this c. 1940 view of Erwin's Clinchfield Drug Store, had taken this job so she could be near her teenage friends. This image reveals the old northern windows, which are now covered over. Today's still very busy lunch counter is now on the opposite side of the building. (Courtesy of Sharlotte Jones-Rynders.)

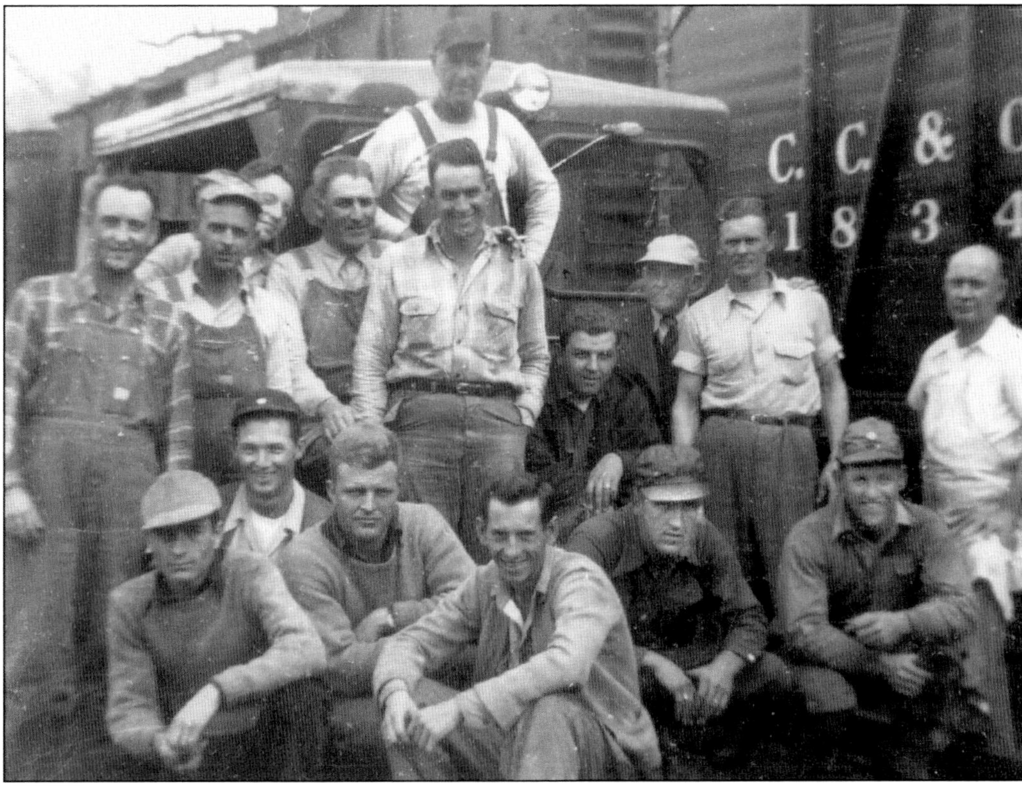

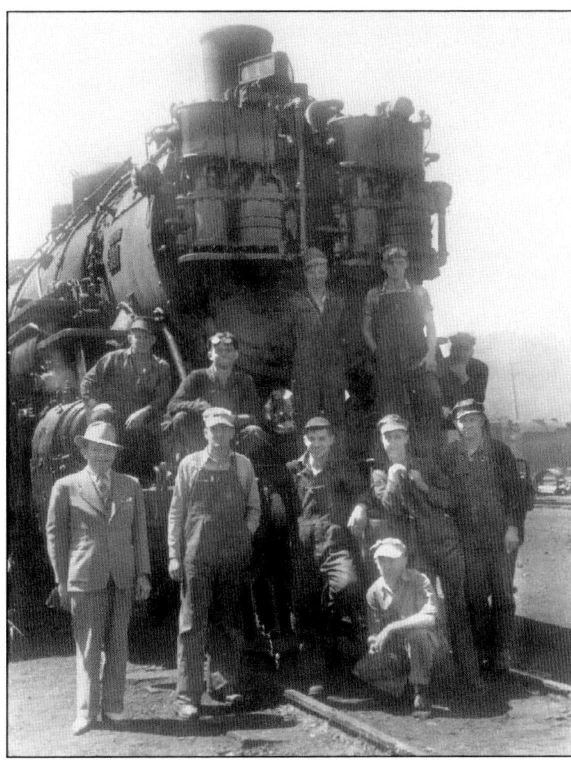

The camaraderie of a small county is evident in the easy familiarity and smiling faces of these Clinchfield Railroad men of the early 1940s. This second generation of railroad men had, for the most part, known each other since childhood, had fathers who had laid the first rails in the mountains or commandeered the old locomotives through the rugged Nolichucky Gorge. Often sharing tall tales and an on-the-rails breakfast of bacon and eggs fried in a fiery-hot coal shovel, these men of the Clinchfield were indeed a brotherhood and the heart and soul of this East Tennessee railroad community. To the right, the Clinchfield Railroad Softball Team gathered for a group photograph in front of a massive locomotive, still wearing the coal dust from their day's work. (Above courtesy of Christine Christy Tipton; below courtesy of Bob Sams.)

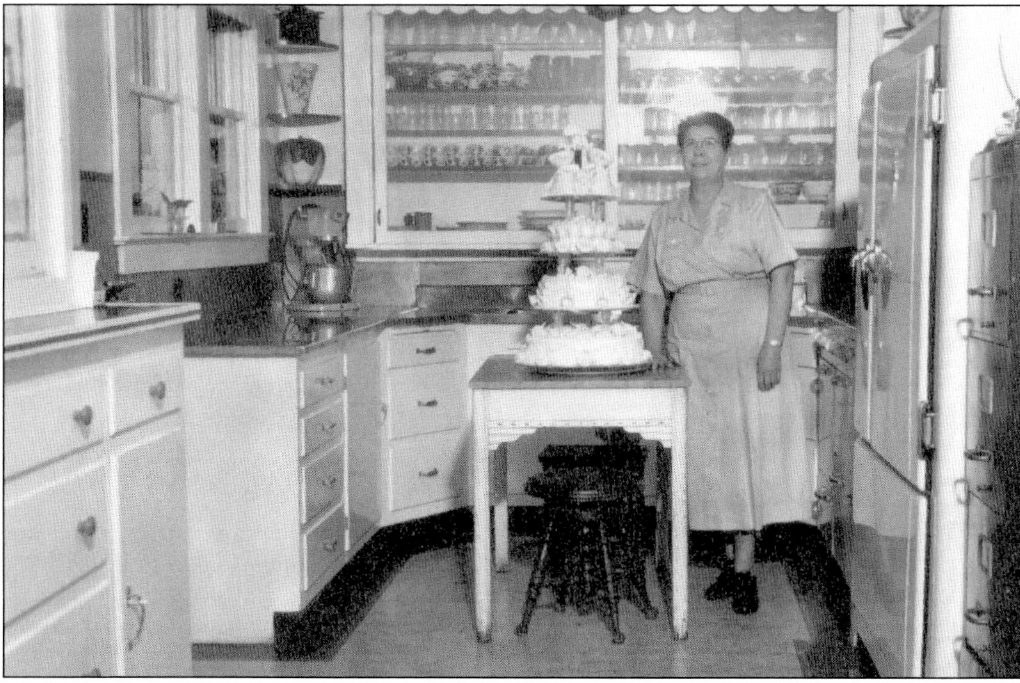

In the late 1930s and 1940s, if a spectacular cake was needed for any occasion, Belle Morgan got the call. Shown in her well-equipped 1940s kitchen on Love Street, Morgan stands proudly beside one of her elaborate confectionery creations. (Courtesy of Martha Brown Stromberg/A. R. Brown collection.)

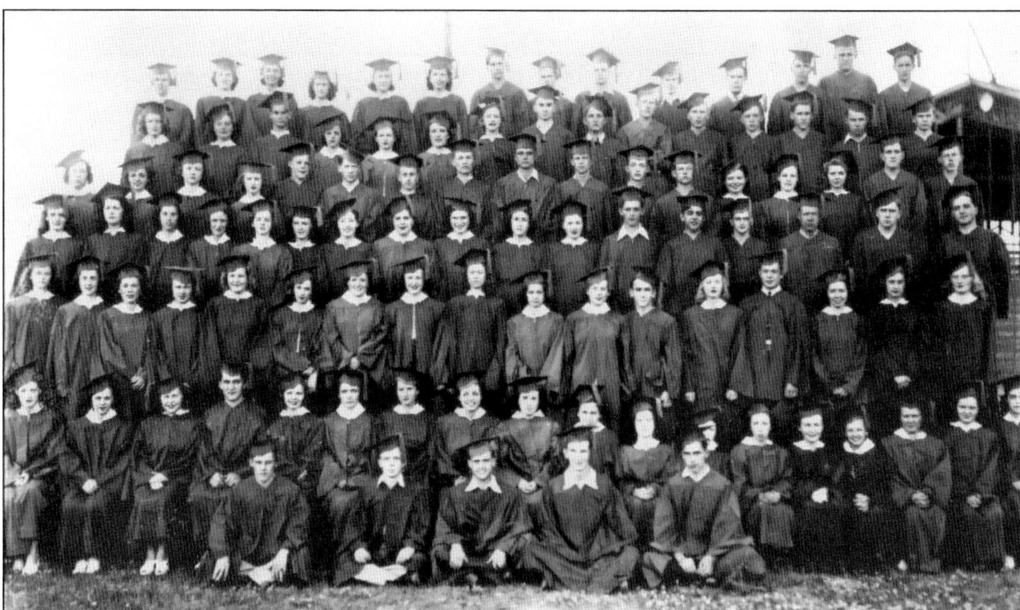

The Unicoi County High School graduating class of 1941 was 103 strong when they mounted the bleachers for this group portrait in cap and gown. Graduation would be spring of 1941, just months before Pearl Harbor would change the lives of these smiling teenagers forever. (Courtesy of the Arnold Williams family.)

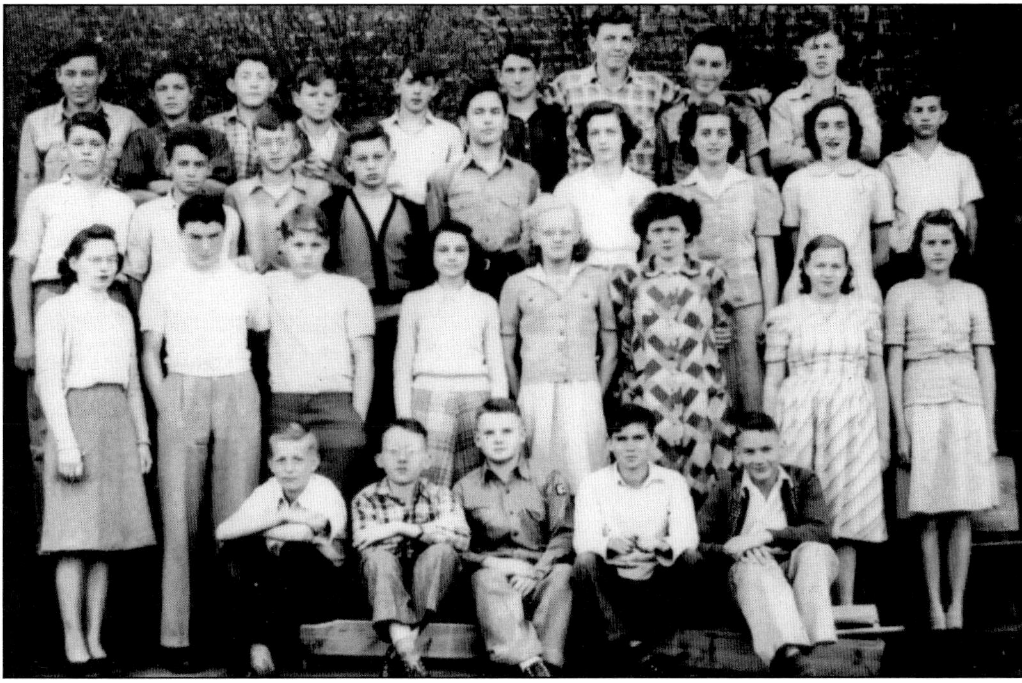

These students of Love Street School were just 13 years old when this class picture was made about 1940. World War II was just over the horizon. James Davis, the serious young man pictured in the back row on the extreme right, went to war as a green, young 17-year-old, returning from the navy in 1945 with wisdom beyond his years. (Courtesy of the Arnold Williams family.)

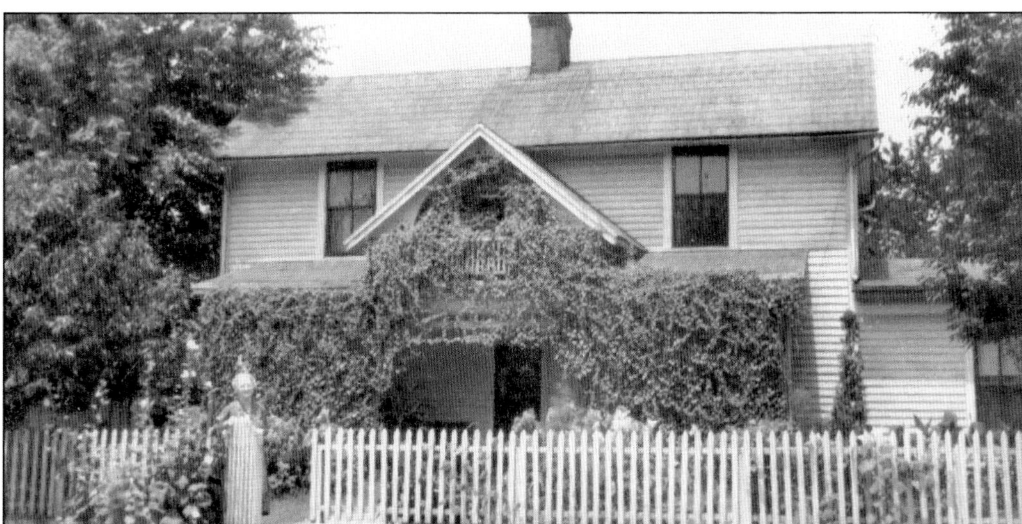

Tuppy Burleson Brown stands at the gate of the picket fence surrounding her home at 241 South Main Avenue in 1944. Known for her abundant flower gardens and the blooming vines that draped her charming old house, Brown also cultivated exotic succulent plants in a picturesque glass greenhouse in her side yard. (Courtesy of Martha Brown Stromberg/A. R. Brown collection.)

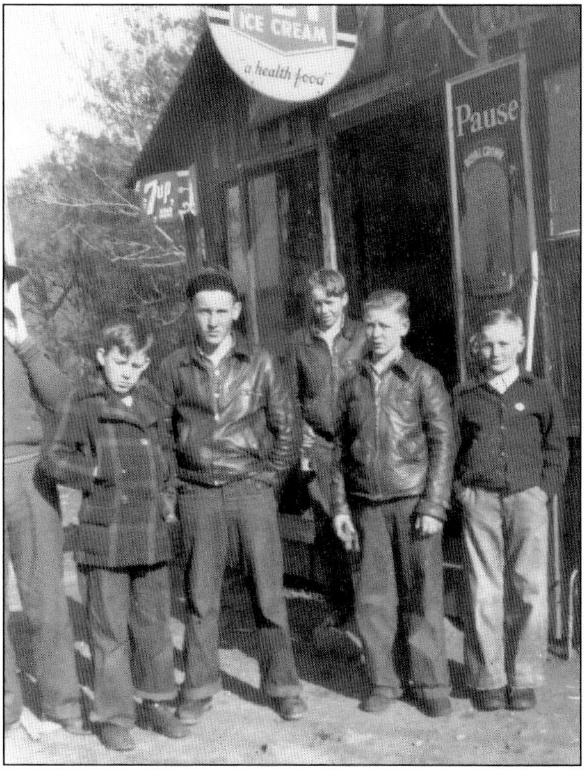

The young men shown in front of Bud Hensley's store in rural Martin's Creek about 1940 all display the self-reliant confidence that marked children of the Depression, who grew up knowing that everyone had to help with the economic survival of the family. John Damon Hensley, second from right, worked in his father's store, and, when necessary, manned the entire business himself. Younger brother Roby stands to J. D.'s right. Below is the famous Ferris wheel that all the kids of Unicoi County had heard about. This amazing contraption, built by J. D. Hensley in the woods near his home on Martin's Creek, stood about 20 feet high. The ingeniously engineered amusement was powered by a hand crank and could seat four riders in the elaborately configured, free-swinging seats. Admission was reportedly a handful of matchsticks. (Both images courtesy of Lucille Hensley Booth.)

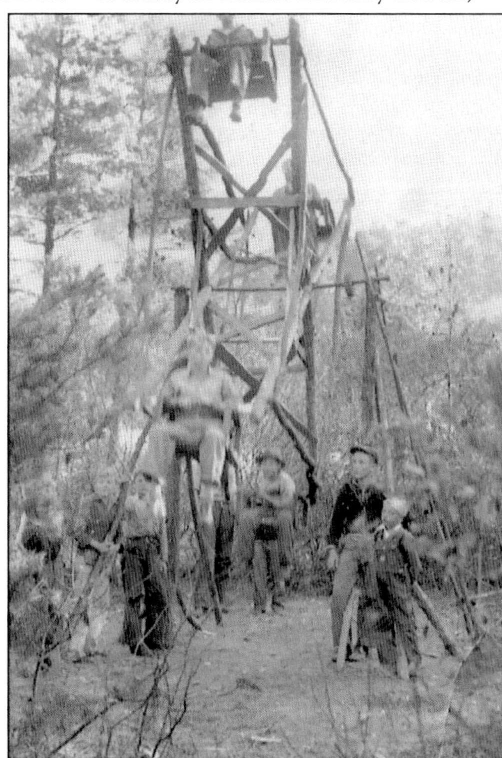

Aunt Bett Morris held the future in her hands—or so some thought. In the 1930s and 1940s, this wizened old lady with the gnarled walking stick and tattered clothes was well-known in the rural Martin's Creek community as a fortune-teller. Her skill was highly suspect. But for a fee, Aunt Bett, or her sister Aunt Nan, would invite eager girls or nervous wives into their cluttered abode, imaginatively foretelling the future from the random scattering of coffee grounds in an old china cup. (Courtesy of Lucille Hensley Booth.)

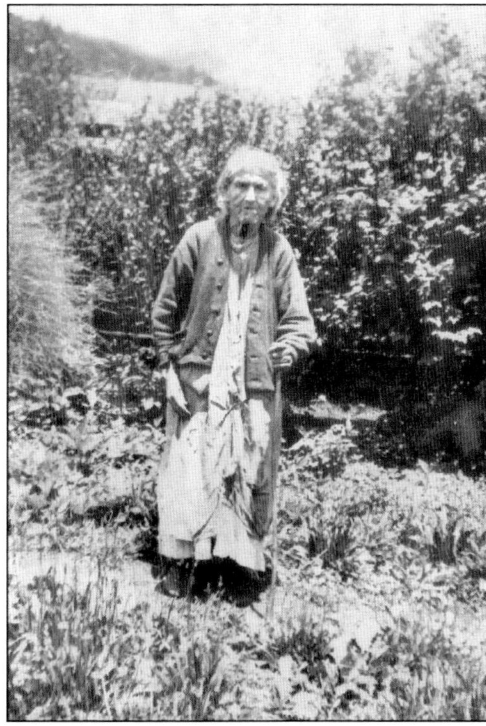

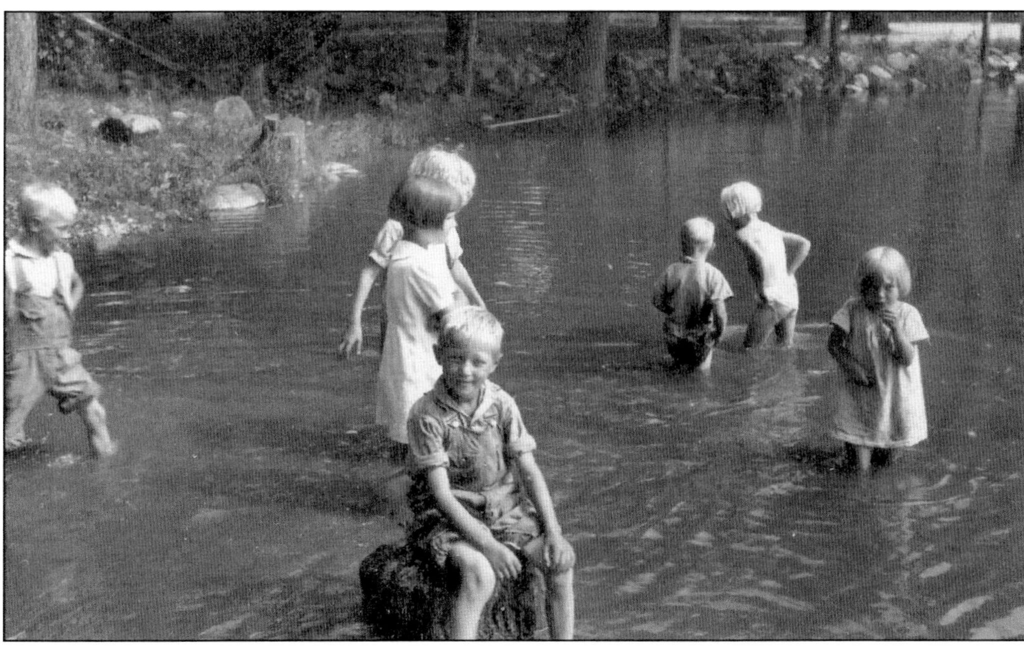

In the early 1940s, Clint Helton built a pond on his property on Martin's Creek Road. This watering hole soon became a gathering place for the children of the Martin's Creek community. Helton's Pond was also used as a place of baptism for the Lily Dale Church of Christ just down the road. The children are, from left to right, Roby Hensley, Louise Helton, Lois Hensley, Ray Banner (on the stump), Ivan Hensley, Eulala Hensley, and Winsie Ingram. (Courtesy of Lucille Hensley Booth.)

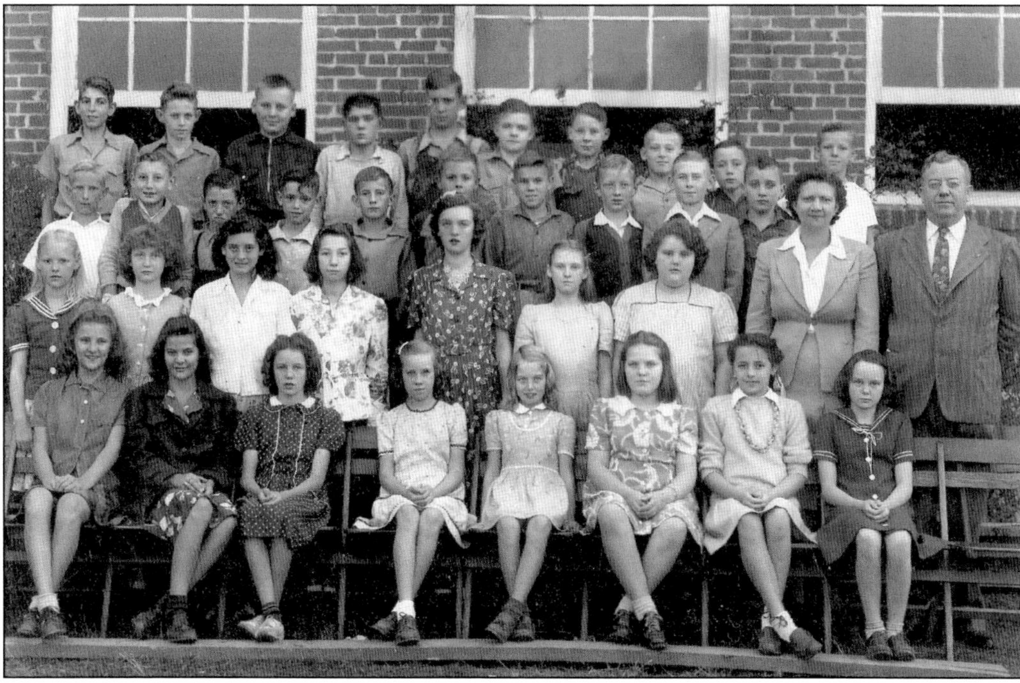

Martin Chapel School served the children of the rural Martin's Creek and Evergreen communities. The original school building burned in the winter of 1930. But in less than a year, the county had allotted $40,000 to construct a new and much-improved school, which included a gymnasium and auditorium, opening in October 1931. Principal Warren Dunbar Sr. poses with this youthful school group about 1944. (Courtesy of Eulala Hensley Davis.)

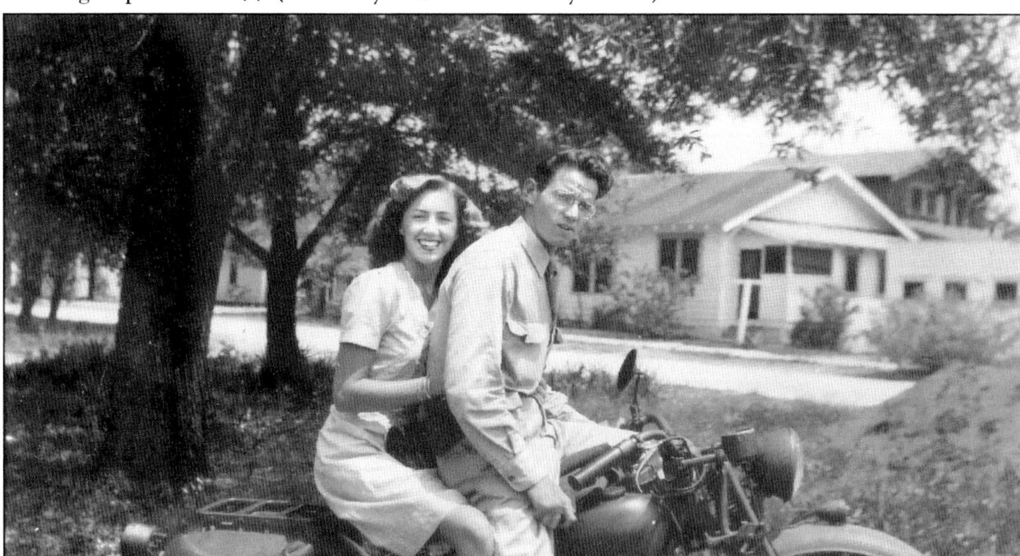

Judy and Dick Moss are the carefree, much-in-love young couple shown on the back of the army-issue motorcycle shortly after their wartime wedding of August 4, 1944. Judy Ferguson had left her Erwin home, answering Dick's impetuous request to be married, traveling alone by train to Tampa, Florida, where Dick was stationed at Drew Field Air Force Base. They have been married now for 63 years. (Courtesy of Judy Moss.)

Mamie Banner Hensley, dressed in her best suit, is shown here in the snowy front yard of her Martin's Creek home one winter's day around 1944. This photograph was made to send to her 17-year-old son Junior who was serving overseas in the Pacific during World War II. The flag with the single star, hung in the window behind Mamie, indicated that this family had a loved one in action in the armed forces. Junior was Mamie's eldest child of 11. Her toddler daughter Alva peeps through the window. Below, Junior Hensley, in his seaman 1st class uniform, was stationed on the USS *Marathon*, a troop transport. He operated a landing craft in the assault on Okinawa, ferrying marines into the battle onshore. Junior's ship was attacked by kamikaze planes, killing his best friend and just missing Junior, who had chosen to sleep topside, where it was cooler. Junior carried his mother's photograph (shown at right) with him throughout the war. (Both images courtesy of Lucille Hensley Booth.)

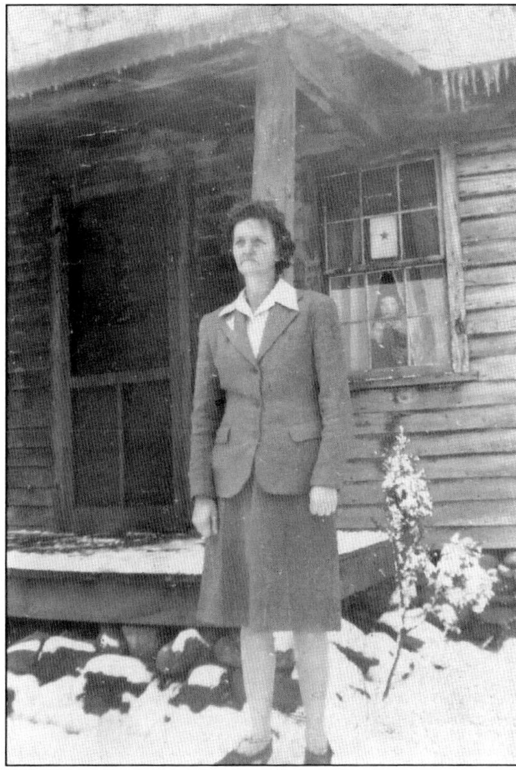

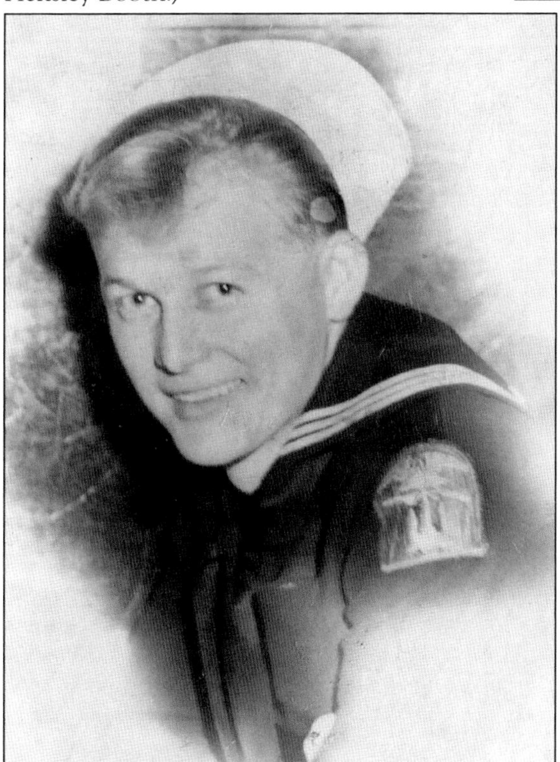

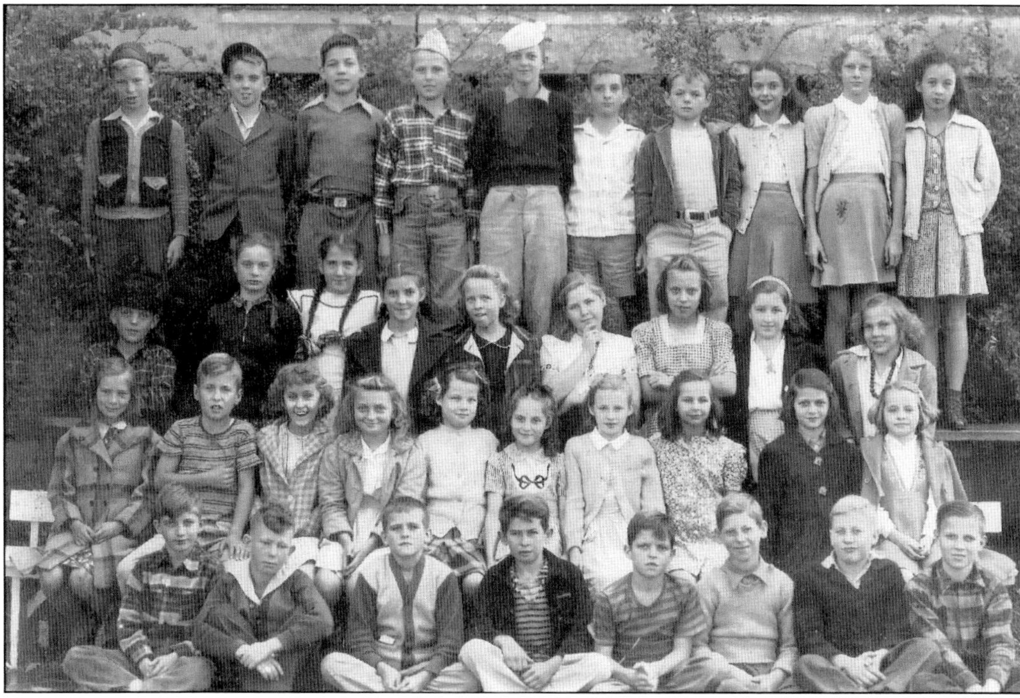

The lively children of this Love Street School class from about 1944 look straight out of central casting and could easily have fit into the 1940s-era *Our Gang* movie comedies—the dainty little girls with their play dresses and hair ribbons and the rough and tumble boys with baseball and sailor caps perched at jaunty angles. The sweet-faced girl in the center with her hand poised delicately at her chin was surely everyone's friend. (Courtesy of the author.)

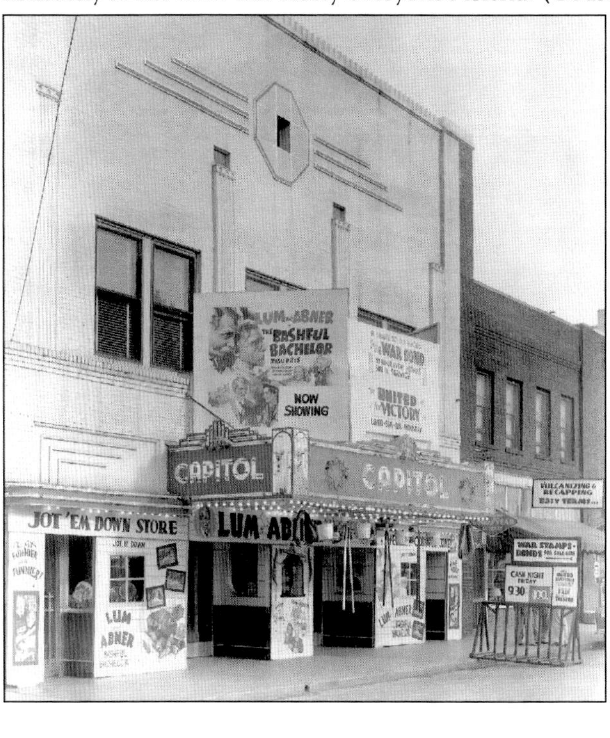

The Capitol Theater, with its "state-of-the-art" Western Electric Sound System opened to the general movie-going public on November 11, 1935. Built and owned by the Hendren Amusement Company, this theater showed all the A-list movies of Hollywood's heyday. Today this art deco–inspired movie theater has become a cultural icon of downtown Erwin and is one of the country's few continuously owned family-operated movie theaters. (Courtesy of Jan Hendren Parsley.)

Four

Victory, Mid-Century, and Beyond

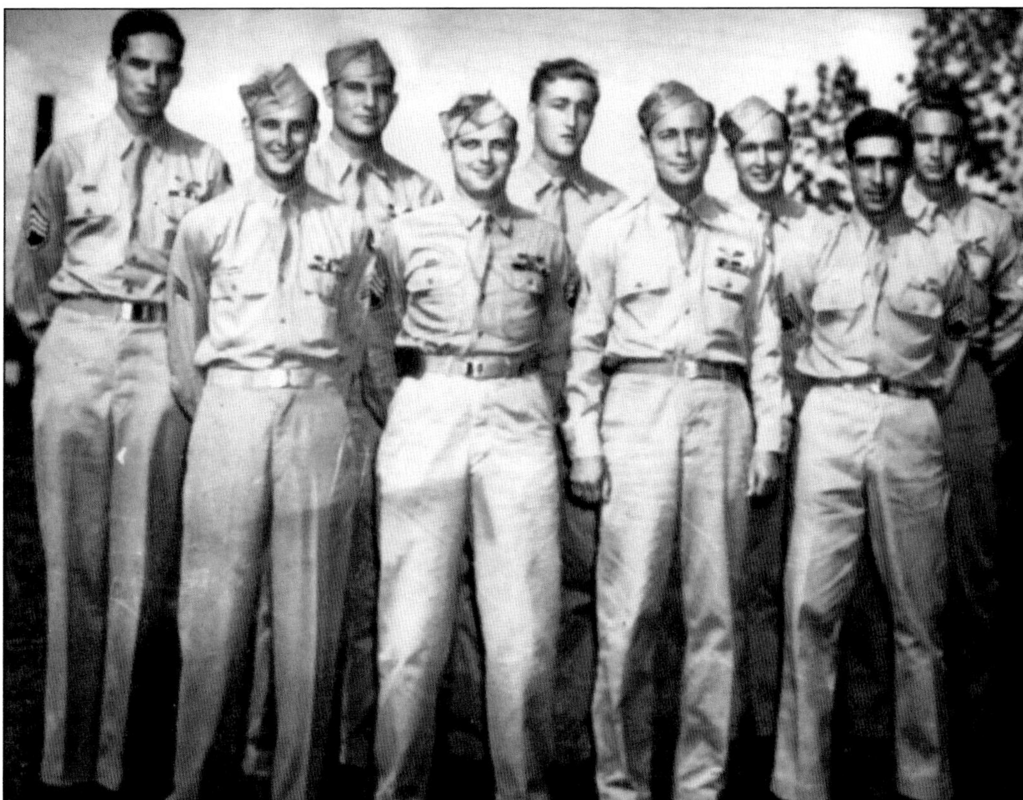

On a sunshiny June day in 1945, nine young men gathered on the grounds of the old Main Street YMCA for a group picture. These soldiers, later known as "The Erwin Nine," were nine young Unicoi County servicemen who all ended up in the same German POW camp together during World War II. Pictured from left to right are Allen Alford, Jim Hensley, Stanley "Homer" Norris, Fred Miller, Richard Edwards, Clyde Tinker, George Swingle, George Hatcher, and Dick Franklin. (Courtesy of George Hatcher.)

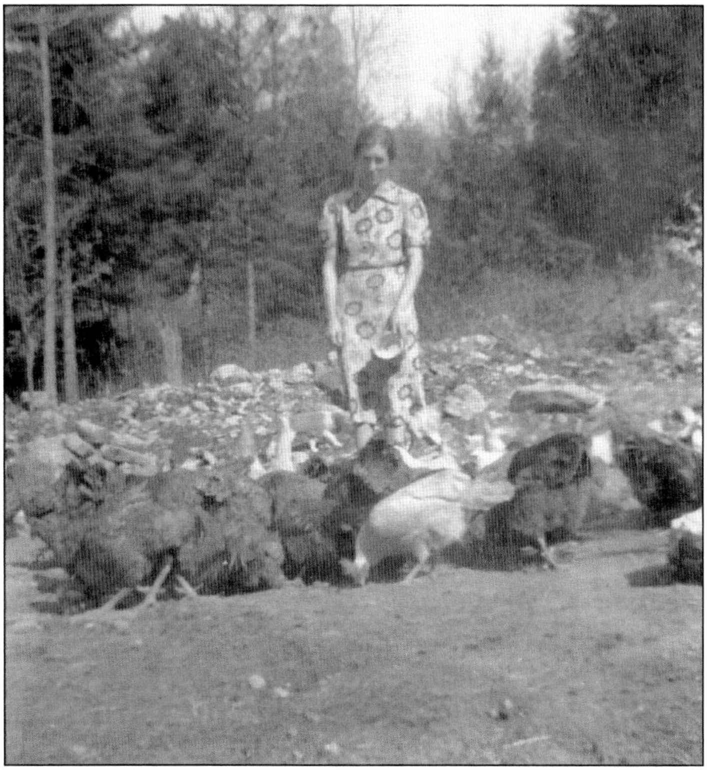

It's obvious why Lydia Tinker Christy referred affectionately to her home at the head of Martin's Creek Road as Gobbler's Knob. Christy was well-known for her fine eggs, which she sold to the community. In this photograph from the 1930s, Christy scatters feed for her busy circle of hefty Rhode Island Reds as the family dog attempts to ride herd on the fowl in the background. (Courtesy of Christine Christy Tipton.)

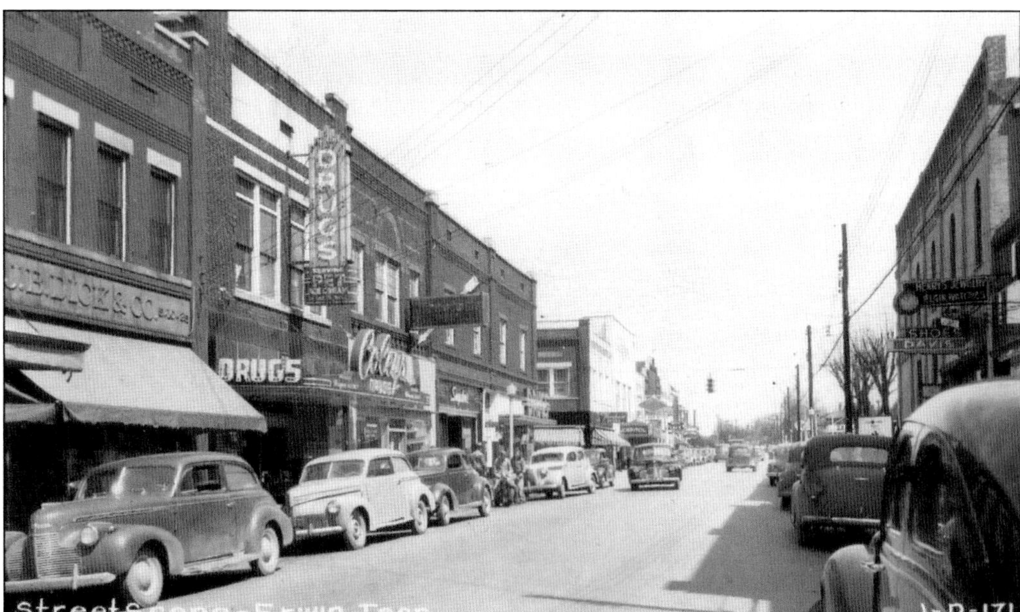

This mid-1940s postcard looks toward the north end of Erwin's Main Street. In the center, at left, is Coley's Drugs, a popular after-school hangout for teens. Up the street was the Clinchfield Drug Store, which had a popular sandwich counter. Coley's is now gone. The Clinchfield is still owned and operated by the Snyder family, and the sandwich counter is still there. (Courtesy of the author.)

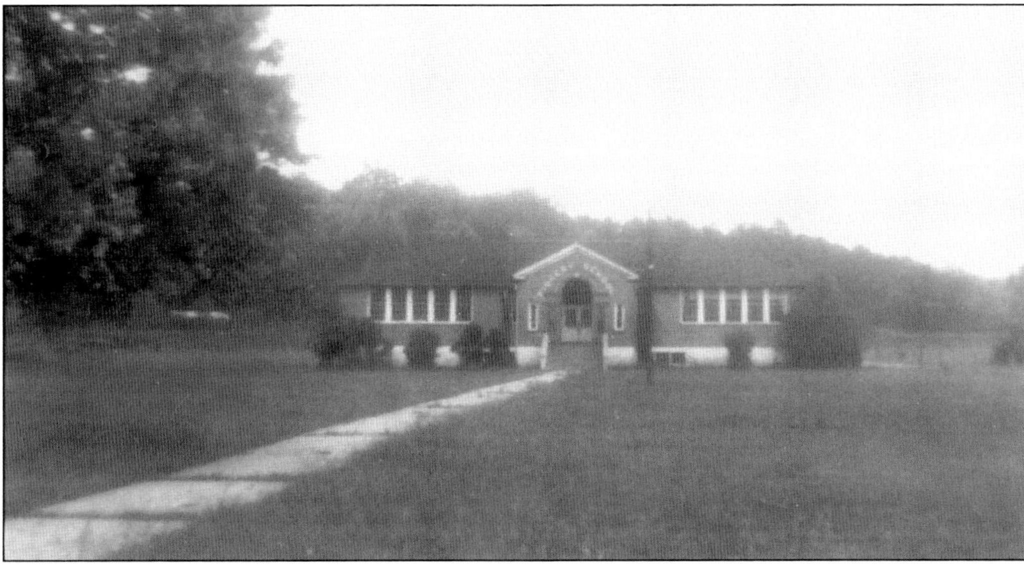

Fishery School, in northern Unicoi County, offered instruction in grades one through eight. It was one of many rural community schools in Unicoi County that persisted well into the late 1970s, when school consolidation was implemented. Lewis Thornberry in his book *Remembering Old Erwin* writes that, in 1946, the average pay for a teacher in Unicoi County was $100 per month and that the highest pay for a teacher with five years experience and a college certification was $139 per month. Below is the 1946 eighth grade graduating class of Fishery School. Pictured from left to right are the following: (first row) Hilda Robertson, William "Bill" Booth, Juanita White, Principal Mary Sams, teacher Merley Guinn, J. P. Campbell, Marie Whitson, and Jim Tapp; (second row) Dorothy Harris, Kenneth Banner, Mae Huskins, Ronald Hensley, Joyce Coleman, Charles Harris, Betty Jo Harris, and Bill Lewis. (Above, courtesy of the Arnold Williams family; below courtesy of Bill Booth.)

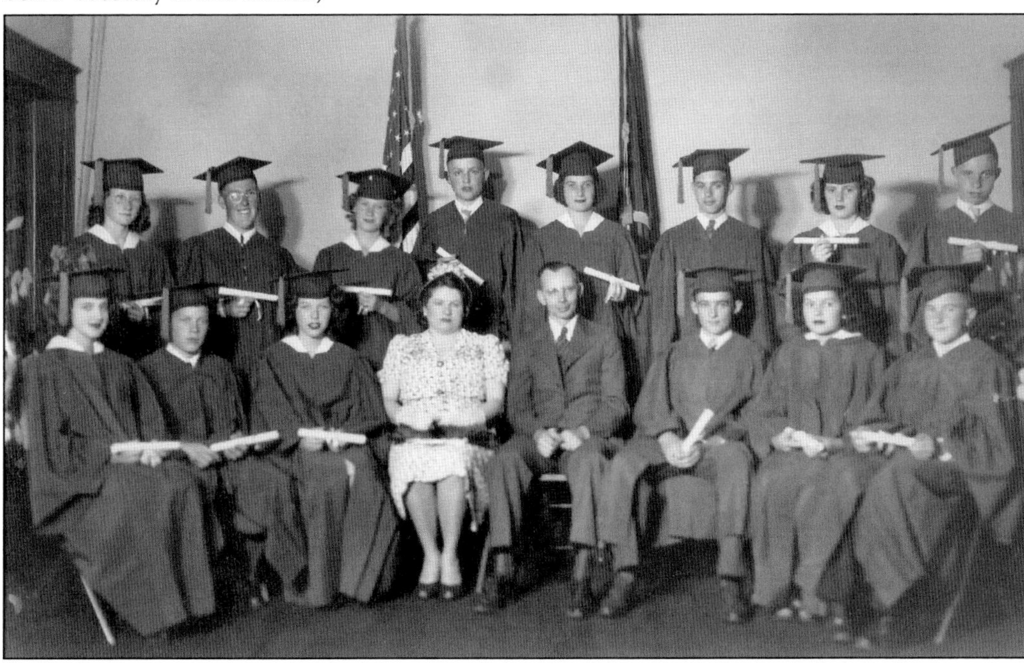

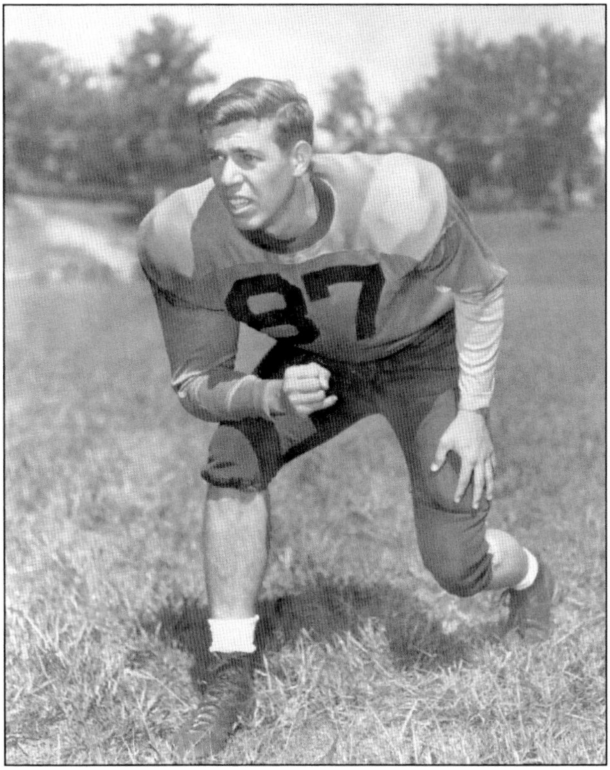

These two 1940s-era Unicoi County High School football players, Frank Gentry Jr. and Phil Prince, were also both outstanding players for Clemson University. Gentry, left, was a member of two bowl game teams. He married and came home to Erwin to manage the family business. Prince, a standout in the memorable Clemson win over Missouri in the Gator Bowl, became president of Clemson University in the mid-1980s. (Both images courtesyof Bert Thompson.)

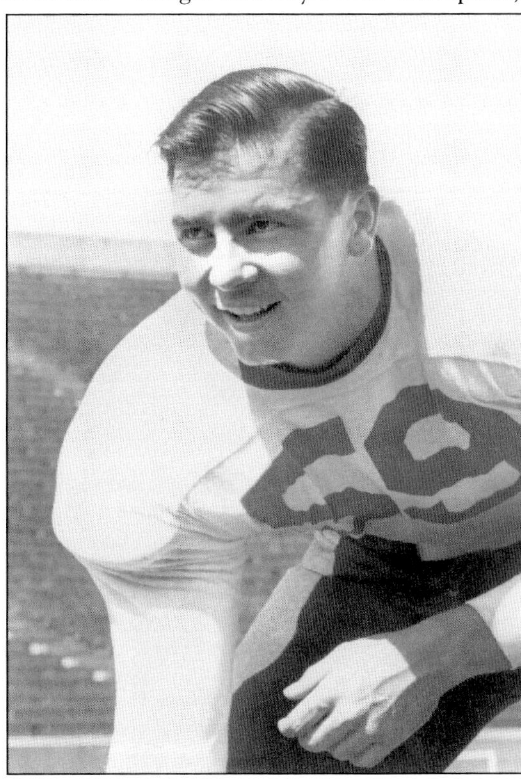

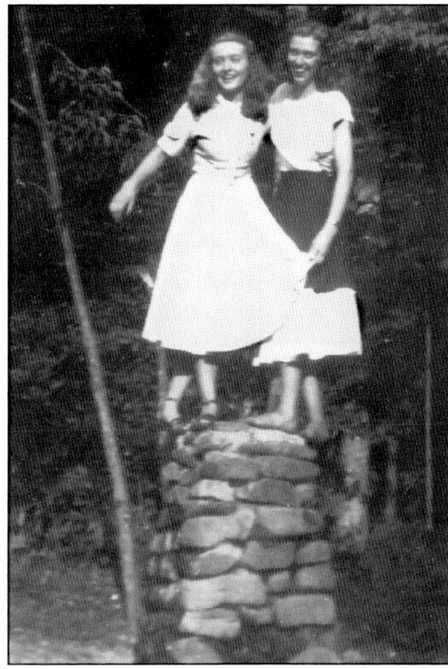

Iris Edwards, at left, and Helen Christy perch precariously atop a rock pillar at Chestoa Springs in the late 1940s. Chestoa Springs, in southern Unicoi County, and Rock Creek Park, in the northeast part of the county, were two equally popular family outdoor recreational areas in the years after World War II. For local teenagers, however, these were the places to see and be seen and just enjoy being young. (Courtesy of Christine Christy Tipton.)

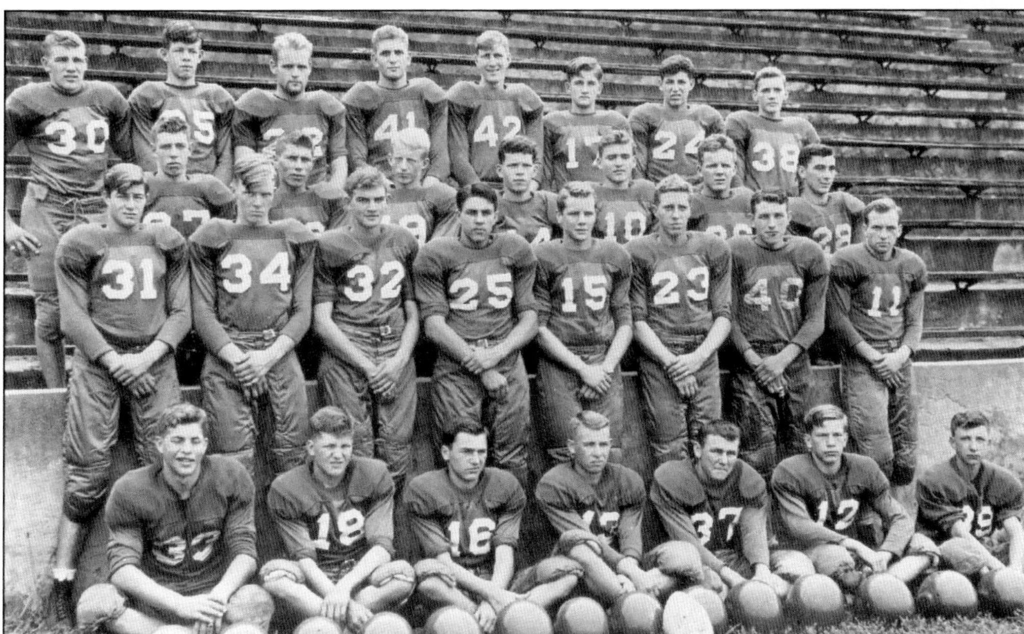

Writer Lou Thornberry described the 1947 Unicoi County High School football team as the "cardiac kids," for their propensity to squeak out a win in the last minutes of a game. The 1947 season was the last for beloved coach and father figure A. R. "Cap" Isbill, who is remembered as a man of integrity and determination. Among the members of the 1947 squad identified were quarterback Bert Thompson, Mick Bergendahl, Russell Brackins, Gene Davis, Robert Boyd, Ray Grimes, Sam Fortune, Don Shell, Ed Thompson, W. A. Wilson, and Howard Ingle. (Courtesy of Bert Thompson.)

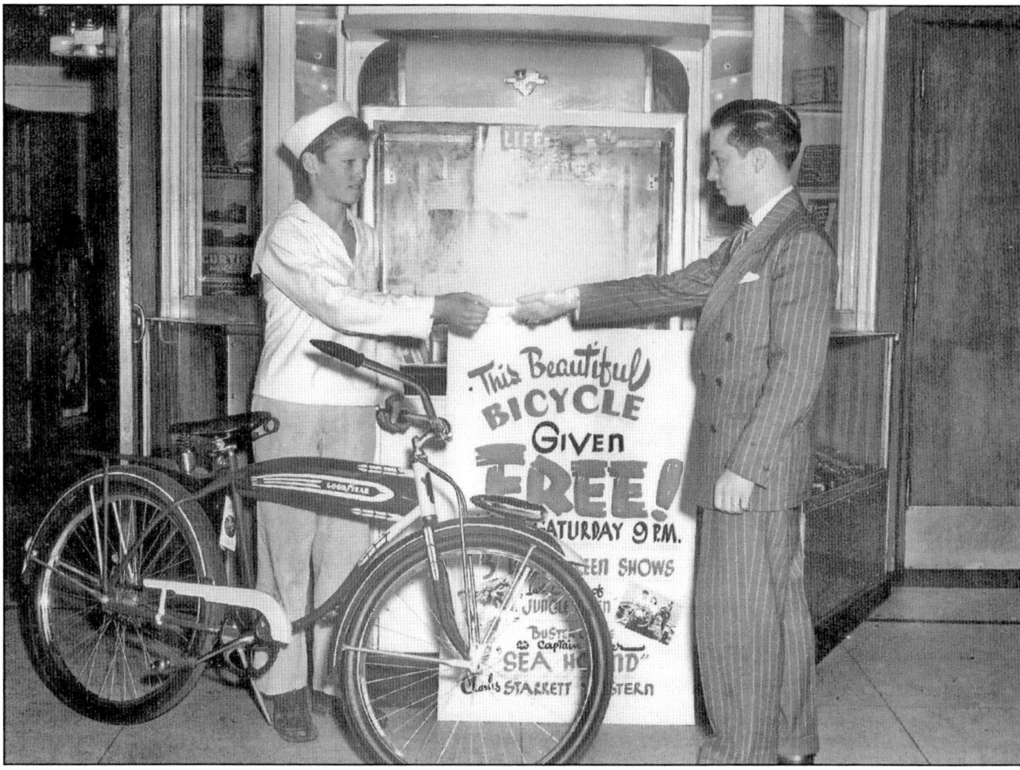

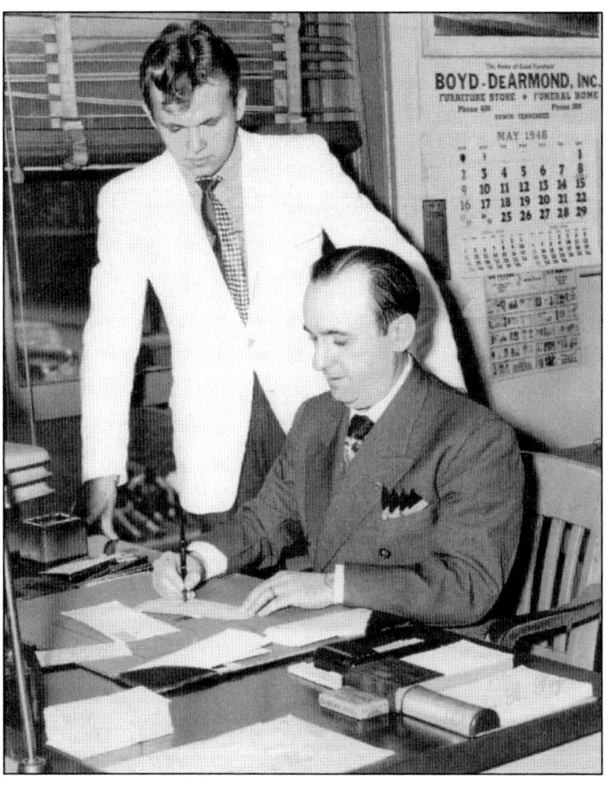

The Lyric Theater was one of Unicoi County's first theaters. Preceded by the Ritz and the Palace Theaters, the old Lyric, located in the western Main Street business block between Union and Love Streets, was the only one of these three early entertainment houses that successfully transitioned from being a venue for vaudeville, to one for silent movies, and finally to one for "talkies." When the more modern Capitol Theater was built down the street in 1935 by theater entrepreneur Earle Hendren, the Lyric, also owned by Hendren, became the official Erwin movie house for B movies and Westerns. An Erwin teenager is shown here about 1948 receiving a promotional giveaway prize of a brand-new bicycle. At left Joe Hendren is shown conferring with his father, theater founder Earle Hendren, in 1948. (Both images courtesy of Jan Hendren Parsley.)

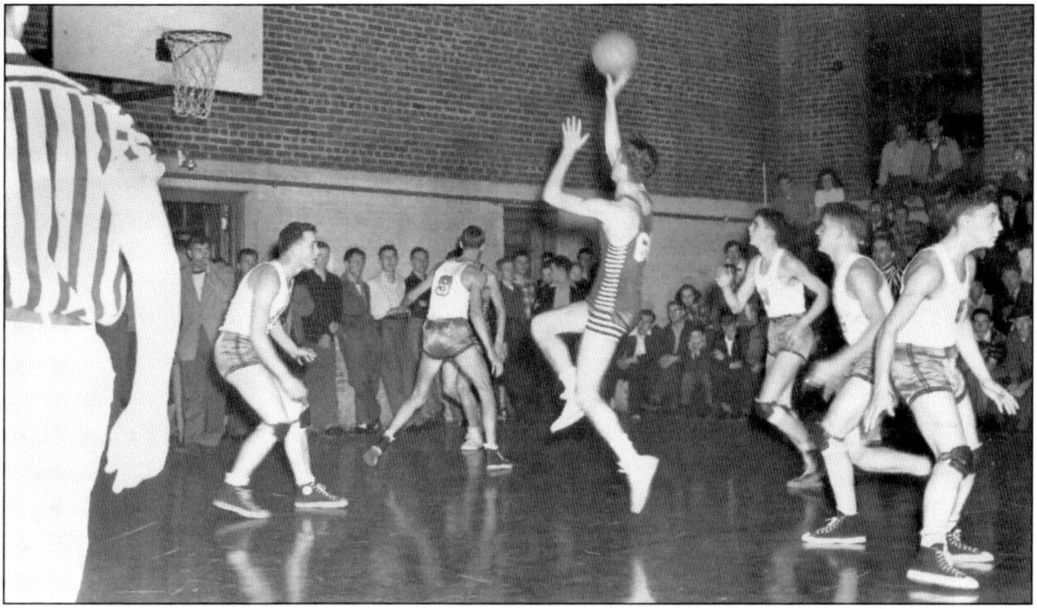

An agile, long-limbed Bobby Sams gains some altitude as he goes up for a two-pointer for the Unicoi County High School Blue Devil basketball team in a game with archrival Kingsport about 1950. Unicoi County's old high school gym was the scene of always-popular, heart-stopping basketball action, as well as doing double duty as a roller-skating rink in the off-season. (Courtesy of Bob Sams.)

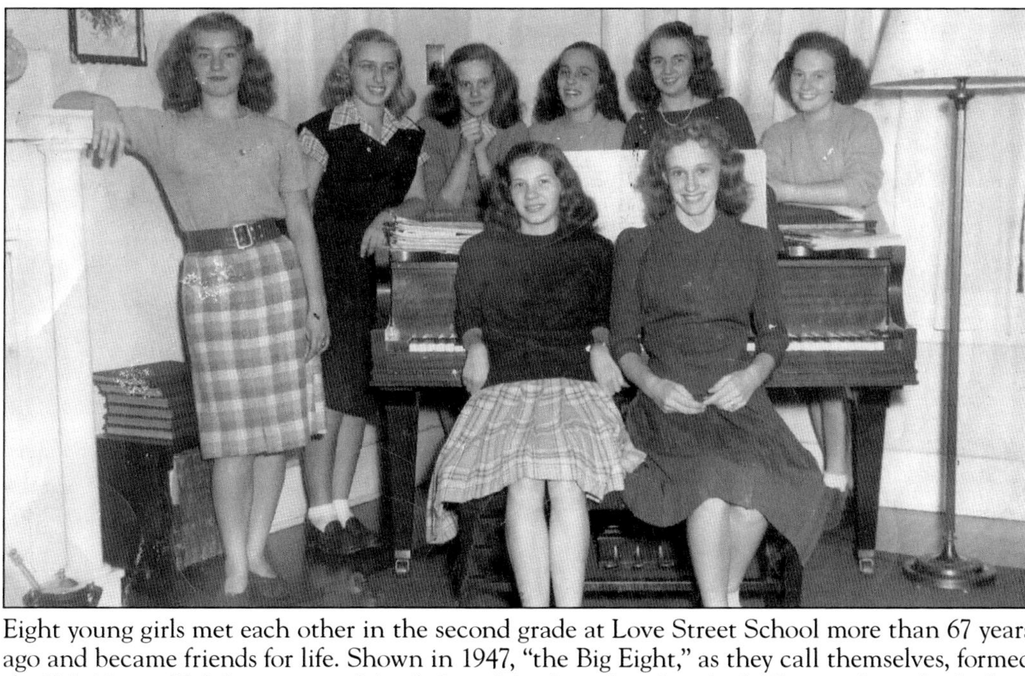

Eight young girls met each other in the second grade at Love Street School more than 67 years ago and became friends for life. Shown in 1947, "the Big Eight," as they call themselves, formed the "No Name Club," meeting in Mandy Long's back yard garden shed. They made crafts, had tea parties, told secrets and formed an unbreakable bond of sisterhood. From left to right are (seated) Betty Sifferd and Susie Ryburn; (standing) Charlotte Gorham, Amanda Long, Mary Sifferd, Betty Jo Isbill, Patricia Wilkinson, and Myra Edwards. (Courtesy of Myra Edwards Sellars.)

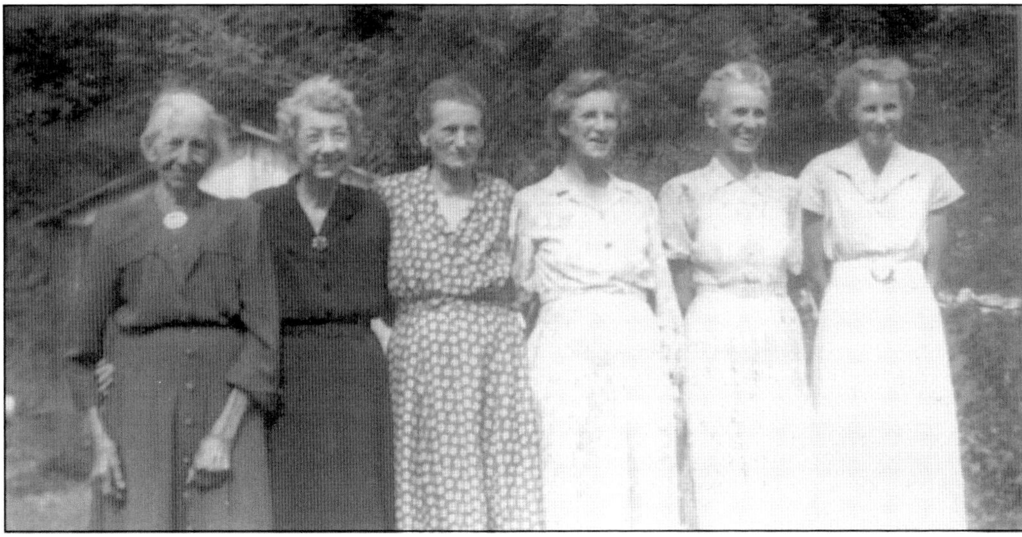

Mame Day of the Rock Creek community was well-known for her kindness and generosity, as well as for her oft-needed skill as a midwife. She delivered many a Unicoi County babe. The sweet-smiling matriarch is shown here in the 1940s with her own five lovely daughters to her left: (from left to right) Eua Kilby, Maude Miller, Ida Ayers, Lola Ayers, and Belle Peterson. (Courtesy of Debbie McInturff Tittle.)

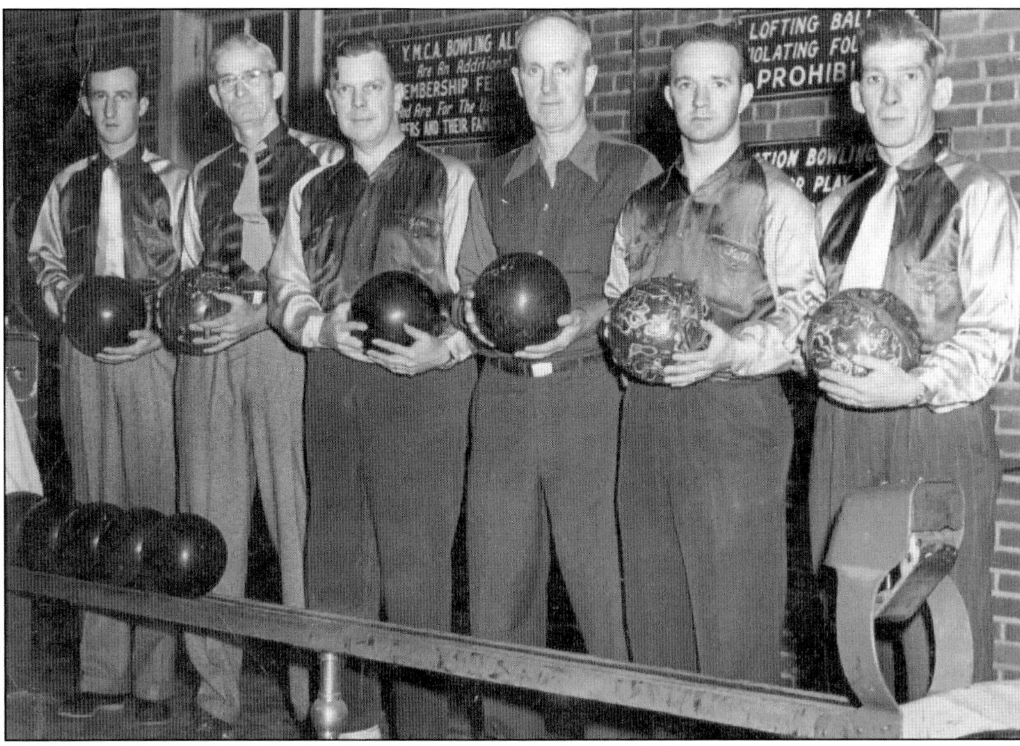

The 1948–1949 Unicoi County YMCA Championship bowling team strikes a pose in matching satin team jackets. Pictured from left to right are Glenn Tilson, Bob Kyle, Harry Baughman, Jim Christy, Bill Boyer, and Johnny Hart. The old YMCA on Main Street had originally started as a club owned by the Clinchfield Railroad. (Courtesy of Christine Christy Tipton.)

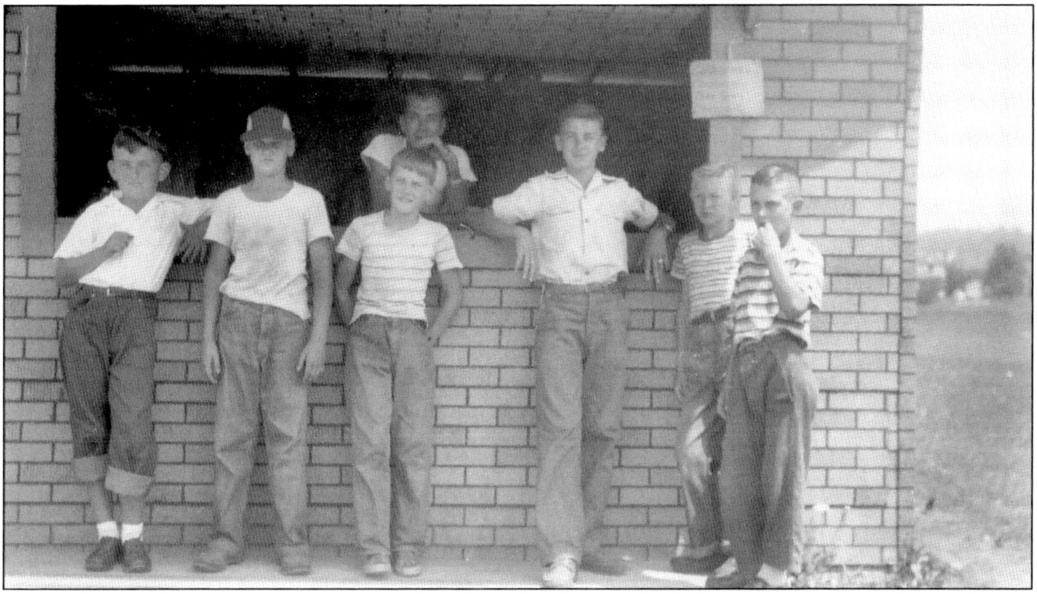

A host of young golf caddies take their leisure between rounds at the caddy shack of the old Mountain View Golf Course around 1951. A plum job for Erwin's preteen boys, caddying could earn one as much as 50¢ for hoisting golf bags around nine holes of play. Above, pictured at left is Lewis Thornberry. Third from right is Charles "C. J." Brotherton. The others are unidentified. Mountain View Golf course was constructed in 1941 on the former Fairview Field. Like many other courses of the period, Mountain View had "greens" of sand that had to be smoothed, or "dragged," after each round of play. Below, young Lewis Thornberry props his Schwinn bike alongside the water trap of the first hole. The old golf course property today is home to the new Unicoi County High School and Unicoi County Middle School. (Both images courtesyof Lewis Thornberry.)

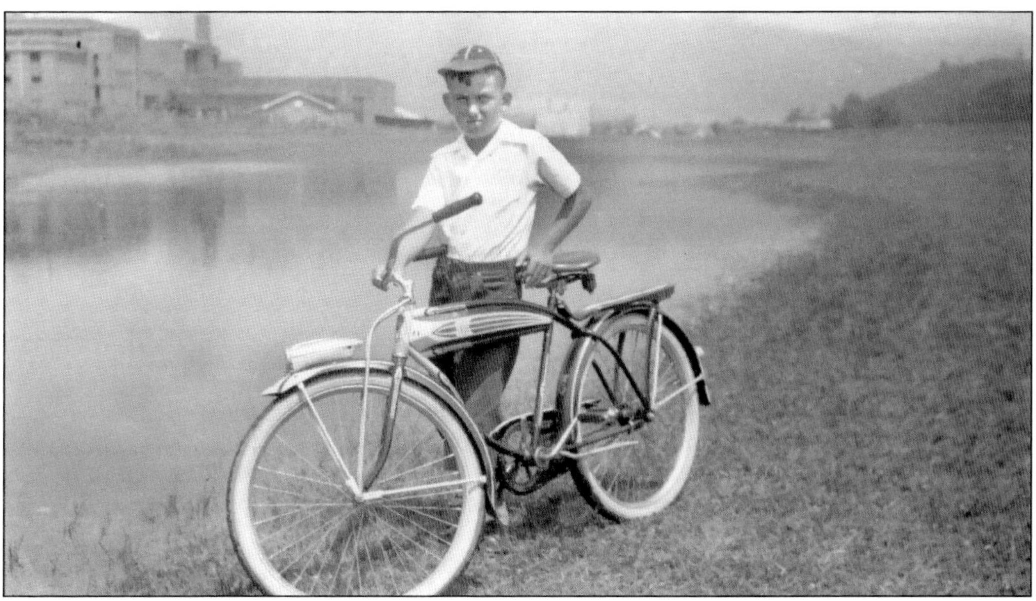

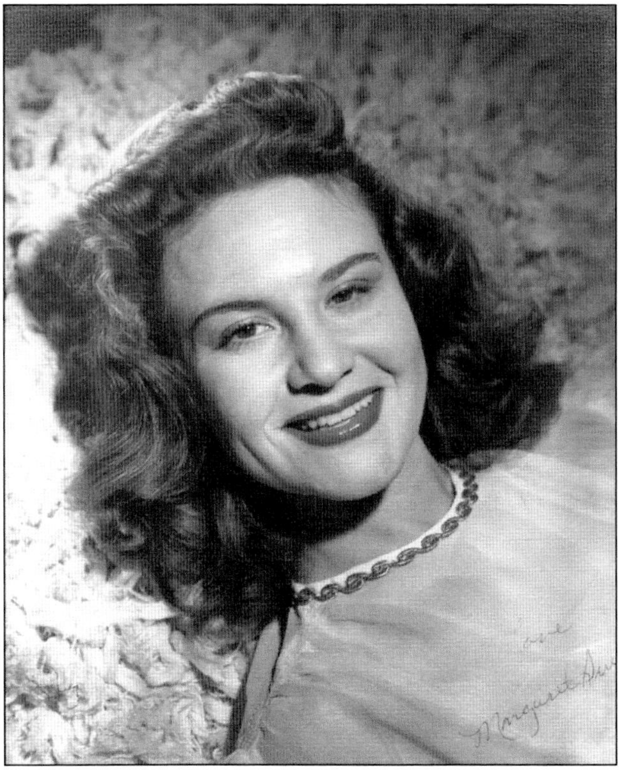

Margaret Sue Range is an entertainment legend in Unicoi County. Shown here in a classic late-1940s "Hollywood Studio" pose, Range began her dancing career as a small child in Erwin. Dressed by her older sister as Shirley Temple, she would dance atop store counters for nickels, much to her mother's dismay. After professional dance study in New York, Range returned to Erwin and opened the Range School of Dance. She and some of her students also appeared in the 1980s movie *Dirty Dancing*. (Courtesy of Margaret Sue Range.)

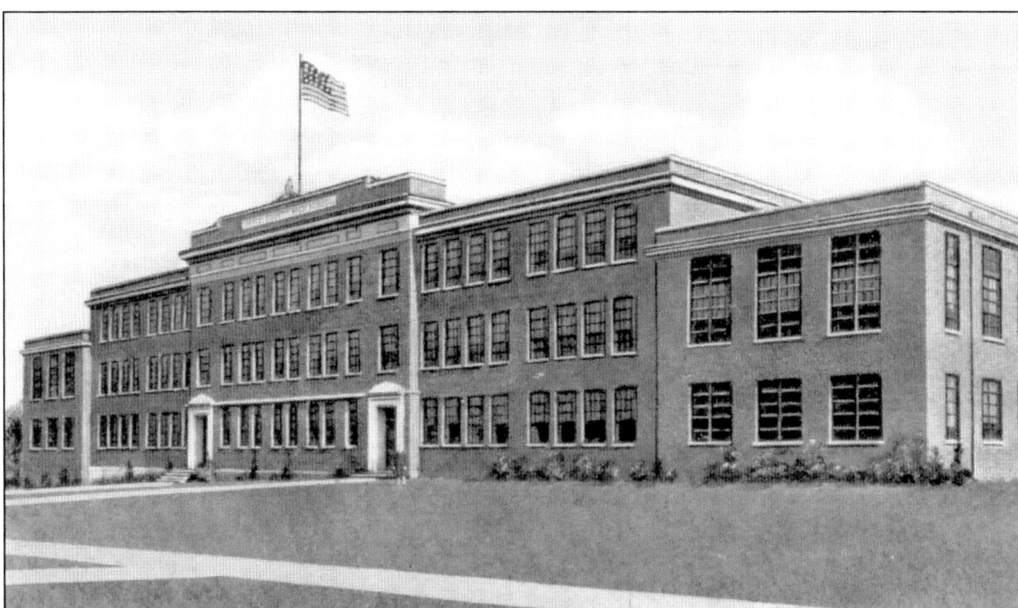

The first official Unicoi County High School was dedicated in November 1929 by Supt. Frank W. Gentry Sr. The fully accredited high school, located on Unaka Way, offered a modern, high-school curriculum, which included a business course, vocational and industrial education, as well as physical education. Regional sports competition also became central to the Unicoi County High School experience. (Courtesy of Lewis Thornberry.)

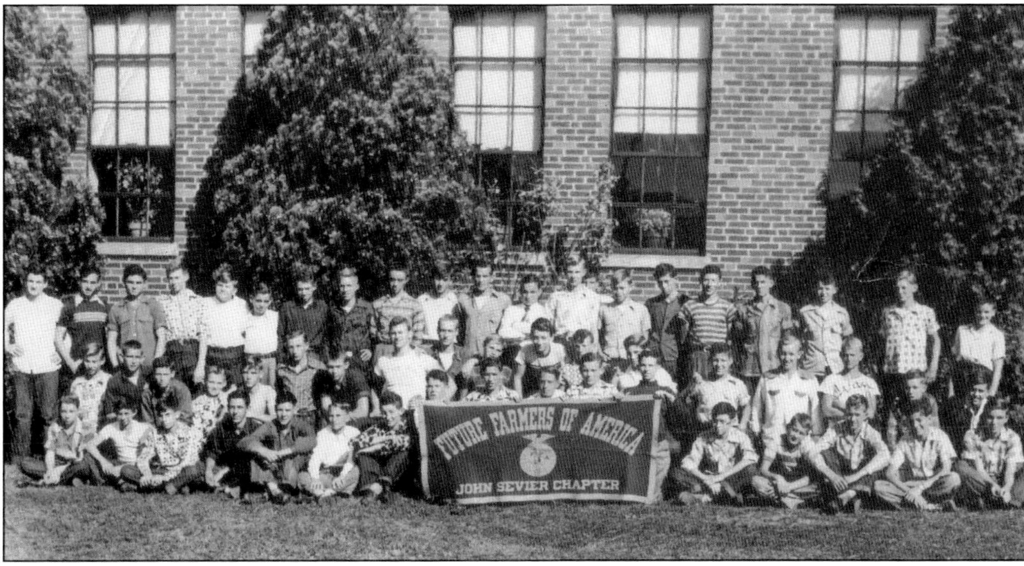

In the 1950s, family farms were still in abundance in largely rural Unicoi County. In this atmosphere, the John Sevier Chapter of the Future Farmers of America was a healthy organization at Unicoi County High School, as seen in this well-attended group portrait from the early 1950s. (Courtesy of Lucille Hensley Booth.)

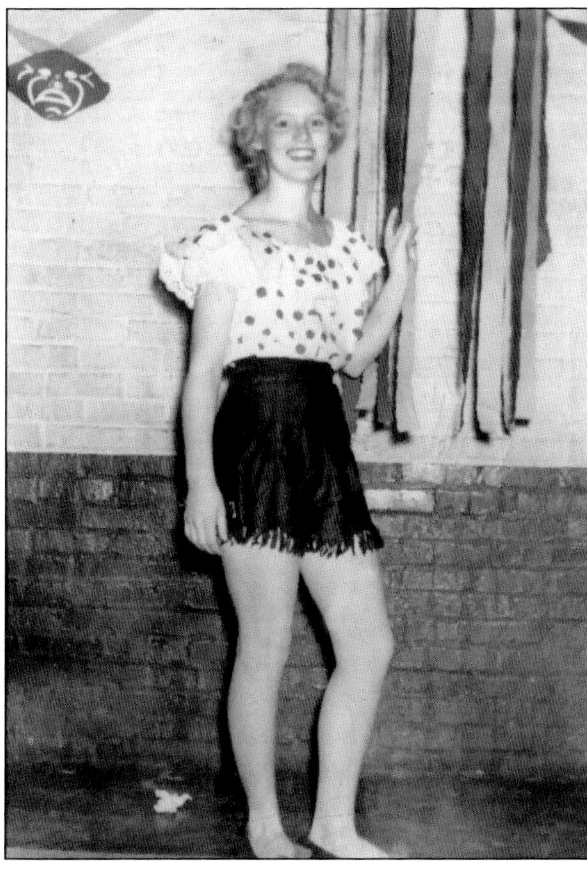

Dressed as Daisy Mae of Dogpatch, from the popular 1950s *Li'l Abner* comic strip, play, and movie, Eulala Hensley poses for her picture at a Unicoi County High School dance about 1951. Her escort was Richard Davis, who naturally portrayed Li'l Abner for his girl. Richard and Eulala married at age 19 in November 1952 after graduation from high school. Eulala had been chosen as the first runner-up in the 1950 Miss Erwin beauty pageant at the tender age of 15. (Courtesy of Lucille Hensley Booth.)

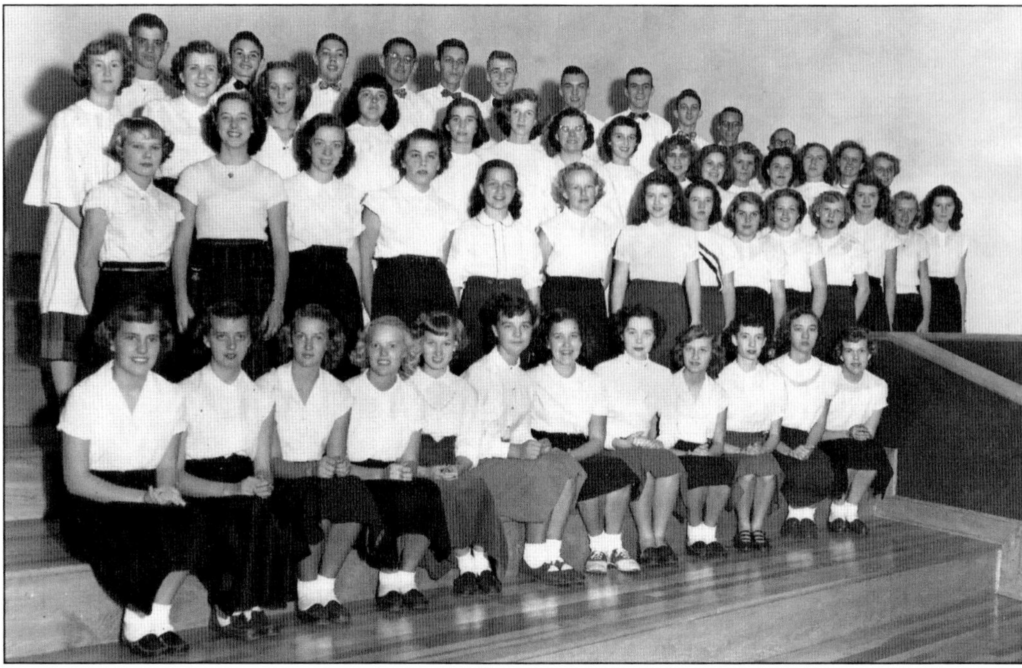

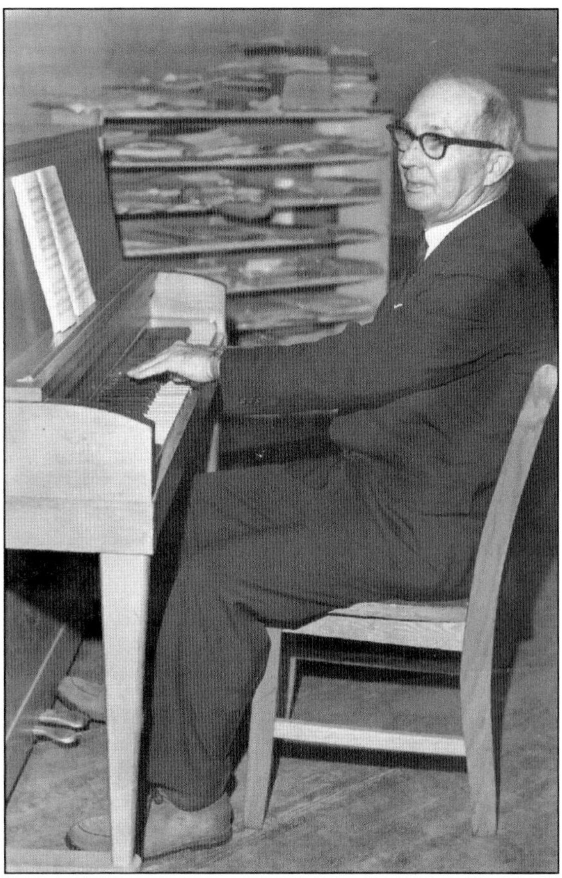

The Chorus of Unicoi County High School in the early 1950s was an energetic group whose melodious performances gained recognition across East Tennessee. The vocally talented teenagers traveled the East Tennessee region, performing under the inspired leadership of Unicoi County music director Pat Alderman, seen below. Alderman was influenced by music from a young age and worked not only as a stellar performing musician and vocalist, but also a writer and historian. In addition to writing the landmark outdoor historical pageant, "The Overmountain Men," first staged in Erwin in 1952–1953 with a cast of Unicoi County natives, Alderman later became the county's official historian, penning *Greasy Cove, in Unicoi County* in 1975 and *Tilson Grist Mill* in 1981. Alderman died in 1984. (Above courtesy of Lucille Hensley Booth; below courtesy of Patsy Alderman Tittle.)

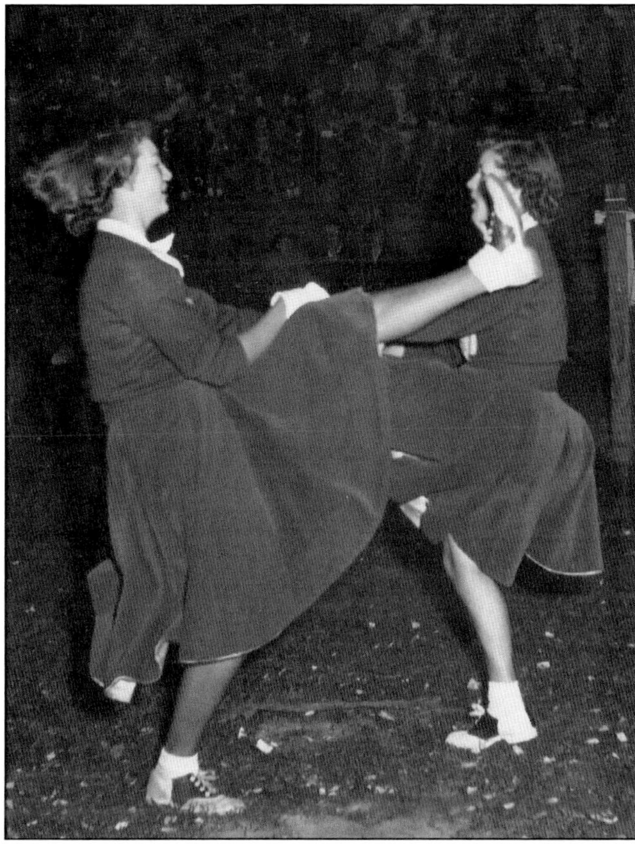

Lucille Hensley (left) and Marie Osborne offer a high-spirited kick that would make the New York City Rockettes proud as they lead a boisterous sideline cheer for the Gentry Stadium crowd at a Blue Devils football game in the early 1950s. Below, the Unicoi County High School cheerleading squad forms a pyramid for the camera about 1951. Pictured from left to right are the following: (first row) Beverly Hawkins, Lowell English, Lucille Hensley, Huey Sizemore, and Anita McFarland; (second row) Joyce McCurry, Eulala Hensley, and Marie Osborne. Little Beau Anne Brummit, daughter of the Unicoi County High School Blue Devils football coach Bo Brummit, was the cheerleading mascot. (Both images courtesy of Lucille Hensley Booth.)

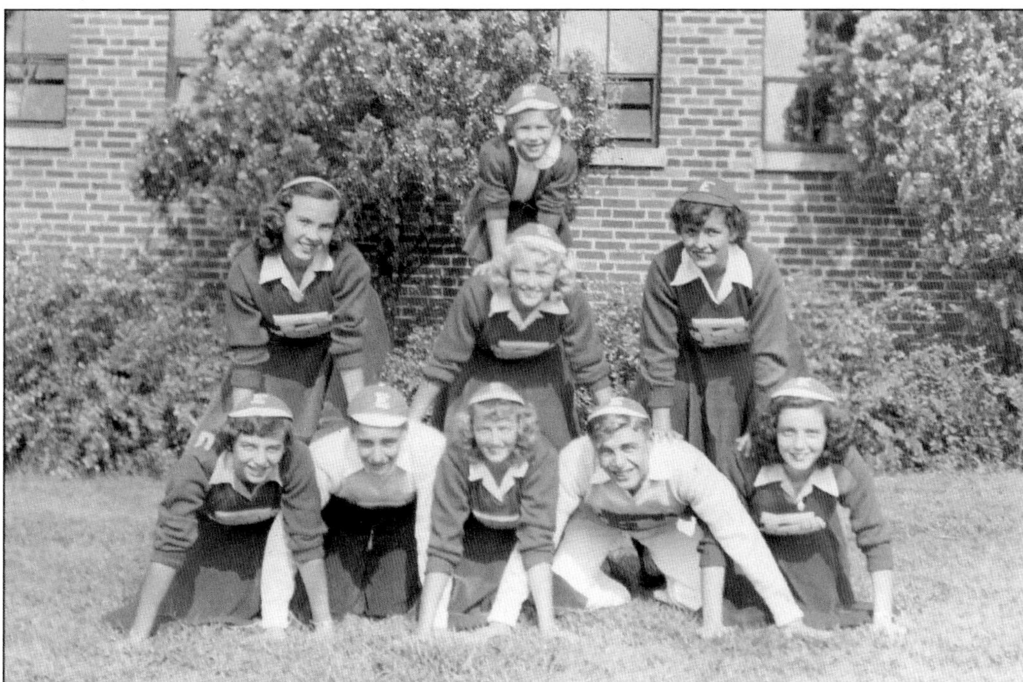

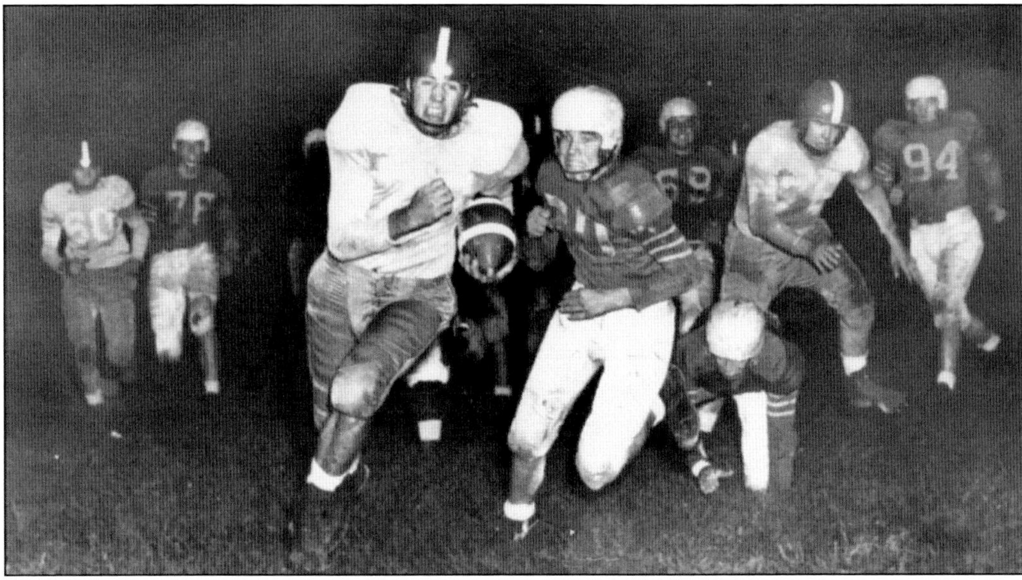

In 1950, Blue Devil halfback W. A. Wilson was known for his lightning runs and his incredible yardage gains, which inevitably led to winning touchdowns. Under the direction of coach Bo Brummit and players like Wilson, Billy Joe Turner, George Hensley, Leo Turner, R. C. Street, and J. B. Salts, Unicoi County High School football was ranked 13th in the state. Wilson was elected to the First Team All-Tennessee squad that season. (Courtesy of Bert Thompson.)

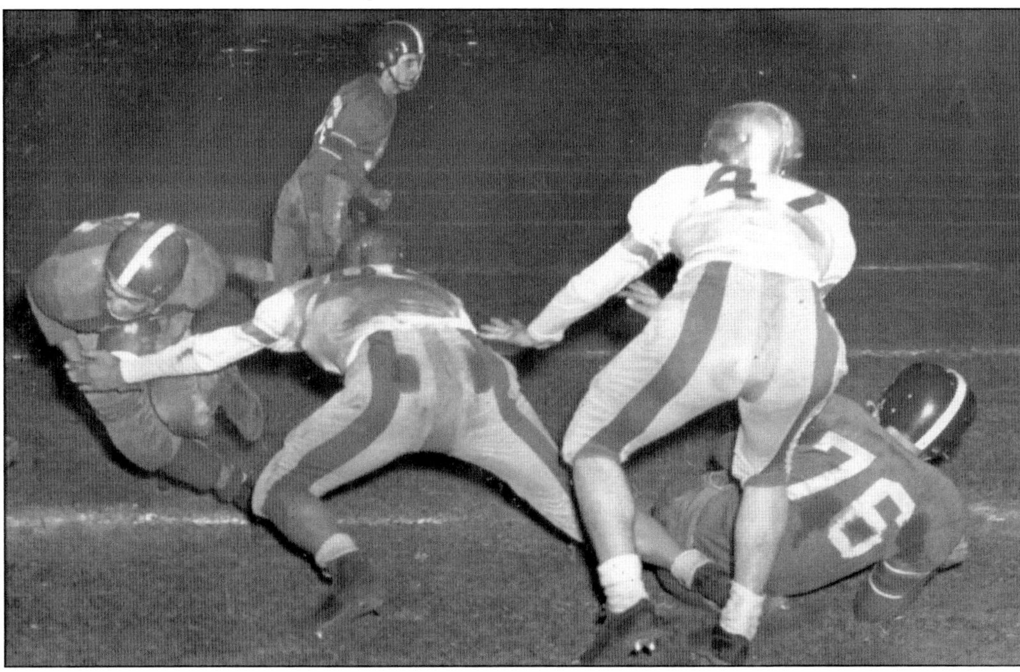

Lanky Richard Davis, in the background, was an unlikely football player at 6 feet 2 inches, but he managed to make the field his own and scored numerous touchdowns for Unicoi County High School. It was said that the opposing team couldn't figure out Davis's running style. His long legs would zig off in one direction and just as quickly zag back the other way. He left his pursuers far behind. (Courtesy of Lucille Hensley Booth.)

Passenger service had always been a central feature of the Clinchfield Railroad. In this photograph from 1954, Clinchfield conductor Bob Davis offers his hand to a Unicoi County matron as she departs the train car. With the increased use of interstate highways in the 1950s, passenger train service declined. The last Clinchfield Railroad passenger train ended in the mid-1950s. (Courtesy of the author.)

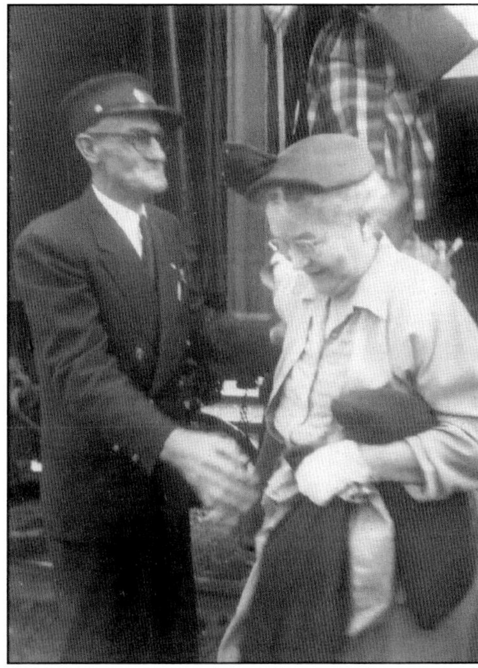

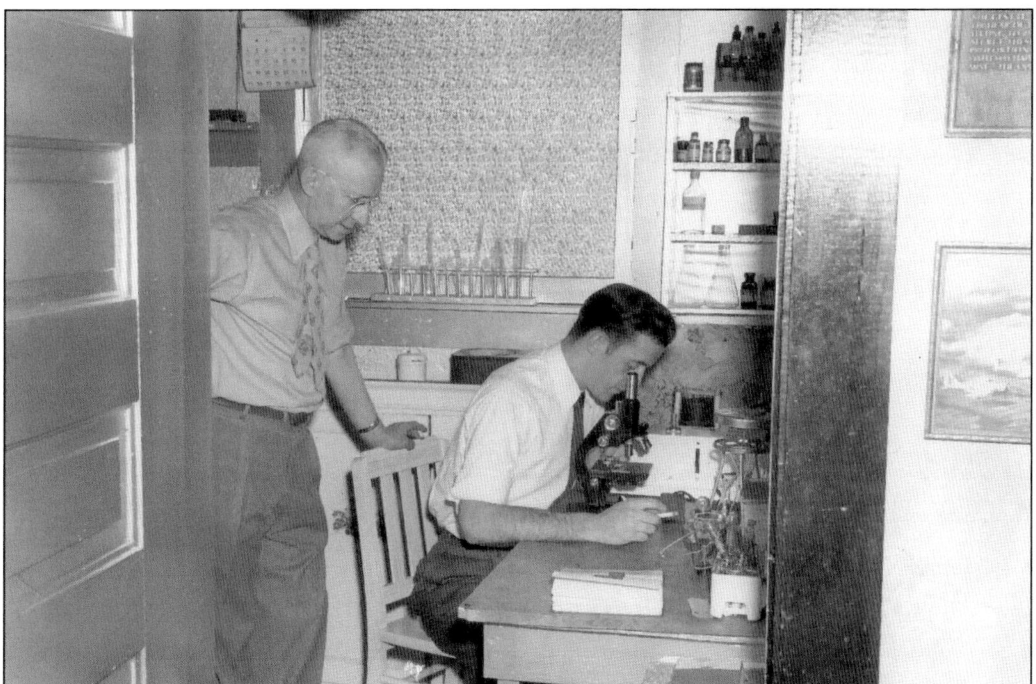

Dr. J. R. Moody and Dr. Earl Peterson are seen in the late 1940s conferring on lab results in their joint medical office located on Vinton Street. Erwin native Earl Peterson took his medical degree at the University of Tennessee at Memphis and then married Dr. Moody's daughter Anne. Dr. Moody, the second-generation son of Irish immigrants, graduated from Vanderbilt and was also instrumental in organizing the county's first public hospital on Academy Street. (Courtesy of Pat Lynch.)

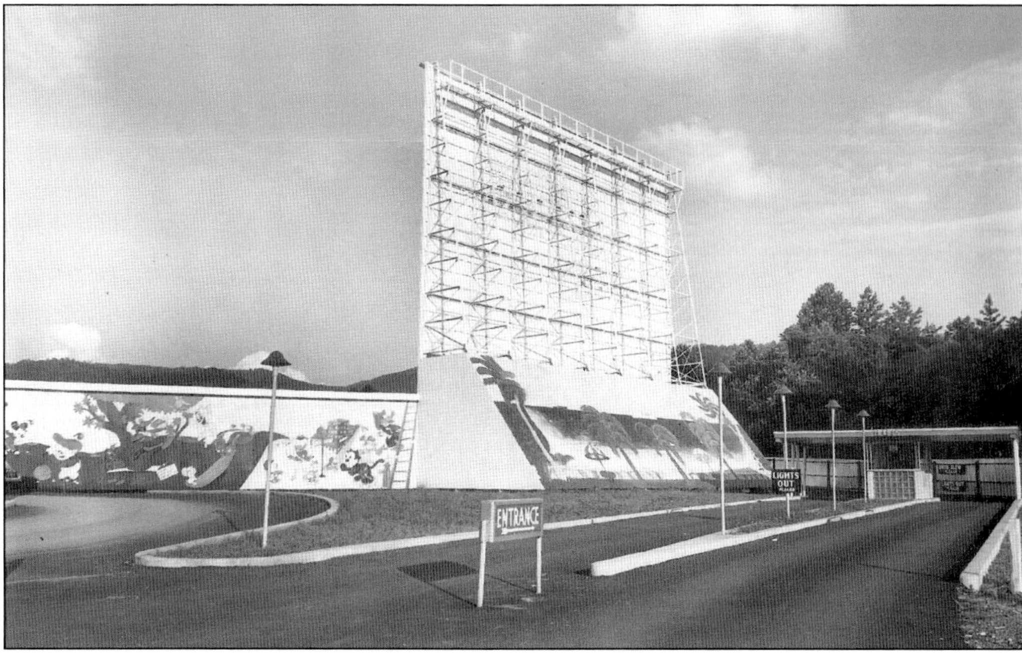

The first wide-screen, open-air feature at the grand opening of the 6-acre Holiday Drive-in Theater on April 2, 1953, was the Technicolor family film *Meet Me at the Fair*, starring Dan Dailey and Diana Lynn. Admission was 50¢ for adults, and children under age 12 were admitted free. Attendants washed windshields to guarantee a better view. The Holiday Drive-in also featured a cafeteria-style snack bar with white-uniformed ladies ready to serve 25¢ hamburgers, hot dogs, Sno-cones, and boxes of fragrant popcorn. A Kiddyland playground situated down front below the 70-foot high screen occupied the kids until it was dark enough to show the movie. (Both images courtesy of Jan Hendren Parsley.)

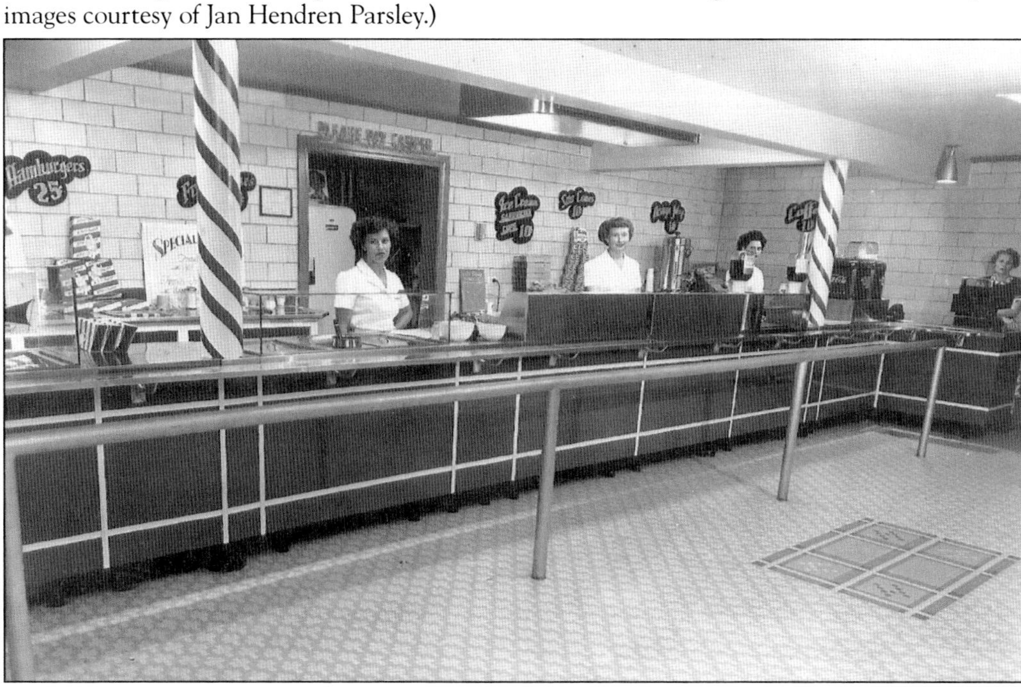

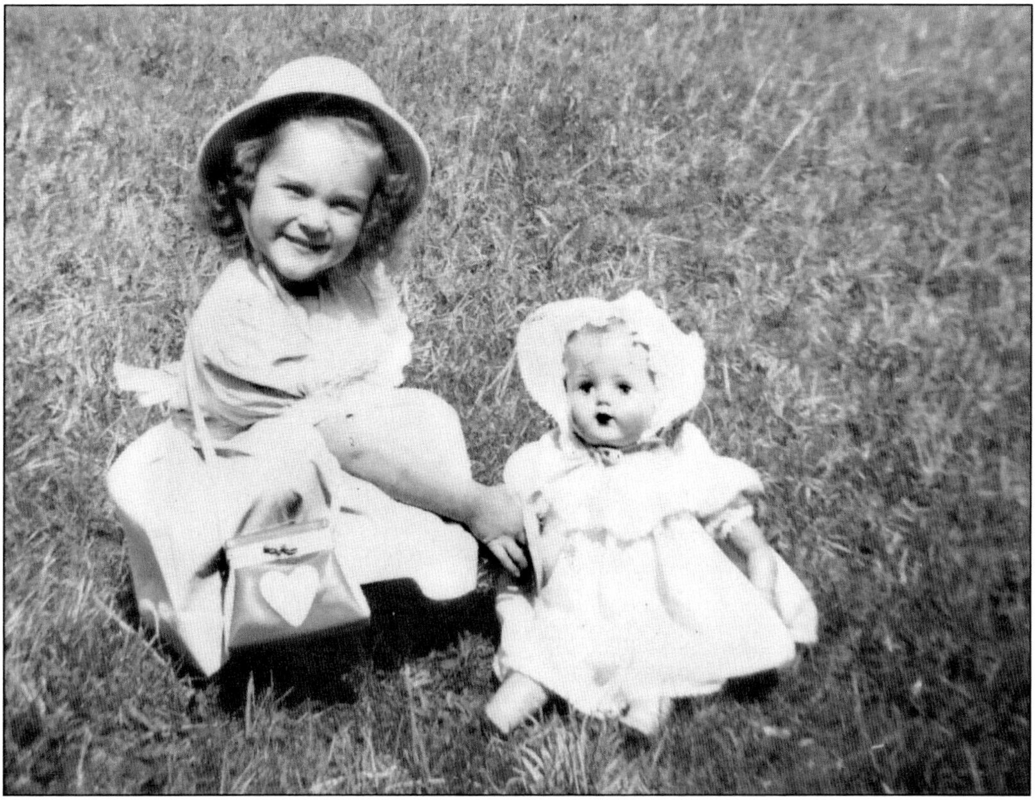

Christine Christy Tipton, known to her family as "Punkin," smiles artfully for the camera in her Easter Sunday best about 1951 in the company of her best baby doll, "Janie Sue." Tipton grew up to become the author of *Civil War in the Mountains*, a stirring account of the little-known Battle of Red Banks fought on a bitter December day in 1864 along the banks of the Nolichucky River in what is now southern Unicoi County. (Courtesy of Christine Christy Tipton.)

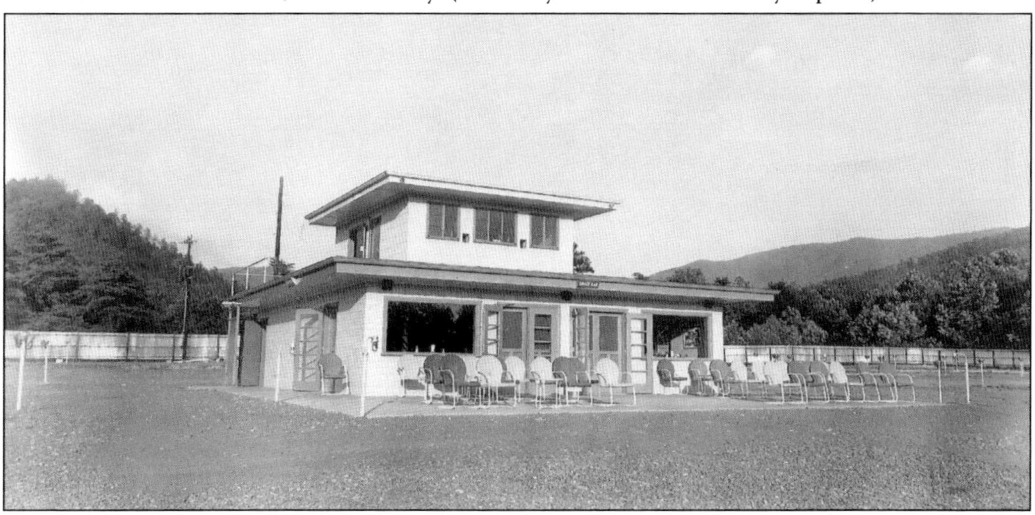

These metal lawn chairs served the walk-in patrons of the old Holiday Drive-in. The proximity to the drive-in snack bar may have been an incentive for the choice of these open-air seats, but the sound quality of the movie may have suffered a bit. (Courtesy of Jan Hendren Parsley.)

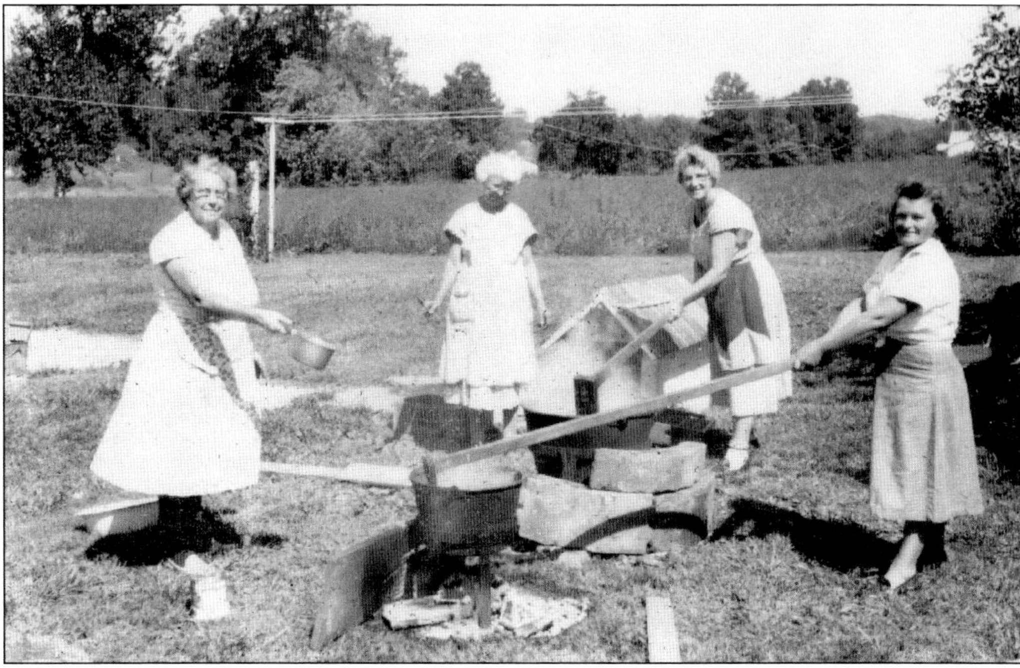

Making apple butter has always been a regular event of the fall harvest season in Unicoi County. In this photograph from the 1950s, Dolly Edwards (extreme right) and four unidentified friends tend the bubbling cast iron pot, which would have been stirred all day until the cooking apples had reached the right consistency for apple butter. Now in its 30th year, the Unicoi County Apple Festival, sponsored by the chamber of commerce, welcomes some 100,000 visitors annually. (Courtesy of Juacquetta Davis Edwards.)

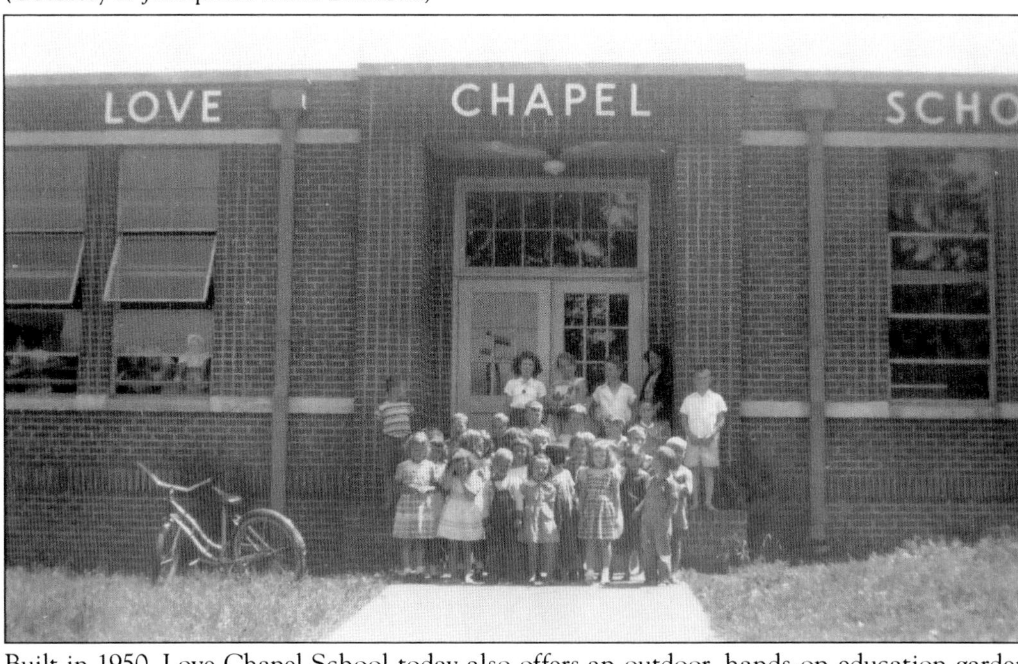

Built in 1950, Love Chapel School today also offers an outdoor, hands-on education garden program. (Courtesy of Dennis and Lillian Foster/Jakie Foster collection.)

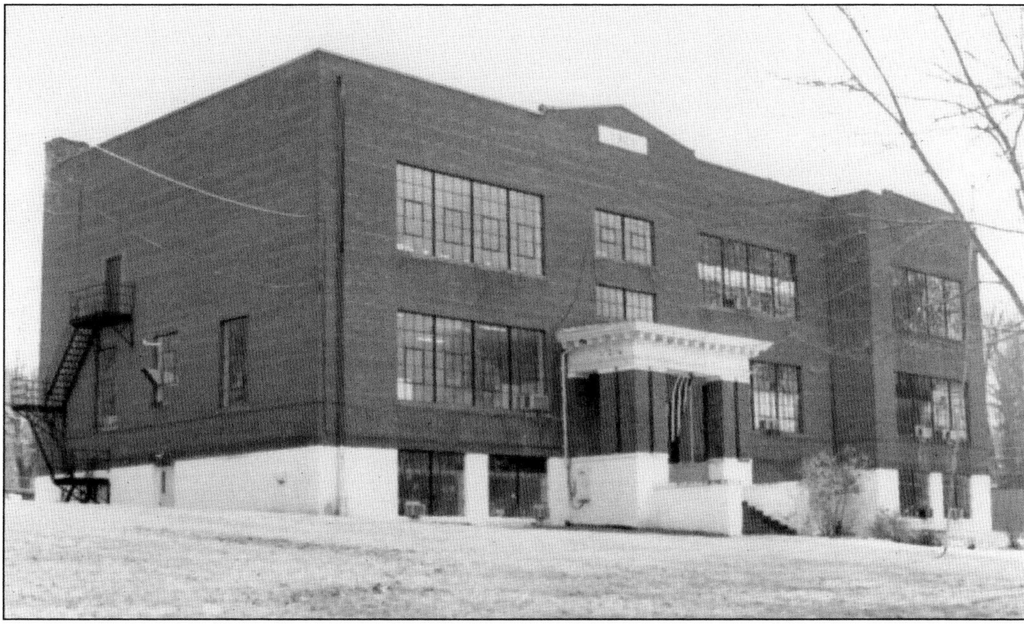

Built in 1922, Elm Street School filled the immediate needs of the booming population of Erwin. County school consolidation in the 1970s eliminated the use of this sturdy, brick building as a schoolhouse and transformed it into the central office of the Unicoi County School System. (Courtesy of James A. Goforth.)

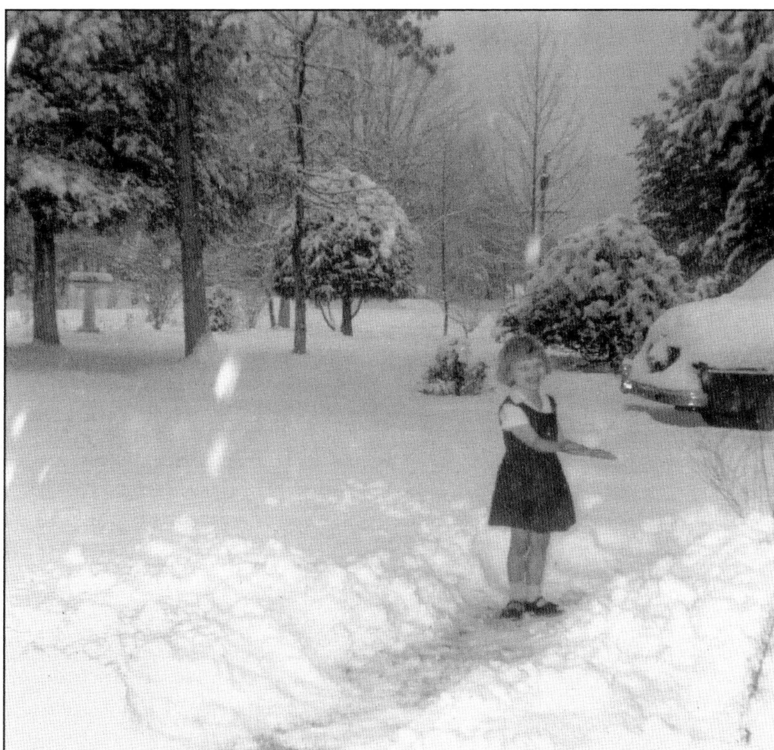

The deep snow from this 1958 photograph was an early spring anomaly. Five-year-old Linda Davis rushed outside at the behest of her Mamaw, Lula Davis, for just a quick snap of her Brownie box camera. Lula and Bob Davis owned what, in 1958, was the last house on the left on Rock Creek Road, just before the entrance to the park and Cherokee National Forest. (Courtesy of the author.)

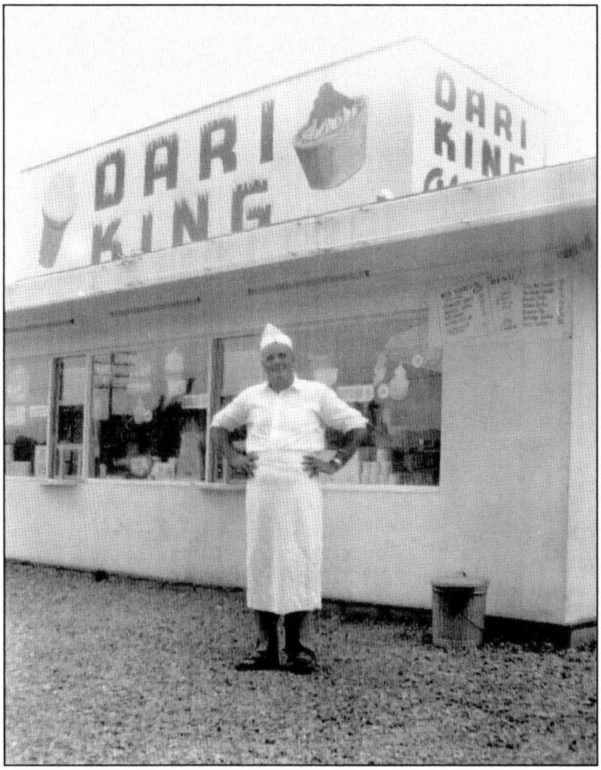

Bill Seagroves and Marjie Deaton met at a tent revival in Erwin and married in 1938. After working in the Baltimore shipyards during the 1940s, Seagroves returned to Erwin in the 1954 with his wife, Marjie, and his four children to take on the challenge of running a drive-in restaurant. The resulting Dari King on the old Johnson City Highway, north of Erwin, was a great success and instantly became a popular hangout for Erwin's teenagers. Curb hops served customers, delivering orders on metal trays with hooks that attached to car windows. Hamburgers were 25¢ and soft drinks 10¢. Orange Crush was a local favorite. The Seagroveses' hot dog, with Marjie's famous chili recipe, was also a hit. Bill opened the Dari-Ace in 1959 on the Jackson-Love Highway and later Seagroves Restaurant up the road in 1964. (Both images courtesy of Dennis Seagroves.)

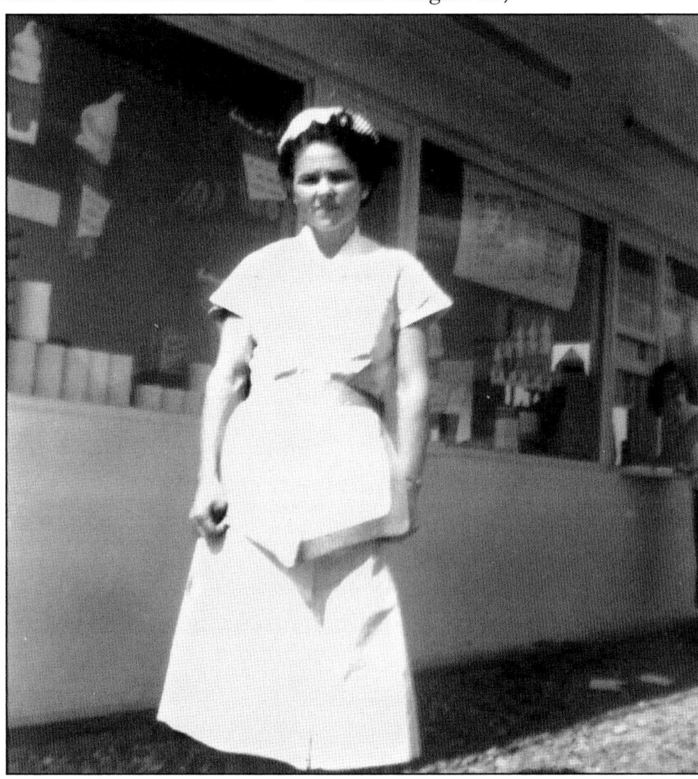

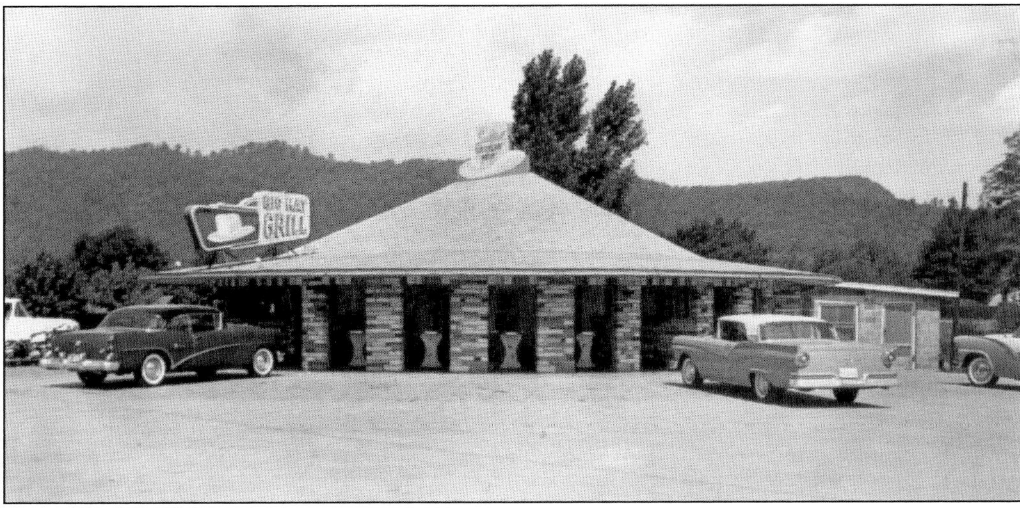

The Big Hat Grill, with its conical roof, was a popular icon of Erwin's post–World War II social history. This 1950s-era restaurant, conceived by local entrepreneurs Conrad Beam and George Hartsock, also featured curb service, as well as an al fresco dining area of wooden booths situated under the arched eaves of the hat brim. The late-1950s menu offered a large T-bone steak for $3.75, pork chops for $1.35, and a charbroiled cheeseburger for 50¢. (Courtesy of Lewis Thornberry.)

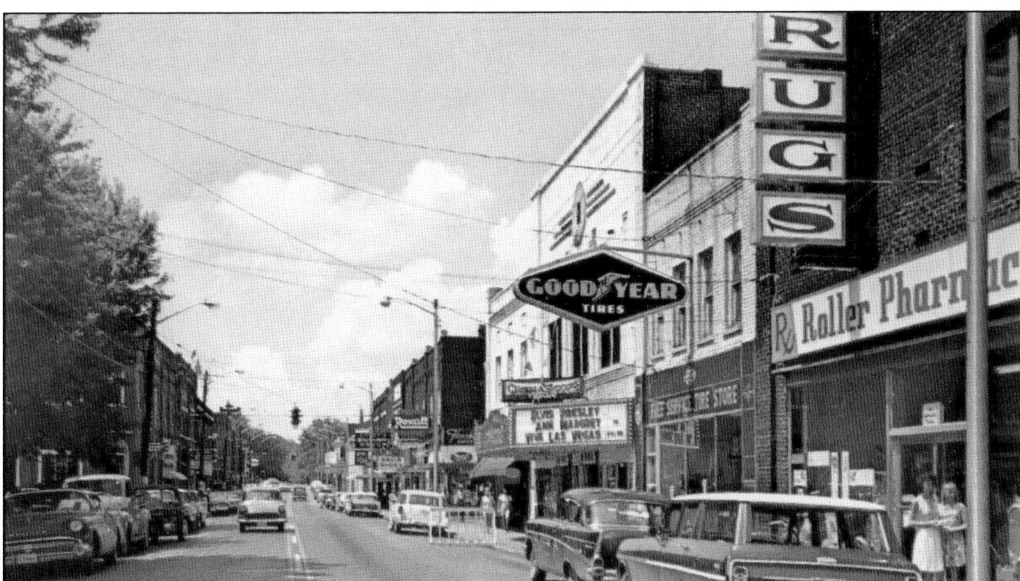

It could be an opening shot from the movie *American Graffiti*, but this scene is, in fact, Main Street in downtown Erwin from a tourist postcard of the mid-1960s. To the right, the movie marquee of the Capitol Theater proclaims Elvis Presley's *Viva Las Vegas* as the featured attraction that week. With the exception of the 1960s automobiles, the view looking south on Main Street is very much the same today. (Courtesy of Lewis Thornberry.)

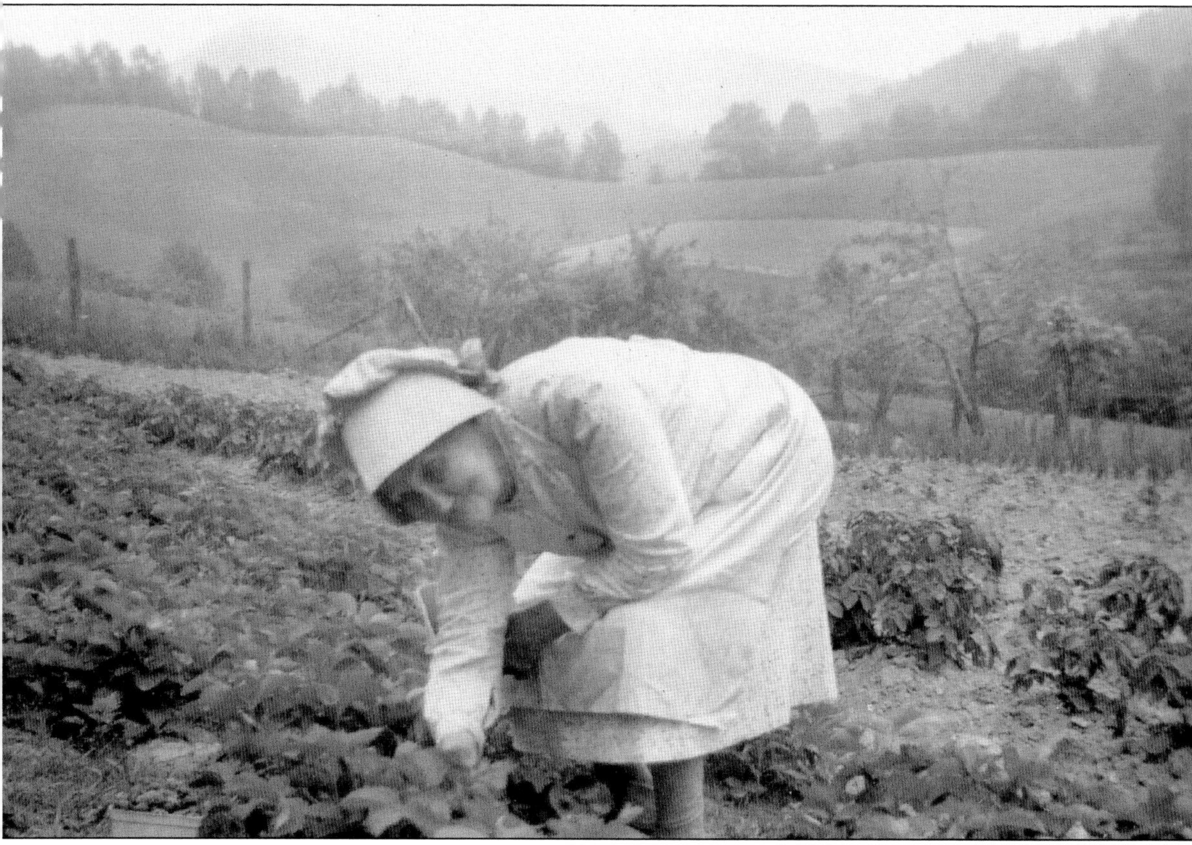

The mountain landscape of Tilson Mountain Road in Flag Pond is much the same today as it was when 97-year-old Martha Tilson Farnor went out in her garden one morning in 1960 to pick strawberries. Farnor lived to age 105. When asked how she had attained such great age, this remarkably mountain-wise, staunchly Republican, and deeply religious woman quoted from the Bible saying, "The wicked shall not live half their days." (Courtesy of Dennis and Lillian Foster/Jakie Farnor collection.)

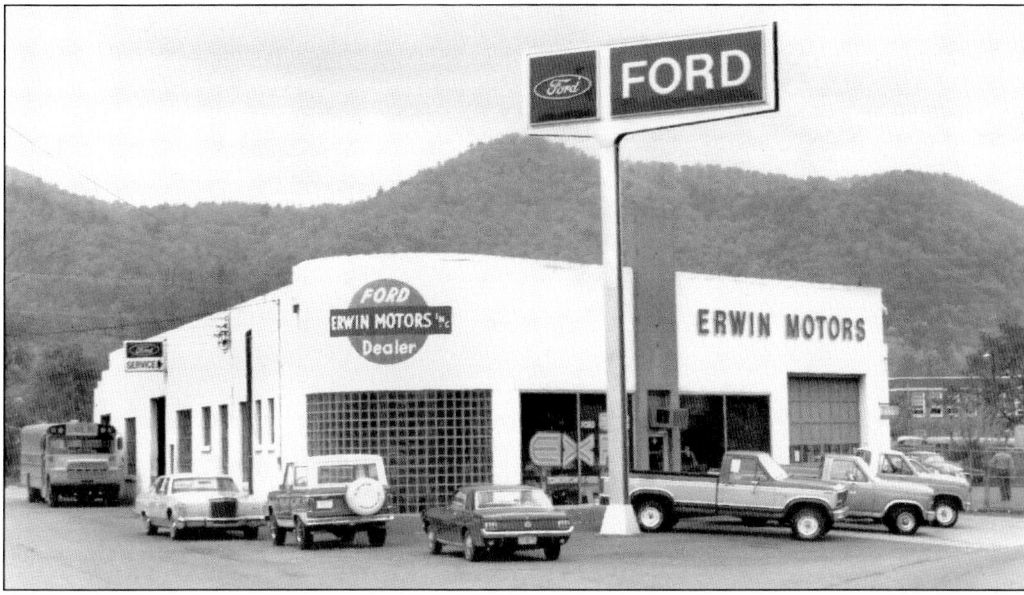

Erwin Motors was a longtime Ford dealership and garage owned and operated by the Love family of Love Chapel in southern Unicoi County. It was located in the triangle created by the intersection of Martin's Creek Road, Mohawk Road, and the Jackson-Love Highway. Below is the extended Love family clan in the early 1960s. From left to right are Theodore Love Jr.; Nellie and T. R. Love, also owners of Love Dairy; James H. Love; his wife, Marie; daughter Janet; John D. Love; his wife, Ernie, and children Amanda, Carol, and David; Stanley T. Love; his, wife Charlotte; daughters Lois Ann and Mary Nell; David M. Love; his wife, Patsy; and daughter Kathy; Clarence S. Love; his wife Jean; and sons Tim, Keith, and John; Robert L. Love; his wife, Opal, and sons Bobby and Bill. (Above courtesy of the Arnold Williams Family; below courtesy of Becky Harvey Love.)

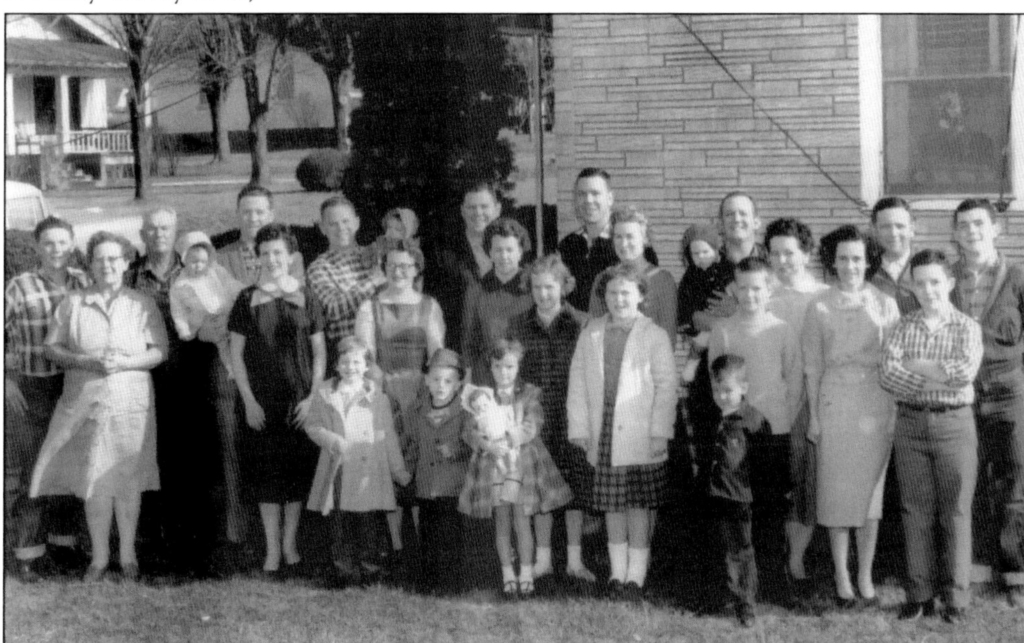

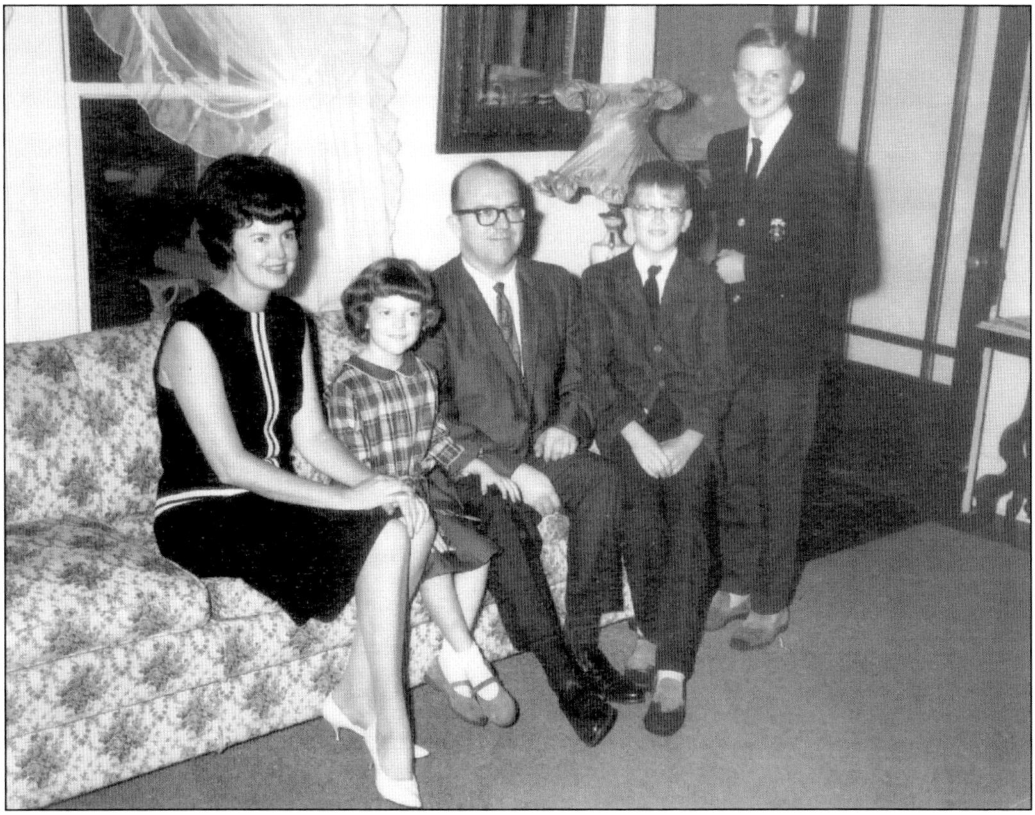

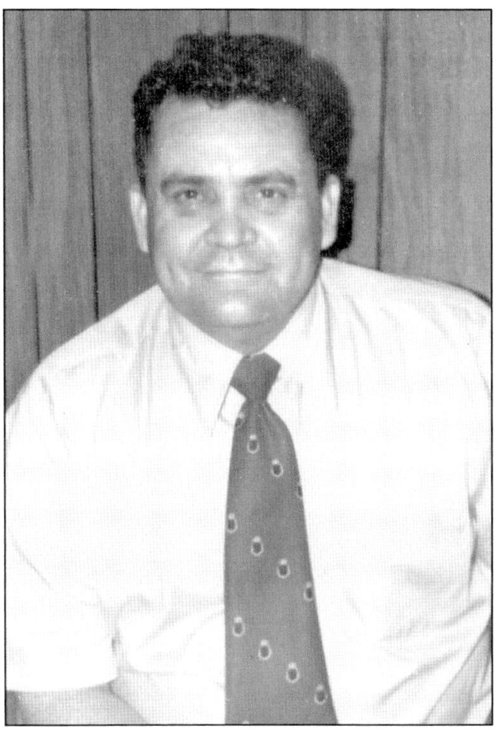

Born in Carter County, Dr. Nat Ed Hyder graduated from the University of Tennessee at Memphis. He entered medical partnership in the early 1960s with Dr. Earl Peterson and later Dr. Harmon Monroe. After more than 50 years as a physician, Dr. Hyder continues his practice at the Dry Creek Medical Center in Unicoi County. He and wife Elizabeth, a former nurse, are shown here in their Erwin home about 1967 with daughter Gretchen, son Mike, and son Nat (standing). The Hyders' son Paul died in 1962, shortly before his third birthday. (Courtesy of Dr. Nat Ed Hyder.)

Dr. Earl Baines came to the practice of medicine late in life, prompted by a life-altering automobile accident that required him to give up dairy farming. Baines completed his residency in Wilmington, North Carolina. In 1965, looking for a good place to raise a family, Dr. Baines came to Erwin to become a partner in Dr. Earl Peterson's medical practice. Later Dr. Baines had a practice on Tucker Street. He passed away in 1986. (Courtesy of Donna Baines Seagroves.)

Dr. Harmon L. Monroe received his medical degree from Emory University in Atlanta, coming to Erwin to practice medicine in 1934. Noted for his involvement in civic affairs, Dr. Monroe served as both mayor and alderman of Erwin. He was also past president of the Kiwanis Club and the American Legion, and served in North Africa during World II. Dr. Monroe was instrumental in the establishment and construction of the county's first modern hospital in 1953.

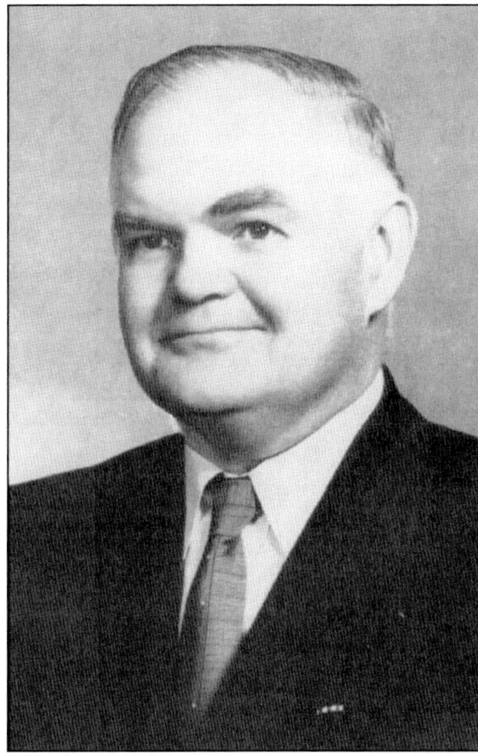

The Southeastern Autorama, headquartered in Unicoi County, is the oldest vintage car show in the State of Tennessee. Begun about 1964 by Big Hat Grill owner Conrad Beam, this eye-catching display of classic automobiles took off immediately as part of local festivals and community parades. Today the late-summer automobile show is a popular destination event, drawing car enthusiasts from all over the country. In this 1967 photograph, a young Boy Scout scopes out the chassis of this 1920s ragtop. (Courtesy of Kim Arwood/ Southeastern Autorama collection.)

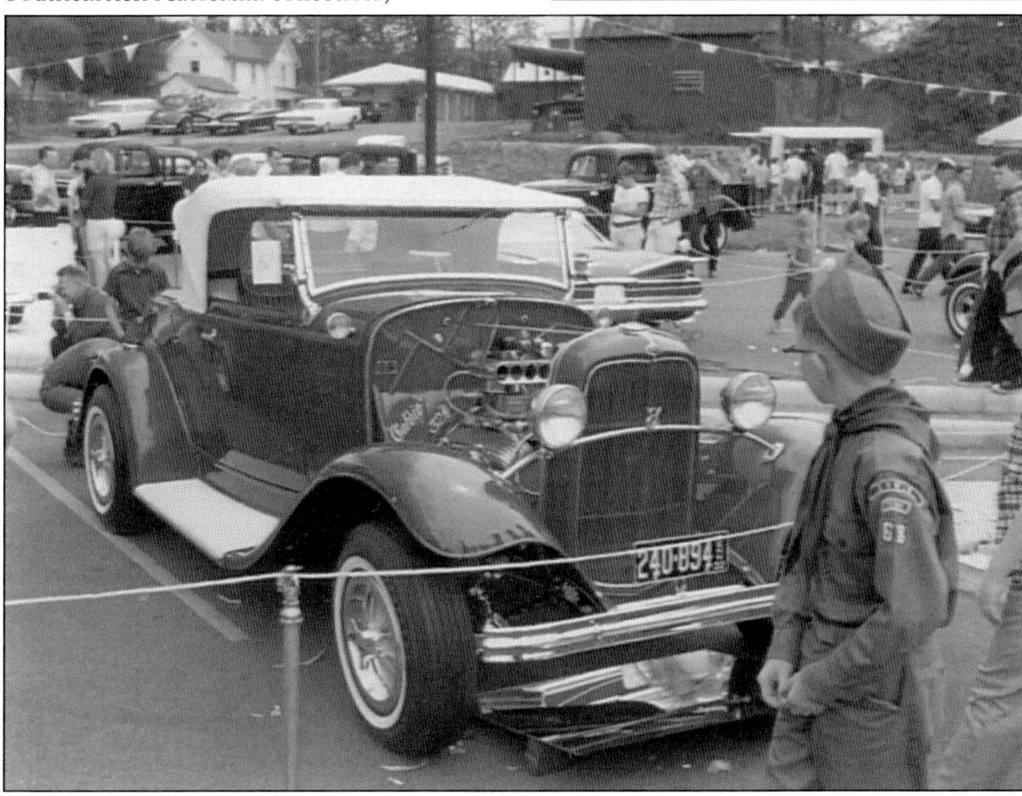

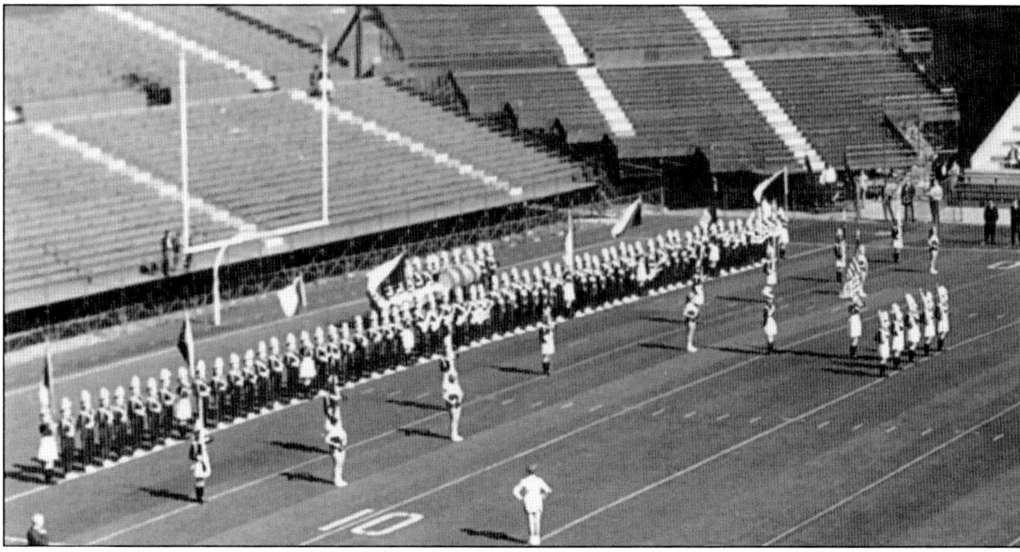

Under the direction of youthful band director Jim Gladson, the Unicoi County High School Marching Band of 1967–1972 experienced a dizzying success and energy that has sustained the high school band program for 40 years. The UCHS Band won numerous awards across the Southeast. The 1968 band is shown in formation on the field at the University of Tennessee. (Courtesy of Jim Gladson.)

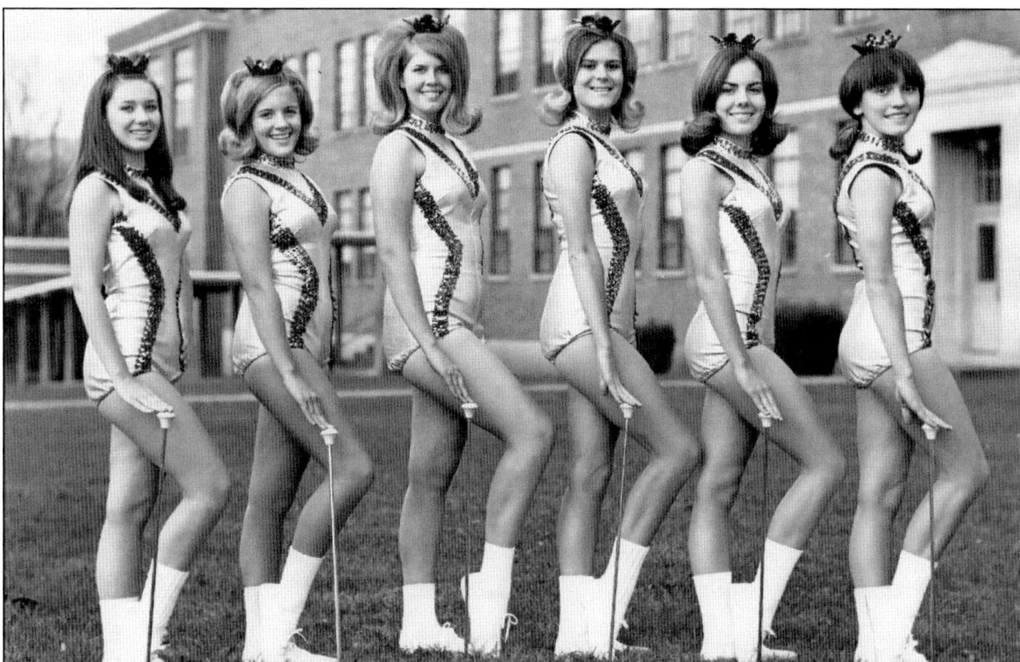

This sterling 1971 majorette squad of the Unicoi County High School Marching Band had to work in sync to achieve the perfection of their intricate twirling routines, something they had become accustomed to since they first picked up batons at the age of five or six as part of Erwin's fabled Miss Jeanne's Majorettes. From left to right are Marcella Davis, Becky Williamson, Debbie McInturff, Lisa Range, Pam Sams, and Cindy Daniels. (Courtesy of Debbie McInturff Tittle.)

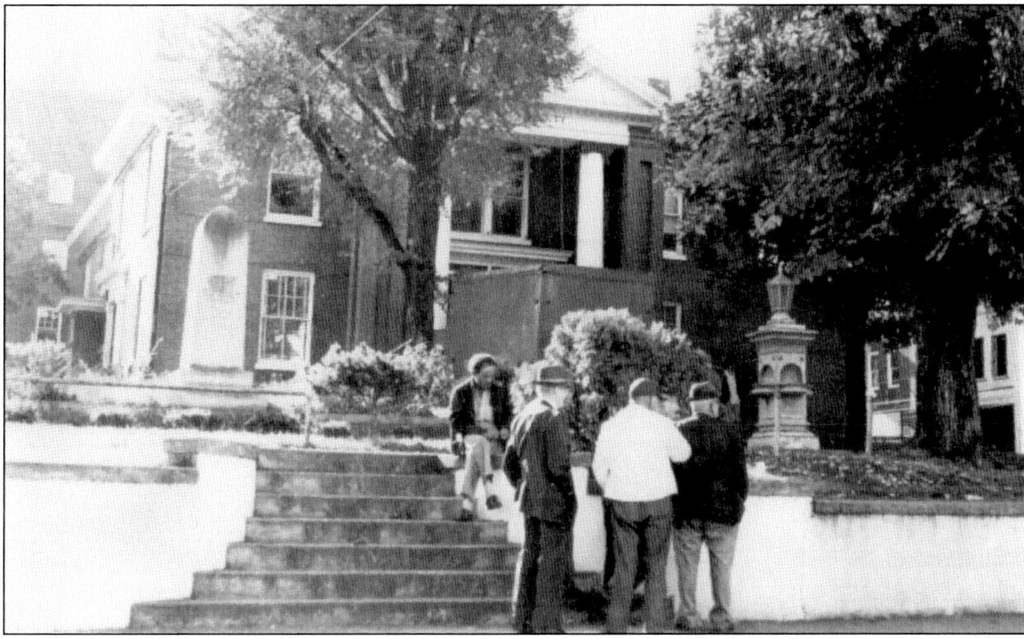

This easygoing scene from the late 1960s reflects the popularity of the old courthouse steps as a gathering place for old-timers. A memorial monument situated on the lawn above the steps saluted the county's World War I veterans, and an ornately carved public drinking fountain donated by Erwin business leader A. R. Brown offered cool drinking water. (Courtesy of the Unicoi County Historical Society.)

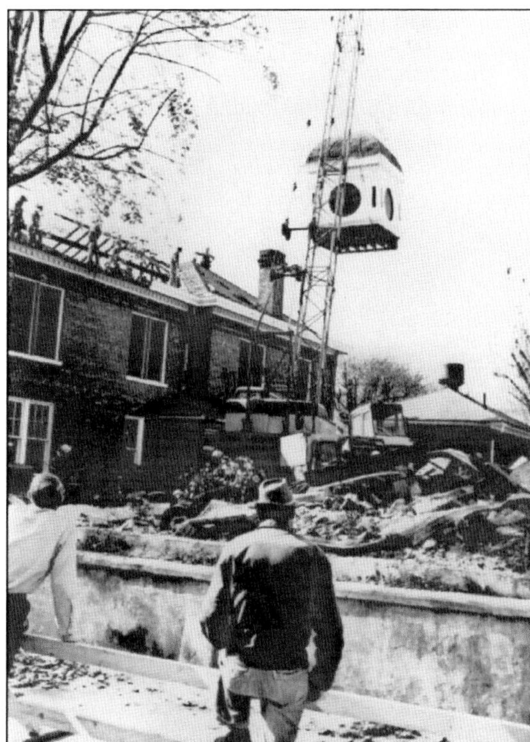

A long-armed crane hoists the familiar bun-shaped cupola of the old Unicoi County Courthouse from its moorings to cle›ar the site for the construction of a new courthouse in 1975. (Courtesy of the Unicoi County Historical Society.)

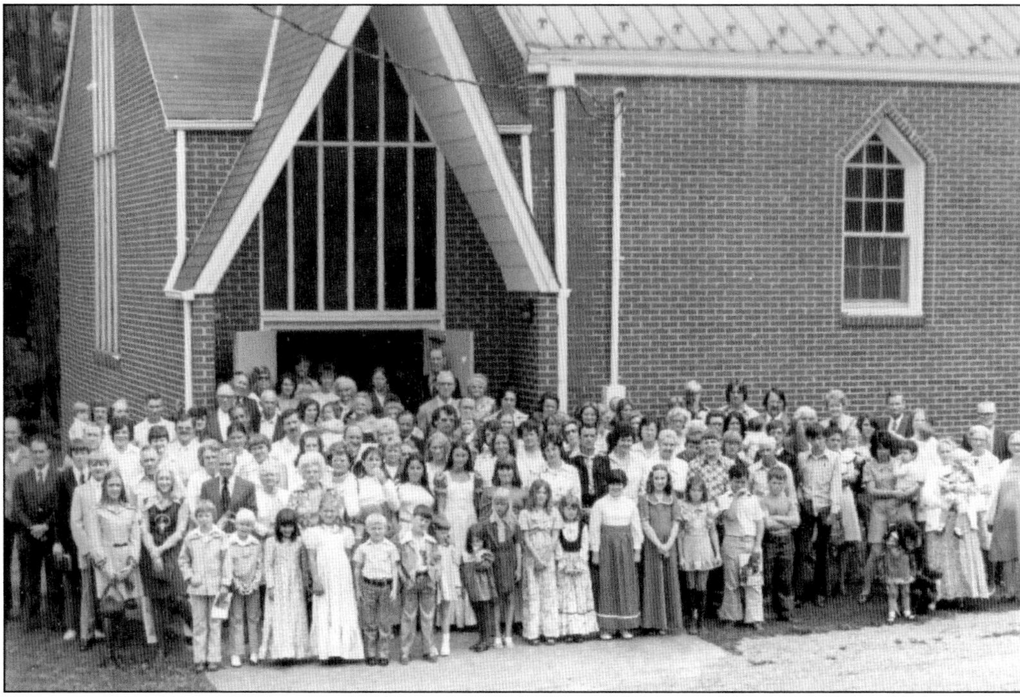

In 1900, lawyer and educator R. W. H. Gilbert constructed a building near his Martin's Creek home for the intended use of the community, calling it "Lily's Dale" for his young daughter. It was frequently used for meetings of the congregation that became known as the Lily Dale Church of Christ, shown in the 1970s. (Courtesy of Lucille Hensley Booth.)

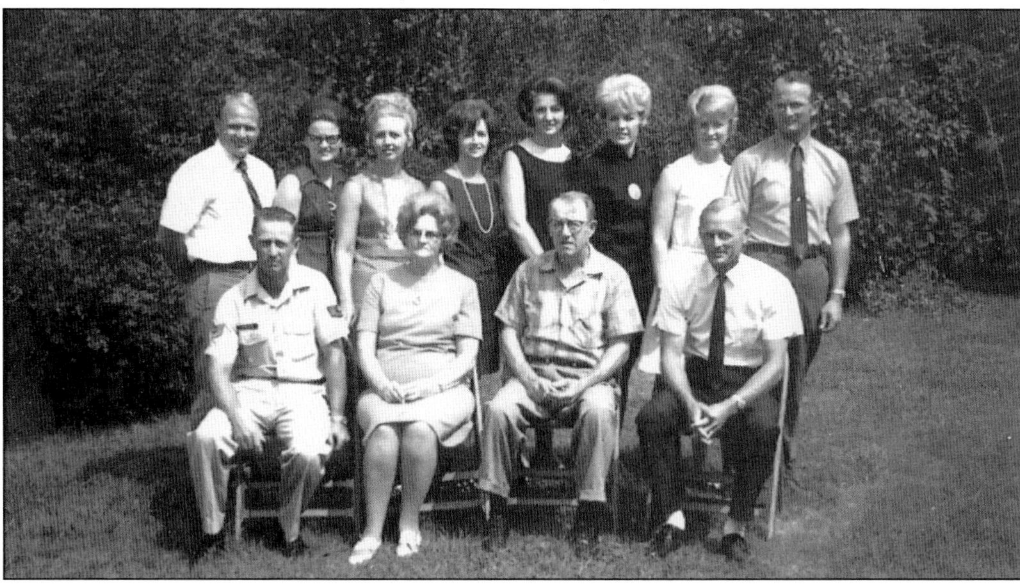

Bud Hensley, from Spivey Mountain, and Mamie Banner, from Martin's Creek, were married in 1924. He and Mamie farmed a large garden that fed a family of 11 children at their home on Martin's Creek. Pictured on the sad occasion of son Roby's funeral in the early 1970s are, from left to right, the following: (first row) J. D., Mamie, Bud, and Junior; (second row) Teddy, Genny, Abby, Mona, Lucille, Eulala, Lois, and Ivan. (Courtesy of Lucille Hensley Booth.)

The late Judge Walter Garland was a tireless advocate for the preservation of the history of Unicoi County. One of the founders of the Unicoi County Historical Society, Judge Garland, at his death, left a massive manuscript documenting the history of Unicoi County to be published by his family. Judge Garland was elected as a circuit court judge in 1966 and was also instrumental in the construction of the modern-day Unicoi County Courthouse. (Courtesy of Kent Garland/Judge Walter Garland collection.)

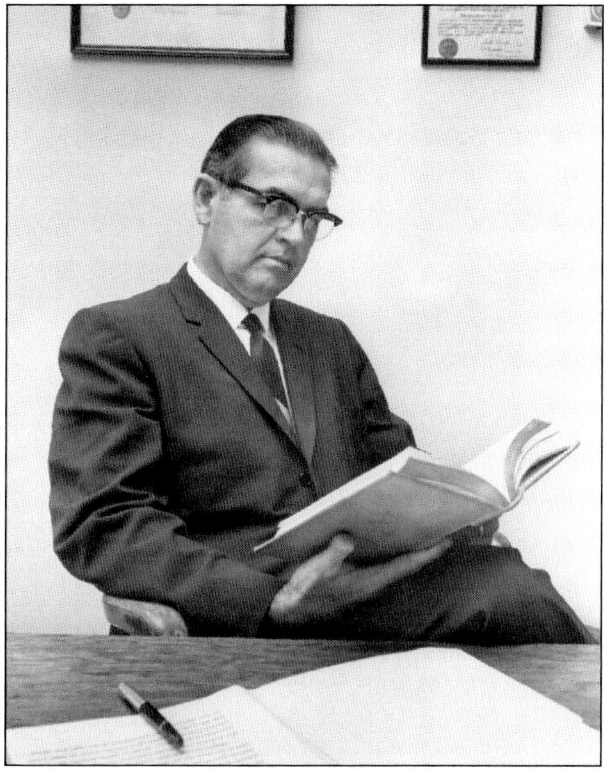

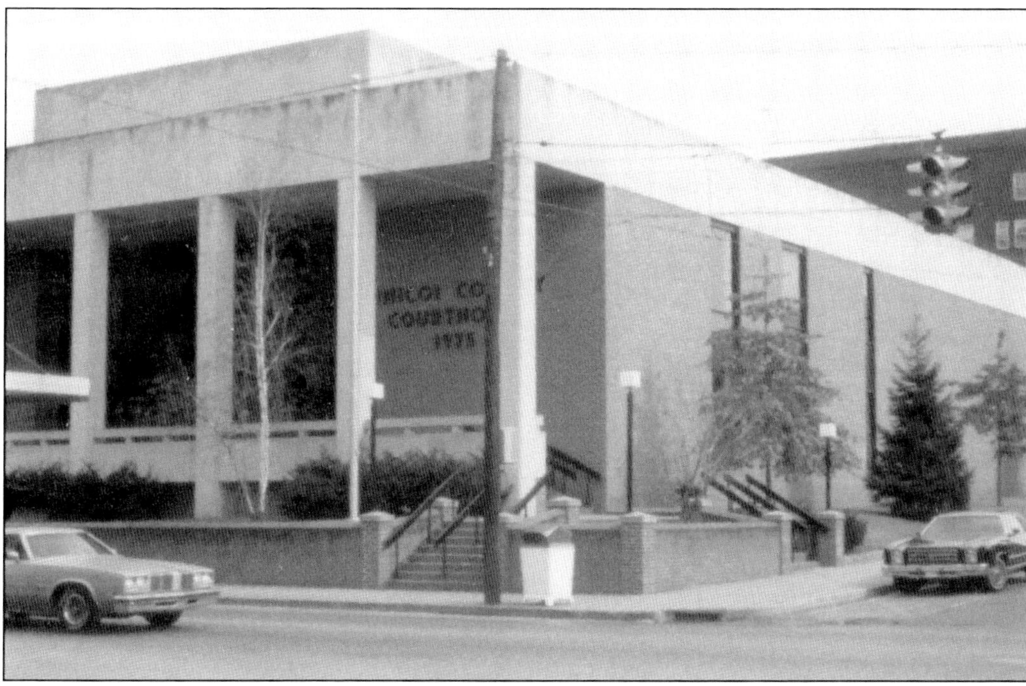

The sleek, multilevel design of the current Unicoi County Courthouse was one of the most innovative in the state when it was built in 1975. Architect-designed, the current courthouse was the solution to the county's ever-increasing need for space. (Courtesy of the Arnold Williams family.)

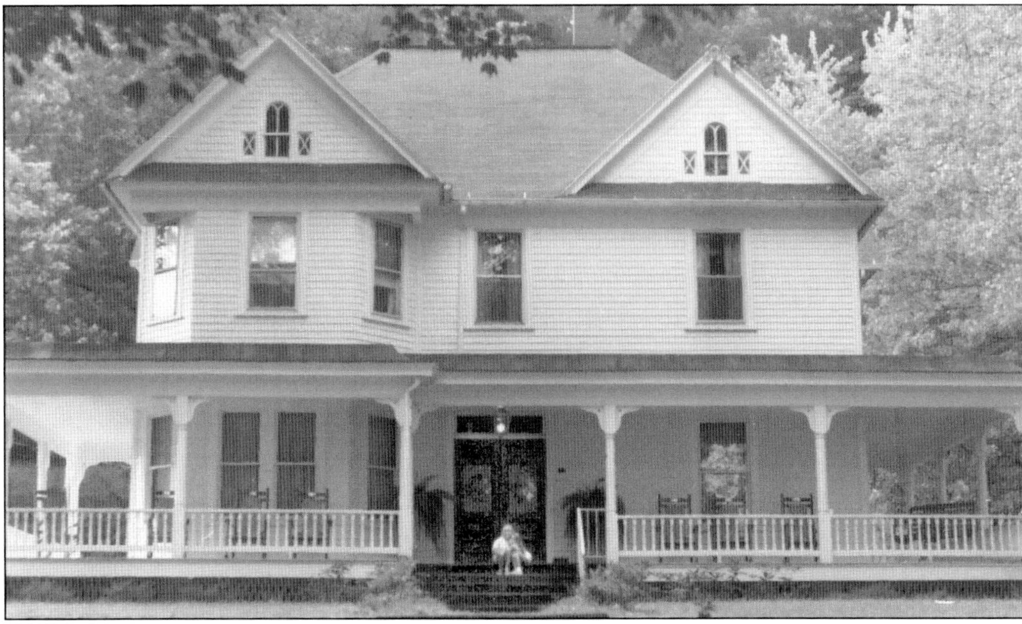

The Unicoi County Heritage Museum, situated on the grounds of the Erwin National Fish Hatchery, was once the official residence of the hatchery superintendent. Built in 1903 at a cost of $4, 454.50, this 10-room, late-Victorian house was home to Supt. A. G. Keesecker and his family from 1905 to 1931. In 1982, community leaders rescued the dilapidated structure for restoration as a local history museum. (Courtesy of the Arnold Williams family.)

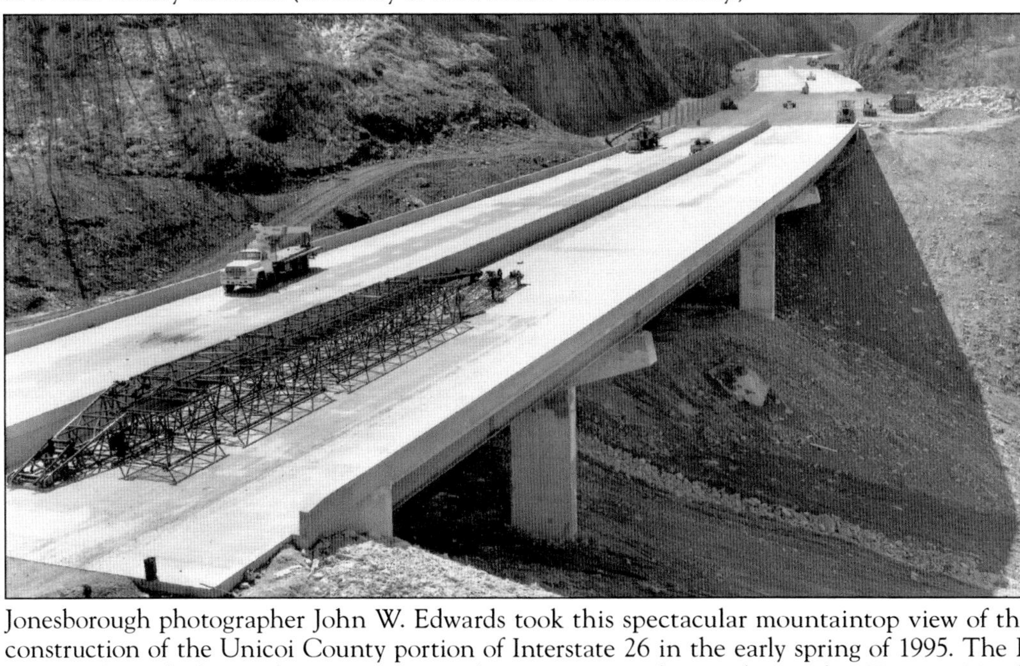

Jonesborough photographer John W. Edwards took this spectacular mountaintop view of the construction of the Unicoi County portion of Interstate 26 in the early spring of 1995. The I-26 span through the southern mountains of Unicoi County has made travel to Western North Carolina easier and more efficient, eliminating the once hazardous, winding two-lane route of hairpin curves and steep mountain grades built a century ago. Tennessee's portion of the I-26 connector opened July 4, 1995. (Courtesy of John W. Edwards.)

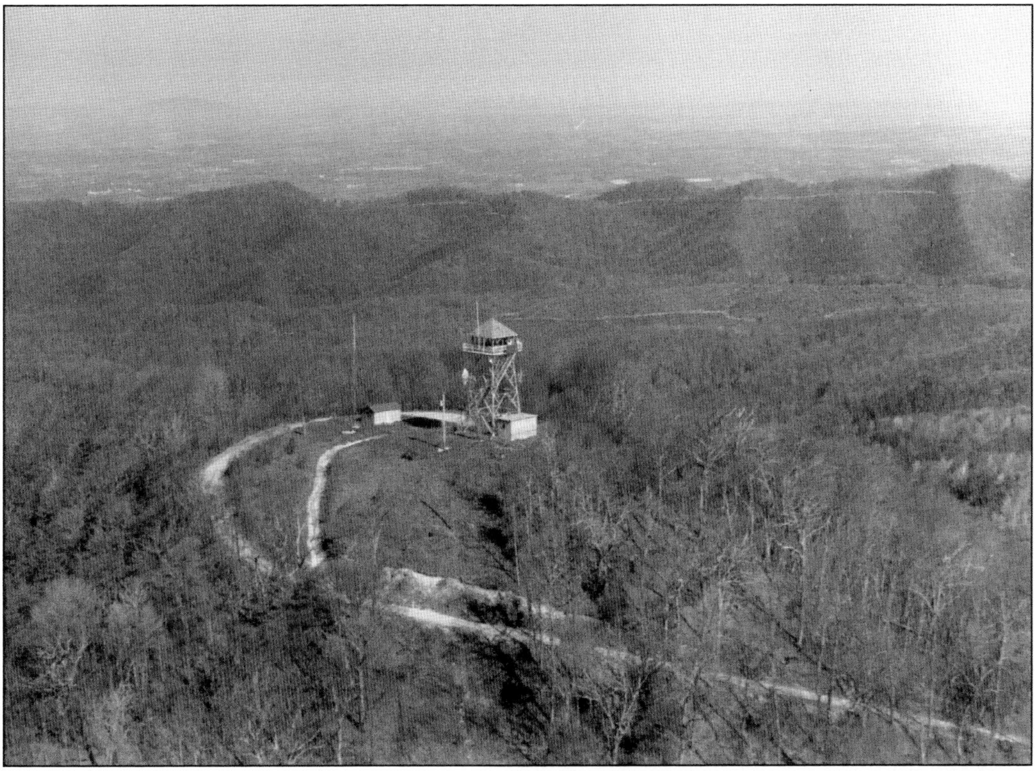

Pinnacle Fire Tower was built in 1931 on Buffalo Mountain in northern Unicoi County. One of the few fire tower lookouts in which living quarters are part of the structure, the decommissioned Pinnacle Fire Tower was deemed a National Historic Lookout Tower in 1998. Today Partners of the Cherokee National Forest are making efforts to secure grant funding to restore the tower and incorporate it into a land-use conservancy for conservation education and public-recreation enjoyment. (Courtesy of Guy Street/ Cherokee National Forest District Fire Management.)

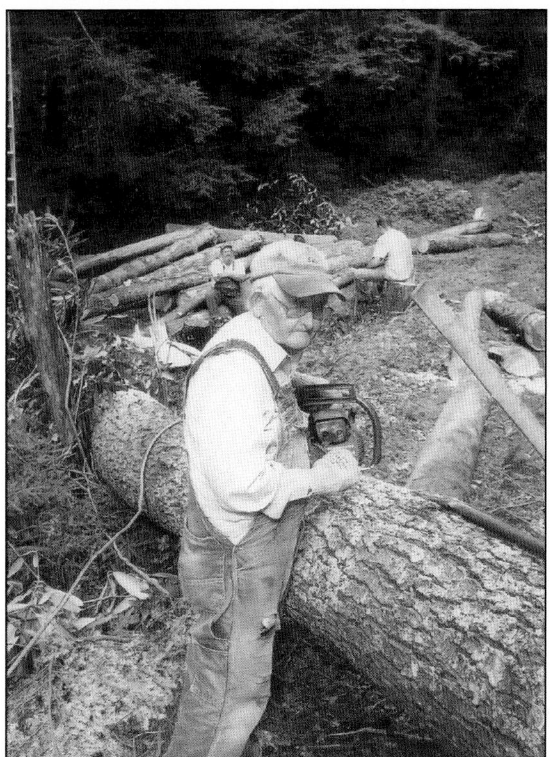

In 2005, eighty-three-year-old Jimmie Clouse of Flag Pond (foreground), neighbor Rupert Brannon (background), and Jimmie's grandson Bennie Clouse (right) surveyed their tree-cutting progress as they helped prepare for the installation of a cell phone tower in the Flag Pond community. (Courtesy of Rupert Brannon/Betty S. Brannon collection.)

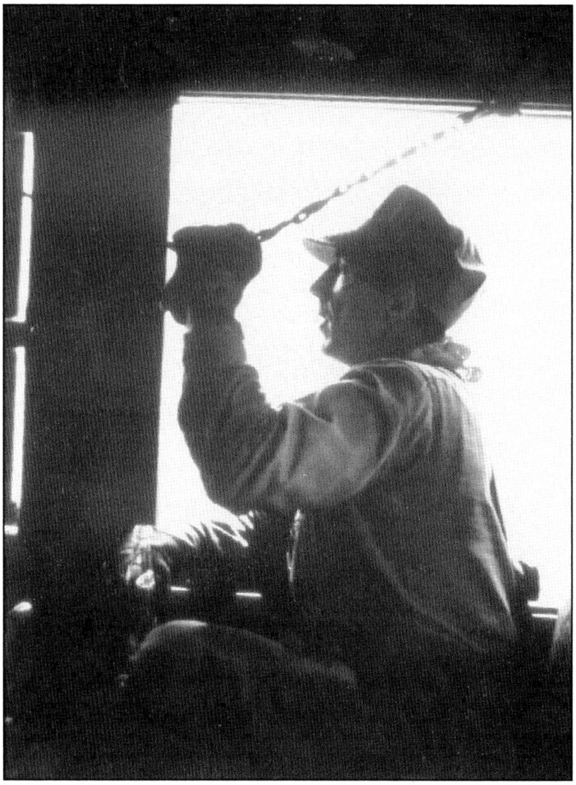

Engineer George Hatcher sits at the head of a speeding Clinchfield locomotive during the 1970s. Hatcher, from a large, loving family, grew up "cross the creek," on the edge of North Indian Creek at the base of Bogart's Hill. He is one of the famous "Erwin Nine" from World War II service. Today, in his 80s, Hatcher exercises every day, walking several miles up and down the hilly streets of his Erwin neighborhood. (Courtesy of George Hatcher.)

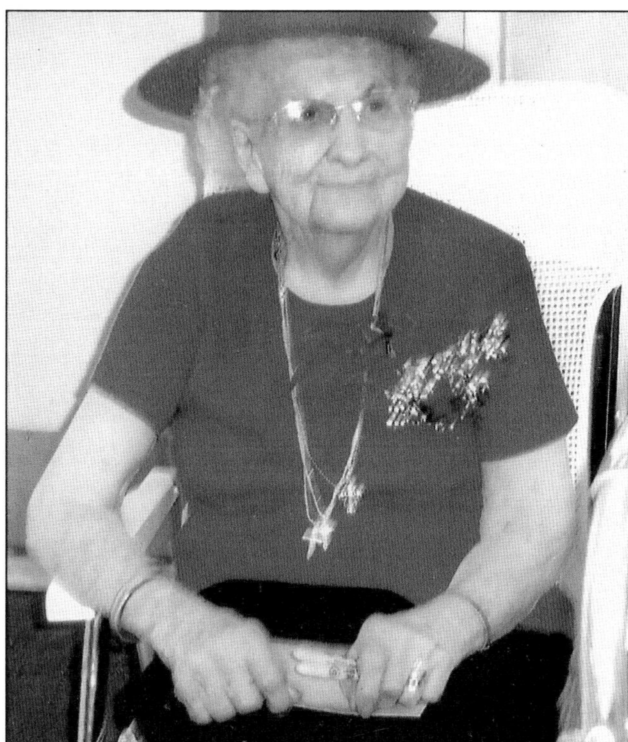

Pauline Cash and her husband, Ray, founded Unicoi County's famous Clinchfield Artware Pottery in 1945—operating from a building situated behind their home on Clinchfield Avenue in Erwin. The Cash Family Pottery—as it was commonly known—produced stylized, highly decorative pitchers, vases, bowls, plaques, and novelty pieces hand-painted by local artisans. In W. Allison Burnette Jr.'s *Collector's Guide to Cash Family/Clinchfield Artware Pottery*, Mrs. Cash recalled, "We dried our first mold in my kitchen oven and mixed the first batch of mud on my back porch in an old wringer washing machine." Ray Cash died in 1987 and Pauline in July 2006. (Courtesy of Lisa and John Pilkington.)

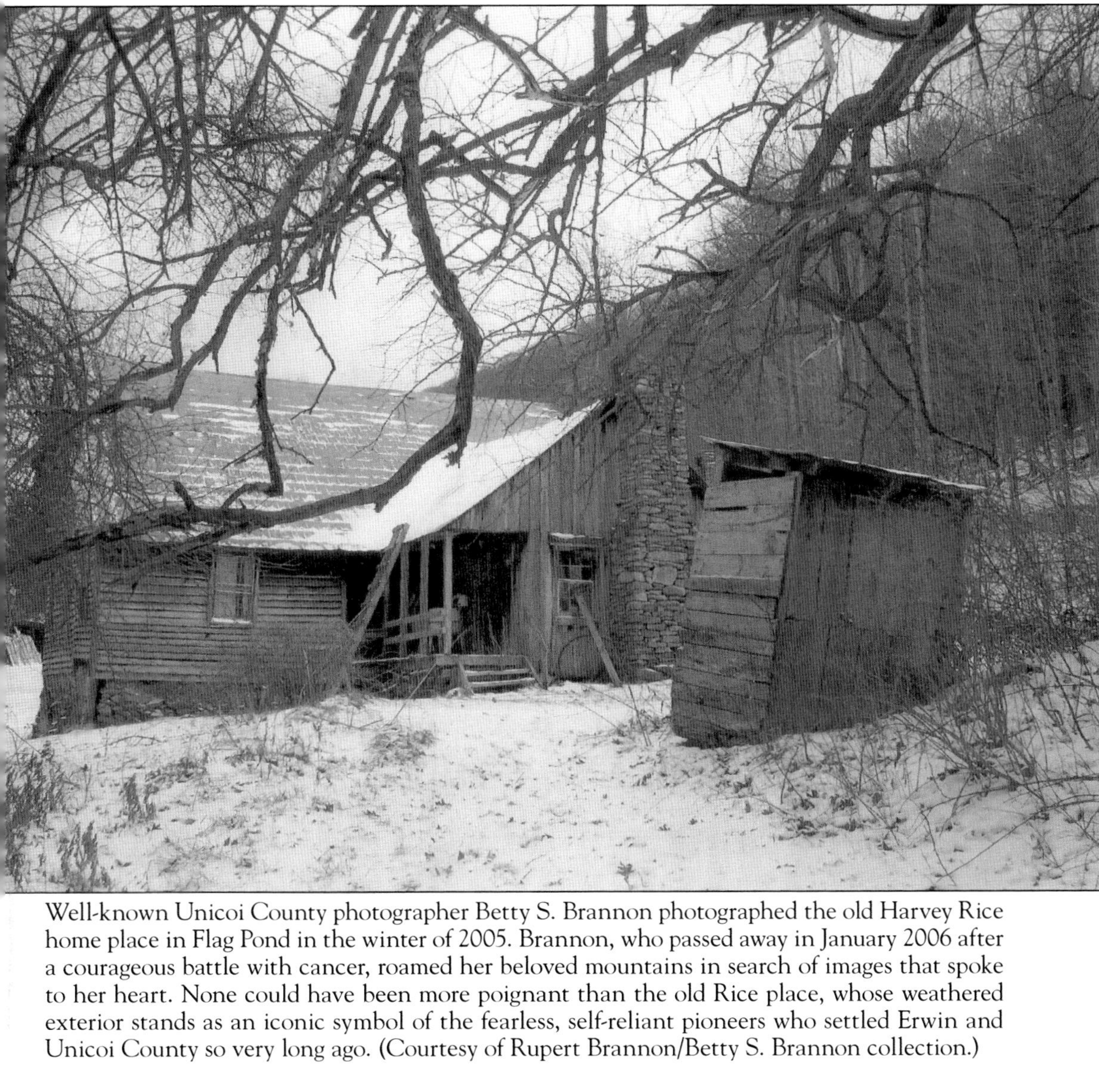

Well-known Unicoi County photographer Betty S. Brannon photographed the old Harvey Rice home place in Flag Pond in the winter of 2005. Brannon, who passed away in January 2006 after a courageous battle with cancer, roamed her beloved mountains in search of images that spoke to her heart. None could have been more poignant than the old Rice place, whose weathered exterior stands as an iconic symbol of the fearless, self-reliant pioneers who settled Erwin and Unicoi County so very long ago. (Courtesy of Rupert Brannon/Betty S. Brannon collection.)

Consistent with our mission to preserve history on a local level, this book was printed in South Carolina on American-made paper and manufactured entirely in the United States. Products carrying the accredited Forest Stewardship Council (FSC) label are printed on 100 percent FSC-certified paper.